Becoming Friends of Ti

Becoming Friends of Time

Disability, Timefullness, and Gentle Discipleship

John Swinton

scm press

This edition published in the UK in 2017 by SCM Press
Editorial office
3rd Floor, Invicta House,
108–114 Golden Lane,
London EC1Y 0TG, UK

SCM Press is an imprint of Hymns Ancient & Modern Ltd (a registered charity)

Hymns Ancient & Modern® is a registered trademark
of Hymns Ancient and Modern Ltd
13A Hellesdon Park Road, Norwich,
Norfolk NR6 5DR, UK

Published in the United States in 2016 by Baylor University Press

www.scmpress.co.uk

British Library Cataloguing in Publication data

A catalogue record for this book is available
from the British Library

978 0 334 05557 0

Printed and bound in Great Britain by
CPI Group (UK) Ltd, Croydon

This book is dedicated to my mother, Janet, because she is wonderful.

Contents

Acknowledgments ix

Introduction: Time, Disability, and the Fragile Brain 1

I. Time and Disability

1 Thinking about Time 21
The Tyranny of the Clock

2 Time and Progress 35
Disability and the Wrong Kind of Time

II. Learning to Live in God's Time

3 Time and Christ 57
A Brief Theology of Time

4 Becoming Friends of Time 67
Love Has a Speed

III. From Inclusion to Discipleship

5 Time and Discipleship 87
Inclusion, Discipleship, and Profound Intellectual Disability

6 Time and Vocation 115
Slow and Gentle Disciples

IV. Reclaiming the Heart

7 Time and Memory 133
Dementia and the Advancement of Time

8 Time and the Heart 147
Affective Remembering

V. The Horror of Time

9 The Horror of Time 165
Acquired Brain Injury and Personality Change

10 The Time Before and the Time After 177
Brain Injury, Human Identity, and the Hiddenness of Our Lives in Christ

11 Time and Ritual 193
Funerals for Friends

Conclusion: Being in Christ, Being in Time 207
Every Body Has a Place

Appendix: Redeeming Time 213
A Lived Funeral

Notes 221
Bibliography 237
Index 243

Acknowledgments

Books are always written by communities. Yes, it is the case that the author sits down at some point and puts it all together, but the ideas presented in any book emerge from a multitude of different sources, conversations, narratives, and perspectives. The author may take all of the credit or the criticism, but a myriad of conversation partners are inevitably central to the depth and richness of any book. I am grateful to the community of friends who have journeyed with me as I have tried to work through something of the complex relationship between disability and time. These friends are timefull insofar as they are people who are aware that recognizing that we live in God's time makes all the difference in the world to the ways in which we see and act in the world. In God's good time, God has chosen to gift me with friends who truly embody something of what it means to be a disciple of the God who *is* love. For such a gift I am eternally grateful.

Thanks must go firstly to Irma Fast Dueck at the Canadian Mennonite University in Winnipeg. It was thanks to her kind invitation to do the J. J. Thiessen Lectures in 2014 that I was provided with an opportunity to think more deeply about issues of time and disability and to share some provisional ideas with a group of people who were both engaged and engaging. Thank you Irma for your friendship and hospitality. Much thanks must go to the people living with disability whose stories are represented in this book. Thank you for the gift of your story. I hope I have represented it faithfully. Thanks to my good friends Medi Volpe at the University of Durham and Jill Harshaw at the Belfast Bible College for taking time to read portions of this book and to give me some wonderful perspectives on theology and what it means to live well with people whom we have chosen to name as profoundly intellectually disabled. Their scholarly thinking, which has emerged from deep personal experiences of the issues discussed in this book, was truly a gift to me. Hopefully they will also be a gift to the readers of this book. My colleagues at the University of Aberdeen Brian Brock and Mike Mawson, as always, provided me with critical reflections and insightful angles indicative of their status as go-to theologians within the field of theological ethics and the theology of disability. It is great to hang around with people who not only are profound thinkers but genuinely care about the issues. Thank you to Stanley Hauerwas for some vital conversations around the issue of time as well as the theology of disability. Stan has been a hospitable guide and a good friend for many years and, I hope, will remain so for many more years to come. Thank you to Jean Vanier for his guidance and mentorship around issues of profound intellectual disability and for his kindness to me over the years. Jean's gentle footsteps provide the basic cadence and the enduring rhythm that guide the movements of this book. I am also grateful for a conversation I had with Hans Reinders a few years ago, which really got me thinking about the importance of time. Hans' encouragement and enthusiasm was much appreciated. Hopefully he will not be too disappointed with what has emerged! I am also very grateful to Tricia Williams, one of my current PhD students, and Dr. Priscilla Oh, a former PhD student and a good friend, for their input into my thinking around issues of dementia. Both of them are deeply embedded in what God is doing within the area of dementia care. I very much look forward to seeing the fruits of their intellectual labor. Thanks also to my good friend and confidante Aileen Barclay for her friendship, support, and wisdom. I have loved working with Tonya Whaley on issues of acquired brain damage. Her story has taught me much about what it means to live well with radical changes to one's identity. Being with her as a person has shown me what it looks like to live faithfully and hopefully with the profound changes that accompany acquired brain injuries. And, of course, I am ever thankful for my wonderful wife, Alison. Only God knows why God gifted me such a wonderful person. I am grateful.

Introduction
Time, Disability, and the Fragile Brain

> Time is the context that gives meaning to everything in this world, and conversely everything that has meaning for us in this world, everything that has a place in our lives, exists in time.
>
> (Iain McGilchrist)[1]

> For at just the right time Christ will be revealed from heaven by the blessed and only almighty God, the King of all kings and Lord of all lords.
>
> (1 Tim 6:15 NLT)

This is a book about time. It is not, however, about any old time. It is about *God's time* and what it means to live one's life faithfully within the time that has been gifted to us. There is no getting away from the fact that time is a fundamental aspect of the ways in which we understand, construct, and try to make sense of the world. As Iain McGilchrist in the epigraph to this chapter puts it, "Time is the context that gives meaning to *everything* in this world."[2] Without time we would be like rudderless ships floating aimlessly around and around in a sea of unending timelessness, beings without direction or meaning, vessels without compasses, maps without coordinates. Time drives us, guides us, and shapes our expectations of what was, what is, and what will be. Time is immovably written large across all of our horizons.

As I write this introduction and glance at my watch, the time is 10:25 a.m. I have been awake for five hours. I had to get up at 5:25 to pick up my daughter, who was returning from a holiday in Cyprus. Her plane was late, so she ended up arriving in Aberdeen very early in the morning. Thus far today I have gazed upon at least *ten* clocks, each of which has helped to orient me in and toward the world in quite particular ways: (1) My alarm clock woke me. (2) The alarm on my iPad reinforced the point! (3) The clock in my kitchen urged me to hurry up and find the car keys as time was moving on and I did not want my daughter stranded alone in a parking lot after a twelve-hour journey. (4) The clock in my car concretized the incessant time telling of the radio DJ. (5) The vision of my daughter pointing at her wrist watch confirmed my culpability. I was late. . . . (6) The clock on my daughter's phone glowed in the fading dawn as she got her fix on Facebook . . . or was it Instagram . . . Snapchat? I imagine by the time this book comes out all these trends will be considered dated, passé: their time will have come and gone.

And that was just the beginning of the day. I dropped my daughter off at home, jumped back in my car, and headed off to work. The DJ spouting forth from my car radio struck me as oddly obsessive-compulsive in her incessant reminders that another few minutes have passed me by. I feel as if my life is slipping away with every announcement. I get to work and park my car. "Morning, Prof," says the friendly parking attendant. "You're in early!" I explain the sad tale of my daughter's return. He smiles kindly and pretends to care. (7) The clock in my office here at the university has kept me on time and told me, with some degree of accuracy, when it was time to head for my first teaching session. (8) The clock in the classroom encouraged me by pointing out that it was almost coffee time and that I should just ignore my students' jaded glances at their phones, PCs, wrist watches, smart watches, and whatever other devices they were using to map out their sorrow, joy, and boredom at my neatly timed teaching performance. (9) As I walked back to my office, the corridor clock caught my eye, and I nodded knowingly as I passed it by. And now here I am with an in-box full of e-mails, all expecting an instant response. I think people assume that the e-mail they sent to me is the only one I have received today! (10) Finally! The clock on my PC reminds me that the day has only just begun. It is only 10:25, and already I am timed out! I haven't even gotten to my voice mails, all neatly timed with precisely when people called me, what they want me to do, and when they would like me to do it and call them back. When we begin to pay attention to time, we very quickly come to realize just how powerful and formative it is for our lives. Time rules over pretty much everything that we do, have done, and are likely to do in the future. Humans are creatures who are ruled by time.

OBVIOUSNESS AND ODDNESS

There is an obviousness and an oddness about these basic observations on the power of time. When we think about the structure of our lives, it is obvious that time plays a central role in the formation of who we are and how we come to see ourselves and indeed to be ourselves in the world. Iain McGilchrist is quite correct: time is indeed the basic and inexorable context for meaningful human experience. That much seems undeniable. Nevertheless, it is rather odd that time should have such power, bearing in mind that we cannot see it, touch it, or even really name what it is in a way that draws out any kind of general agreement. Time rules over us, but what exactly is it that we think our multiple clocks actually capture? In his *Confessions*, St. Augustine asks a similar question:

> For what is time? Who can easily and briefly explain it? Who even in thought can comprehend it, even to the pronouncing of a word concerning it? But what in speaking do we refer to more familiarly and knowingly than time? And certainly we understand when we speak of it; we understand also when we hear it spoken of by another. What, then, is time? If no one ask of me, I know; if I wish to explain to him who asks, I know not.[3]

We know what time is because we experience it all around us as it shapes and forms us and gives our lives meaning, purpose, and a framework for direction. However, if we are asked to break it down and explain precisely what it is, the solidity of time seems simply to melt away and slip through our fingers.

THE MYSTERY OF TIME

Part of the problem is the fact that there are dimensions of time that are deeply mysterious. Certainly we can measure "it" and hypothesize about what "it" may or may not be. Depending on whether you are a scientist, a philosopher, an anthropologist, or a psychologist, you will have your own particular theory of time. It is, however, unlikely that you will find much consensus between or even within these disciplines. Time eludes consensus. A mystery is something that is hidden, something that is not clear or obvious to everyday logic. Mysteries evade our usual abilities to explain using the ideas, concepts, assumptions, and capacities that we might draw upon to solve an everyday dilemma. For example, the doctrine of the Trinity is inherently mysterious. The suggestion that God is one and yet simultaneously three—Father, Son, and Holy Spirit—is one of the deepest and most profound mysteries within the Christian tradition. It is central to Christian faith, yet it eludes and exhausts human reason and rationality. The mysterious nature of the Trinity does not mean that we can know nothing about God, only that we cannot know everything about God and that even that which we do know is gifted to us in and through the Spirit: "The mystery that has been kept hidden for ages and generations, but is now disclosed to the Lord's people" (Col 1:26 NIV). Theologically, mystery pertains to knowledge that is both hidden and revealed:

> At that time Jesus, full of joy through the Holy Spirit, said, "I praise you, Father, Lord of heaven and earth, because you have hidden these things from the wise and learned, and revealed them to little children. Yes, Father, for this is what you were pleased to do." (Luke 10:21 NIV)

For something to be mysterious does not mean that the subject of inquiry is either impenetrable or so esoteric as to be meaningless. Naming something as a mystery, in this sense, serves to point out the limits of human reason, the centrality of divine revelation and the gifted nature of human knowing. Naming something a mystery does not mean that it cannot be vital and transformative. Augustine considers time to be mysterious, unnameable, and owned by a God who inhabits time as a timeless, impassive Creator rather than as a time-bound sentient creature. Despite his claim not to know what time is, he nevertheless goes on to dedicate a significant section of his *Confessions* to wrestling with the nature of time. Time can be mysterious and at least partly accessible at precisely the same time. The key is to recognize that dealing with mystery is not simply a matter of logic, empirical evidence, and clever argument; it fundamentally involves humility, faith, and a willingness to accept divine gifts that one may not be able fully to comprehend or fully articulate.

A PRACTICAL THEOLOGY OF TIME

With this way of thinking about time as a basic foundational perspective, in this book I intend to offer a practical theological perspective on time.[4] As such, the book will seek both to reflect theologically on the issues concerned *and* to explore what they look like as they work themselves out within the individual and communal lives of the people of God. The underlying presumption is that thinking about God—theology—is intended for the service of God and ultimately is a way of enabling human beings to love God and one another more fully. The *Westminster Shorter Catechism* informs us that "the goal of human beings is to glorify God and to enjoy God forever."[5]

We might say something similar for the goals of theology: theology, properly focused, should be perceived as having the goal of enabling human beings to glorify God and to enjoy God forever. If God is love (1 John 4:8), then theology is all about the purposes of such love.

HOLDING THEORY AND PRACTICE TOGETHER

The problem, of course, is that theology is quite often *not* seen in such a light. Stephen Pattison astutely observes that

> over the last century and more, western theology has turned to the human and seen its task increasingly as understanding the creators of the ideas and discourse of theology rather than God God in God's self.[6]

This is a helpful observation. As one peruses the bustling market of theological books, there is clearly a propensity to see theology as reading *about* and *looking at* the ways in which people talk about God. Whether one is a Barthian, a Bonhoefferian, a Wesleyan, a Calvinist, or a Hauerwasian, the temptation is to spend time looking at the ideas of such scholars and reflecting on what they have to say about how we should understand and respond to God quite apart from whether such ways of thinking impact upon the faithfulness of our bodily lives. We can easily end up thinking like Barth but failing to act like Jesus.

The academic separation of systematic theology from practical theology functions as an example of the split between those who, it is perceived, talk and think about God and those who engage with the world where God is presumed by both to be acting. Within the academy at least, there is a tendency to downgrade anything that is prefixed by the word "practical." I frequently hear well-meaning colleagues telling me that they think the split between systematic theology and practical theology is nothing but an (over)reaction against certain strands of esoteric theological thinking. They tell me that I should really just be called a theologian. I rarely if ever hear systematic theologians telling me that they should actually be called practical theologians!

And yet Jesus informs us quite clearly that the center point of the Christian life is love. The most important love is our love for God, our Creator and the one who loves us first. This love compels us to love one another:

> "'Love the Lord your God with all your heart and with all your soul and with all your mind and with all your strength.' . . . 'Love your neighbour as yourself.' There is no commandment greater than these." (Mark 12:30-31 NIV)

Love is not a concept or an idea. The idea of love cannot be separated from the practice of love. True, conceptualizing love is an aspect of learning what love is. As we will see as this book moves on, our intellectual formulations matter, just as long as they serve the purposes of love. In a social context where love has multiple and contradictory meanings, it is important to have clarity of thought around what Christian love is. However, love is first and foremost a practice; it is something we do with the whole of our bodies, not just our minds. Love demands to be seen and felt before it can be believed. In a hypercognitive and often practical academic theological environment, it is easy to downgrade practice and experience. But to do so is to make a fundamental mistake: the experience of God's love *precedes* our understanding of it. God, who *is* love, loved the world long before the world knew it was loved.

> For he chose us in him before the creation of the world to be holy and blameless in his sight. (Eph 1:4 NIV)

The love of God is something we live into, not simply something we reflect upon. It is the subject of our lives, not life's object. If theology is for the purposes of love, propositional knowledge should not be separated from embodied practice.

In this book we will attempt to hold the center between theory and practice by bringing key theological ideas into critical conversation with the human experience of disability. In this way the book will take seriously insights from systematic theologies but locate them within a particular context that will test them and enable them to participate faithfully not only in the practices of the intellect (important as such practices are) but also in the practices of love as they are worked out by and within the whole people of God. The call to listen to experience and view individual theologians as aspects of a larger, more complex divine interaction among theology, church, and the contemporary world is a much more interesting prospect than simply knowing for knowing's sake. It is also much closer to the ethos of Jesus' command to love God, self, and neighbor that forms the heart of the gospel and surely forms the heart of the theological task.

To be clear, practical theology is not in any sense anti-intellectual. Throughout, the book will draw upon a variety of complex theological and philosophical ideas and perspectives as a way of understanding key issues pertaining to time and disability. The point is that such intellectual knowledge requires embodiment if it is faithfully to participate in the practices of love.

> Whoever does not love does not know God, because God is love. (1 John 4:8 NIV)

TIME AND DISABILITY

This book is about time, but it is also about human disability. As will become clear, the two are intricately interconnected. The language and imagery that people use around disability are replete with time-based metaphors and descriptions. Within medicine, time is central to the ways in which illness and disability are named and understood:

> Chronic fatigue, intermittent symptoms, frequency,
> incidence, relapse, prognosis, acquitted, congenital,
> developmental delay, terminal, acute.

Terms such as these place disability (and illness) within quite specific timelines, with assumptions and judgments being made in accordance with the temporal sensibilities of the physician and the implicit and explicit ways in which medical knowledge locates disability within time. Importantly, such timefull descriptions lay out an understanding of what normative progress in human beings *should* look like.

Disability theology, disability studies, and time

It is not just medicine that presumes a close relationship between disability and time. Both disability studies and disability theology draw on a variety of temporal discourses in their attempts to explicate the political and theological implications of disability. Take, for example, the idea of people being *temporarily able bodied.* Alison Kafer, speaking from a disability studies perspective, argues that the idea of temporarily able bodied people is designed

> to reveal "nondisabled" and "able-bodied" as temporal, and temporary, categories; think here of the "TAB" tag (temporarily able bodied), intended to remind nondisabled people that the able/disabled distinction is neither permanent nor impermeable. Disability studies' well-rehearsed mantra—whether by illness, age, or accident, all of us will live with disability at some point in our lives—encapsulates the notion suggesting that becoming disabled is "only a matter of time."[7]

Kafer correctly identifies the centrality of time for the idea of temporarily able bodiedness. All of us will grow into disability as time moves on (disability is only a matter of time). That being so, there is no fixed category that separates disability from so-called able bodiedness. The implication here (and the critical political point) is that disability issues are not only of interest to people living with disabilities; they are of interest to *all* people because at some stage all people will become disabled. It is just a matter of time.[8]

Are there disabilities in heaven?

Likewise, some of the key arguments within disability theology pivot on issues of time. Those who would argue that a person's disability is part of who they are and that they will carry them over into the eschaton work with a particular argument about time. The discussion revolves around the value of disabled bodies in-the-now and whether that value and these particular bodily or psychological features will be preserved in the eschaton—that is, the time of Jesus' return, a time when time as we know it will end.

> And God will wipe away every tear from their eyes; there shall be no more death, nor sorrow, nor crying. There shall be no more pain, for the former things have passed away. (Rev 21:4 NKJV)

For some disabled people such as the sociologist and theologian Nancy Eiesland, some of the former things, namely her disability, will not pass away in the eschaton. Quite the opposite; for Eiesland it is vitally important that her disability remains with her in her resurrection body. Without it, she believes she could not recognize herself.[9]

> My disability had taught me who I am and who God is. What would it mean to be without this knowledge? Would I be absolutely unknown to myself in heaven, and perhaps even unknown to God?[10]

As will become clear in chapter 11 of this book, the idea that anything about us is determinative of who we are is theologically questionable. Nevertheless, Eiesland perceives her disability as a formative, vital dimension of who she is. Without it she cannot imagine who she would be. Healing would make her a stranger to herself and to others.

There are no disabilities in heaven

If the "are there disabilities in heaven" conversation is timefull, so also is its opposite: "disability should be healed." Those who choose healing as an appropriate response to the presence of disability exhibit a desire to get rid of disabilities (eradicate what was) to create a "new person" in-the-present (radical pre-eschaton transformation), in anticipation of that time when we will all be transformed (what will be). From this perspective, healing rejects the meaning and significance of the past, provides the person who lives with a disability with a new identity and a new future. The general assumption tends to be that what was before—that time when the disability was with us—was meaningless and has been overpowered and eradicated (through healing), in order that a new era can come upon the (formerly) disabled person wherein we can live without the burden of disability in anticipation of the ultimate transformation that will occur in the eschaton. We can now act as if the "then person"—the disabled person—is inferior to the "new person." We celebrate the passing of the disabled person and welcome the new (temporarily) able-bodied person.

The problem with such a perspective, of course, is that it does not take seriously Eiesland's key point: *disability is a meaningful and formative aspect of who a person is*. It is not as easy as it may seem simply to discard a person's disability as if one were somehow lancing a boil. Disabilities, like many other bodily aspects, are identity forming. As a man, for example, the fact that I exist in a testosterone-saturated body is not a by-the-way. It shapes my sense of being in the world in deep ways. Take that from me, and I am in a real sense quite different. Eiesland's point about the connection between our bodily form and our self-perception is important and not confined to issues of disability. We may not, as we shall see, be wholly identified by our bodies or our minds, but they certainly affect our perceptions of who we are in quite profound ways.

Frances Young draws out this point nicely in her reflections on her son Arthur, who has a profound and complex intellectual disability. Thinking through whether healing makes any sense within the context of Arthur's life, she ponders:

> There is no "ideal Arthur" somehow trapped in his damaged physical casing. He is a psychosomatic whole. . . . What sense would it make to hope for "healing" in cases like this? . . . There are twenty-two years of learning process that he has missed out on. In what sense could we expect normality, even if the physical problems were sorted out? . . . Arthur has personality at his own limited level. . . . Healed he would be a different person.[11]

Arthur is Arthur. Taking away his disability and implanting a whole new set of abilities would make him someone else, a person with no meaningful memories, no past, and a very difficult and confused present and future. Unless his new, healed brain came with a set of preconceived memories, he would have absolutely none of the skills that time alone brings. He would be unable to think, walk, talk, or function in any way that someone of his age would be expected to. All of this would have to be learned. If one were to argue that God might implant a whole new set of capacities and a whole new set of memories and ideas into Arthur, then one would be left with Young's dilemma: In what sense would this new person be Arthur? It would seem that some of the central arguments in disability theology are inextricably linked with time.

TIME AND THE SOCIAL MODEL OF DISABILITY

The issue of time is also a dimension that seems to be oddly missing from current conceptions of the social model of disability. Susie Parr, Kevin Paterson, and Carole Pound have pointed out that "the disabling nature of time, and the fact that the rearrangement of social space [as per the intentions of the social model] is not always the answer to every problem faced by disabled people."[12] They suggest that the social model of disability requires a temporal dimension. Their point is that the way in which society uses time and the presumptions that it makes about time can be deeply inhibiting for the life possibilities of people with disabilities. Indeed, our practices of time can be deeply oppressive and excluding in terms of the barriers they create. Parr et al. observe the ways in which the lives of people with disabilities are ruled and deeply affected by implicit and explicit temporal codes and norms that frequently serve to disadvantage and exclude them. Take, for example, the "simple" act of conversation:

> Conversation can take a variety of forms (small talk, chat, discussion, gossip and so on). Each has a specific timescale for participation based on the communication style of non-disabled people. . . . There is what might be described as an *etiquette of timing* that structures everyday social encounters.[13]

Everyday conversation styles and expectations are based on certain assumptions and a form of etiquette (manners) that assumes a degree of conformity to temporal norms and an ability to understand time, speed, pace, and timing. If someone is either too fast or too slow according to these implicit and explicit conventions, they are judged "socially incompetent":

> One must keep in sync with the tempo and pace of a conversation. Any interaction that flouts these conventions is viewed as an embarrassing failure. People with communicational impairments are often excluded from conversation and chit chat because the etiquette of these situations does nothing to allow them time to express what they wish to say. . . . [T]he taken for granted nature of the rhythms and pace of everyday life helps to bring about a disability.[14]

Communicational disabilities exist in time and find their construction and meaning within the social construction of time. It is remarkably easy to wander into what we might call "casual disablism," wherein simply by responding to one another according to the timing of accepted social mores and intuitive norms we exclude people with certain forms of disability. The almost irresistible desire to finish the sentence of someone who is perceived to be "slow of speech,"[15] to walk quickly ahead of those whose bodies move slowly, or to downgrade and ignore (not find time for) those considered to be "slow in thought" is indicative of the way in which perceptions of time tempt individuals, communities, and cultures to demand certain tempos, rhythms, cadences, and timings as criteria for worth, value, meaningful participation, and belonging. The connection between time and disability is fascinating, vital, and obvious when we begin to notice it.

TIME AND THE FRAGILE BRAIN

This book might best be conceived of as an extended meditation on what it means to live faithfully within the time that God has gifted to us. In the light of the experiences of people living with certain forms of neurological disability, the book seeks to offer a theological reimagining of the nature and purpose of time and in so doing offer some pointers for faithful living and the development of genuine communities of belonging. The primary focus of the book will be on forms of disability that emerge from some kind of damage to the brain. The reason I have chosen to focus on various forms of brain damage is important. At a personal level, I have spent a good deal of my professional life working with and alongside people with brain damage. As a nurse working in the area of mental health, I frequently encountered people whose lives and personalities had been radically changed through stroke, encroaching brain tumors, or traumatic brain injury. The question of who they were after their incident or accident and the continuity with who they are now was always a source of uncertainty, tension, confusion, and grief. For people of faith, such uncertainty could be excruciatingly painful. Christine Bryden's plea "Who will I be when I die?"[16] pretty much sums up the lament of both the sufferer and those who are forced to watch others suffering.

Similarly, when I moved into the field of intellectual disabilities, the issue of damage to the brain or a lack of neurological development once again filled my horizons. As I spent time with people living with profound and complex intellectual disabilities—those people for whom words and symbols, the primary ways in which many religions communicate their understandings of God, meant nothing—I often wondered what it might mean to encounter God without words and what it might mean to be wordless in a world where words seem to be central to most of what we do. Part of my problem, of course, is that I am a Presbyterian. For Presbyterians everything comes through words. Some have suggested that the Word became flesh and then became words again in Presbyterian worship! Being with people who have no words was the beginning of my conversion to the fullness of God's love and the wonder of God's communicational possibilities.

As a hospital chaplain, I spent many hours alongside people whose brains were deteriorating such that memory and cognition were no longer central to the way in which they encountered the world. As I watched people with advanced dementia sing and worship, I could not help but be caught up in the deep mystery of what it might mean to worship Jesus when you have forgotten who he is. Holding the hand of someone with advanced dementia and coming to realize that they are not someone who "used to be," but someone who is important in the present and indeed has a vocation that will lead them into the future was, to say the least, humbling, challenging, and quite beautiful.

I did not then know about the deep connections between these experiences of brain damage and the redemptive power of God's time, but I did come to know that damage to our brains does not take away our humanness. Quite the opposite, it sometimes provided me an opportunity to expand my understanding of what it means to be human. I began to realize that who we are is not the sum of our neurological configurations. There is a sense in which this book is working out formally ideas that I already knew intuitively.

Hypercognition and Neuromania

There is another important reason the book focuses on issues around forms of disability that emerge from changes within the brain. Brain damage (or a lack of development of the brain) does not simply have to do with neurology. The social model of disability informs us that disabilities are not free-floating "natural kinds" that occur in the same way in every place and time. A significant portion of the experience of disability is shaped and formed by the context within which a person experiences their particular form of impairment. Each society and each context a person encounters raises specific disabling issues for people who are perceived as somehow impaired or different. Within post-Enlightenment Western cultures, the brain has come to take on a particular set of meanings that clearly transcend the particularities of individual neurological change. Intuitively, we might assume that brain damage in all of its different forms has primarily to do with neurological damage: our brains are damaged, and therefore we cannot do certain things that others can do. At first sight such impairment seems obviously biological and clearly rooted within the individual's particular neurological configuration. However, when we place this experience within what Stephen Post has described as a *hypercognitive culture*[17]—that is, a culture that has a tendency to value individualism, autonomy, rational thinking, speed of thought, memory, and cognition over such qualities as love, connection, community, slowness, dependence, and vulnerability—it very quickly becomes clear that neurology is not the only story in town.

The brain has come to acquire a quite particular cultural meaning, a meaning that assumes that this particular organ is somehow superior to any or all of the other organs of which human beings are comprised. The brain has become the center point not only for our understanding of the neuromechanics of bodies but also for certain understandings relating to the essence of who and what we are as human beings. It is stating the obvious to observe that our brains are important. The computing power of our brain is startling. Its ability to process information via billions of neurons and synapses that fire, connect, and reconnect as we are configured and reconfigured in ways that both mirror and shape our experiences is, to say the least, quite amazing. As our knowledge of neurology has developed, we have been able to peer into the deepest, most intimate regions of the brain. Neurotechnology can provide us with detailed pictures of the brain that show exactly which part of the brain is deemed responsible for particular actions, specific experiences, particular thoughts, and individual feelings and emotions. We have even been told that such science has revealed to us the origins of God: the so-called God spot within the brain that, if we believe the hype, processes those experiences that we consider to be religious and spiritual.[18] Everything, including our sense of self, our identity alongside our perceptions of the divine, it is argued, is located within the brain. The explanatory power of this "big story" of the brain can easily lead us to succumb to the presumption that somehow "we are our brains" or "our brains are us."[19] Raymond Tallis has described this way of thinking about the brain as *neuromania*: the tendency to see the brain as the only path to understanding.[20] When this happens the feeling that one should equate humanness with neural soundness becomes almost irresistible.

This "big story" of the brain feeds neatly into the cultural narrative that informs us that such constructions as intellect, reason, and cognition are central to what it means to be a worthwhile human being. Descartes' dictum *cogito ergo sum* (I think, therefore I am)[21] has had a profound influence on Western perceptions of what constitutes the core of humanness. *We are because we think, and we think because we have brains*. Of course, the idea that "I think, therefore I am" is not neutral. We have to be able to think in quite particular ways: to remember items in sequence; to articulate our thinking in ways that are publicly understandable and acceptable, that is, to be able to use particular forms of language; to be logical and coherent in our thinking;

and to retain the same style of thinking over time. If I still think the way I did when I was four, then I may well think and therefore be, but culturally my being will not be valued in the same way as those whose thinking has progressed over time. "I think, therefore I am" as a principal for humanness is heavily weighted against certain forms of thinking and inevitably against certain thinkers. This combined with ideas of radical individualism, inviolable autonomy, and a form of economic competitiveness that presents value in terms of effective use of time and measurable productivity sets a very particular social, cultural, and anthropological setting for experiencing brain damage. Such a culture inevitably constructs brain damage in a quite particular way: *negatively*. Damage to the brain easily becomes perceived as damage to our humanness. The conversation around brain damage turns out to be a conversation around what it means to be human. The stakes are high.

This book will make an attempt to displace the centrality of the brain as the essence of our humanness and replace it with the centrality of Jesus. *We are not our brains!* Brains may be a necessary aspect of being human, but they are certainly not sufficient. Damage to the brain is not damage to our humanness. Quite the opposite. Theological reflection on the experience of those living with damaged brains can be a way of enhancing our understanding of what it means to be a human and to live humanly. The key to such transformation lies in a reimagining of time, an undertaking that forms the central task of this book. In God's time all things look different, including our brains.

CHAPTER OVERVIEW

In chapter 1 we will explore the power of the clock and examine the roots of "clock time" and how and why it has come to have so much cultural power over Westerners. Here we will explore some of the ways in which time has become fragmented and dislocated from its religious roots. Time has become a commodity to be bought and sold rather than a gift to be received, cherished, and valued. It has come to be valued for its own sake rather than for the sake of love. Within such a temporal context, those who cannot keep up with the demands of time become vulnerable.

Chapter 2 explores the cultural and historical roots that underlie the justification of euthanasia for people with advanced dementia and abortion and prenatal testing for disability. It draws out the ways in which such attitudes find themselves deeply immersed in a quite particular understanding of time that emerges from a complex social history that is deeply rooted in thinking about time. Through an exploration of the social and evolutionary roots of perceptions of disability, the chapter shows that changing perceptions of time were central to changing perceptions of and responses to disability. This complex social and cultural history underlies many contemporary perceptions of and responses to disability. The way that we have come to understand disability is fundamentally a matter of time.

In chapter 3 we develop a brief theology of time. Beginning with Augustine's suggestion that time is a creature—that is, that time comes into existence when God creates the world—the chapter develops a theology of time that presumes that the gift of time is in fact a gift of love. Time is intended for love and indeed is an aspect of God's love for God's creation. However, time has fallen. The abusive and oppressive nature of time is indicative of its status as a fallen creature. Time requires redemption. In Christ the redemption of time has been initiated. The chapter draws out the radical differences between clock time and God's time. God's time differs significantly from the time of the clock. It is not linear or progressive in the way that clock time is. It is mysteriously simultaneous. Past and future intermingle in ways that are dissonant and glorious. "Jesus Christ is the same yesterday and today and forever" (Heb 13:8 NIV). The time of the clock is linear and unrelentingly progressive, moving forward toward a goal that has no name. God's time is holistic, all embracing, mysterious, and ever present. This chapter lays down a foundational understanding of the nature and purpose of God's time that guides the remainder of the book.

Chapter 4 begins to explore the ways in which engagement with disability can help to transform our understanding of time. Chapter 3 lays down a theoretical understanding of God's time; here we begin to see something of what such a theology of time *looks* like as it is revealed in and through the experiences of people living with different forms of disability. In opposition to the scheduled, controlled, and fast time that is brought to us by the time of the clock, we discover that living in God's time looks and feels quite different. In Christ, time is being redeemed, and redeemed time has a particular shape and form. God's time is created, gifted, slow, generous, gentle, and designed to enhance the purposes of love. God's time does not seek to burden people with schedules, deadlines, targets, and competition. The tradition of Sabbath reminds us that God is a God who rests and commands rest, not a god who thrives on busyness, anxiety, and exhaustion. God's time dictates the speed of love; it refuses to race past those who are moving more slowly. It always finds time for people. In clock time people who are slow of thought or awkward in movement are likely to find others passing them by on the other side of the road. In God's time there is always time to sit together and learn the meaning of love. When we begin to understand what it means to reside within God's time, we are opened up to a whole new way of being in the world, a way that not only respects the differences that disability brings but, in a sense, requires it. In God's time the difference that disability brings is perceived quite differently.

Chapter 5 begins to examine what the developing practical theology of time and disability looks like as we engage with the lives of people with profound and complex intellectual disabilities. It argues that we need to move beyond inclusion to discipleship. The inclusion agenda is helpful in that it enables people to be present within a variety of communities. However, inclusion does not make any demands on people to relate or ultimately to love those who have been included. By moving the conversation from inclusion to discipleship, the chapter seeks to answer the question, What does it mean to be a disciple of Jesus and not, at least cognitively, to know anything about Jesus? The chapter offers a deep challenge to hypercognitive models of knowing God and being a disciple and in so doing opens up space to the body of Christ truly to be Jesus' body, a place where there is "no Gentile or Jew, circumcised or uncircumcised, barbarian, [able bodied or disabled], Scythian, slave or free, but Christ is all, and is in all" (Col 3:11 NIV).

Chapter 6 builds on this shift into discipleship and draws it into the developing theology of time through an exploration of providence, vocation, and calling. The idea of vocation is a profoundly timefull concept. To discover one's vocation is to come to understand what it means to participate faithfully in God's providential movement toward and within creation: to find your place in God's time. Providence relates to God's storying of the history of creation and making sense of what it means to participate in God's time. The chapter argues that people with profound intellectual disabilities have a vocation and a call from Jesus that enables them to participate in God's redemption of time in quite particular ways. The body of Christ is called to ensure that the nature, substance, and texture of that calling is recognized and operationalized.

Chapters 7 and 8 explore the significance of time within the context of advanced dementia. By reflecting on the experiences of people with advanced dementia, these chapters push strongly against any suggestion that people somehow disappear when they begin to forget. It offers a rethinking of standard accounts of memory and offers an alternative to the view that memory has to do with recalling experiences from the past and bringing them into the present with a view to pursuing particular futures. The chapters offer a different model of memory. Recall memory assumes the presence of an autobiographical self. But memory is much more than recalling events. Memory has to do with the ways of the heart, and the heart is not bound by time or damaged neurology. The chapters reframe memory and offer a radically new approach—the memory of the heart—which emerges naturally from within the simultaneity of God's time.

Chapters 9, 10, and 11 focus on the theological and timefull issues that emerge from the experience of acquired brain damage. Dietrich Bonhoeffer reflects that the horror of time is that you can never go back. Once something has happened, you cannot "unhappen" it. The previous chapters develop a positive perspective on time. These chapters explore the more difficult and tragic dimensions of time. The horror of time is well illustrated in the sometimes radical changes that we encounter when our brains are damaged through trauma or change. Chapter 9 draws on the experience of Floyd Skloot, someone who encountered a virus that so damaged his brain that he felt he had become a different person. The chapter lays out the contours of the experience of brain damage and the practical implications of the various changes that people endure.

Chapter 10 picks up on Hans Reinders' temporal dynamic of change from "before" to "after" in the context of acquired brain damage. It argues that the simple temporal movement from before to after is deceptive. Who we were during the time before our accident or incident is not quite as straightforward as it might at first appear. Likewise, the time after is practically and theologically complicated. Working with Paul's assertion that who we are is in fact hidden in Christ (Col 1:26) alongside Karl Barth's idea of soteriological objectivism—the suggestion that our identity is never defined by who we think we are but rather by who we are in Christ—the chapter develops a theology of identity that indicates that within God's time the differences and personality changes that accompany brain damage look very different than they do in models that view such experiences from within linear clock time.

Chapter 11 begins to draw out what such theological reflection on acquired brain injury might actually look like in practice. This chapter is written with my friend and colleague Tonya Whaley, who has gone through the experience of traumatic brain damage and personality change. The chapter explores the ways in which ritual can provide a way of bridging the gap between who persons perceived themselves to be before their brain damage and who they might perceive themselves to be now. Ritual is deeply timefull, drawing the past and the present together and enabling the creation of a new future. Ritual is a way of enabling people to enter into God's time and find timefull healing and restoration as they realize that they are safe and held gently in Christ.

WRITING FROM THE HEART

Before we begin our exploration of time, it is worthwhile to reflect for a moment on the style of this book. A good deal of academic theology is clearly oriented primarily toward the more rational, propositional aspect of our humanness. There is, of course, nothing wrong with approaching theology from this perspective, unless one assumes that this is all that theology is. I have previously suggested that that there is a basic split within theology between theory and practice, a split that requires bridging. Systematic theology tends to focus on propositional knowledge, and practical theology has a tendency to focus on experiential knowledge. An overemphasis on either leads to distortion. To pay proper attention to the subject of theology in relation to disability and time, this split has to be bridged. One of the intentions of this book is to explore ways in which these two approaches to looking at and doing theology might be brought together in a manner that holds the center and offers genuine possibilities for a holistic theology of disability and time. I have therefore deliberately written this book in a way that takes seriously both theology and practice. The style of writing used in the book will therefore endeavor to stimulate and blend formal logical orientation to the issues involved with the experiential, narrative, creative, imaginative, and evocative attention that is required if we are to succeed in our task of loving God, neighbor, and self. I hope and pray that the center can hold.

I

TIME AND DISABILITY

1

Thinking about Time
The Tyranny of the Clock

> I am the Alpha and the Omega, the First and the Last, the Beginning and the End.
>
> (Rev 22:13 NIV)

Time is an elusive concept. Despite its centrality to all that we do, there is no real consensus as to what it is. Philosophy, science, theology, psychology, anthropology, medicine, and personal experience all create and narrate different stories about what time may or may not be. For Aristotle, time was movement; if there is no movement, there can be no time. Time is interactive; it requires a mover.[1] According to this view, God is the unmoved mover, the one who moves other objects without being moved by any prior action. Sir Isaac Newton believed that time should be viewed as an external, universal entity that runs along independently without any human involvement or interference. Absolute time and absolute space exist as independent aspects of objective reality.[2] In opposition to Newton, Albert Einstein argued that time is relative and not absolute. If we travel fast enough, time slows down. In principle, one person who had traveled very quickly but under the speed of light would have lived through several days. The one who had not been traveling at such speed would have lived out several minutes. Their experiences of time would have occurred at *exactly the same time*. In Einstein's theory, the faster one travels, the slower time passes relative to someone who is not traveling at such speed. It is interesting to notice that were one of them to have traveled at the speed of light, time would cease and the traveler would be trapped in eternal timelessness. Einstein could never comprehend why other physicists did not accept the idea of timelessness.[3]

Within the world of anthropology, we discover that time is not only relative to speed, but is also relative to culture. Time means different things for different people across cultures. The way that time is understood in Guatemala is quite different from the way it is understood in Manhattan. Time has a different meaning in industrialized cultures, where the rhythm of the clock provides the shape and form of people's lives, than it does in certain agricultural societies that are much more in tune with the movement of the sun and the changing of the seasons.[4] Within the area of mental health, psychiatrists and researchers point to the ways in which time slows down when one is depressed,[5] speeds up when one is manic,[6] and seems to move ever more quickly as we age.[7] For many of us, time as we experience it day by day at a personal level is simply the way in which we pattern and structure our lives in order to help us make sense of the daily flow of our existence. Most of us have a fairly pragmatic approach to time: it is there to be used. It does not make much difference what time *is* in and of itself; what matters is what time *does*—that is, the ways in which it affects our lives, structuring our days, guiding our plans for the future, and properly placing the past in ways that make our present and future clearer. Although, in our more reflective moments, we may be curious as to why spending time with someone whom we love seems to pass so quickly and what it is about hanging out with boring people that makes us feel we are trapped in never-ending time, many of us do not spend much time thinking about time, at least not in dislocated conceptual terms.

It seems clear that time is not a fixed and obvious concept that is agreed upon by everyone. Time is a flexible concept that tends to find its meaning and definition according to the particular disciplinary or epistemological context within which it is being observed, lived out, or reflected upon. Our understandings of time are scientifically and philosophically diverse, hermeneutically complex, culturally bound, and deeply value laden, reflecting a variety of worldviews, morals, standards, plausibility structures, and learned assumptions. In a very real sense, there is a variety of kinds of time.

THE TIME OF THE CLOCK

Within Western cultures and those cultures influenced by the West, one particular kind of time has been particularly influential and formative of perceptions of time: *the time of the clock* (o'clock). The time of the clock has quite distinct features. It is assumed to be *linear, dynamic, and forward facing* (constantly moving forward), *measurable* (observable and open to quantification), and *controllable* (open to commodification, manipulation, and management). Time is assumed to be something that can be broken down into small, practical components that can then be used as currency within various "marketplaces," be they economic, political, relational, psychological, or spiritual. Time is perceived as fragmented, commodifiable, scheduled, and, above all, instrumental. Benjamin Whorf describes this perception of time as *Standard Average European Time* (SAET). Standard Average European Time contains a number of key features, including

> an insistence on punctuality (that one be "on point" on the timeline, as they have promised), synchronicity (the coordinated positioning of several people simultaneously on the timeline), historiography and paleontology (the exact locating of past events on the timeline), and, most revealingly, a plethora of behaviors like "wasting time" (as one might waste perfectly good food), "selling" and "buying" time (as one would sell or buy apples or wheat), and "saving time" (by shortening the distance travelled on the timeline to accomplish a task). All of these in turn imply a capacity to "measure" time (as one would measure any object with extension) by counting off seconds, minutes, or hours.[8]

Rather than life being viewed as a continuous, meaningful whole wherein each moment latches seamlessly onto and into the next, SAET separates and compartmentalizes the various aspects of our past, present, and future lives. This mode of time creates the impression that time is fragmented: we have family time, leisure time, market time, study time, prayer time, quiet time, devotional time. Time is created as a series of dislocated fragmented moments held together by the transient necessities of human desire. The temporal anticipation of external meaning and eschatological hope so central to religious perceptions of existence are presumed to belong to a different age, a different time. The link between the units of time that SAET and its derivatives create is not devotion to a creator God who holds all time in God's hands and is steering creation toward redemption: "My times are in your hands; deliver me from the hands of my enemies, from those who pursue me" (Ps 31:15 NIV).

Instead, the link between fragments of time is shaped and determined by human desire and the incessantly moving hands of the clock. The rhythm of our lives is regular, mechanical, and, above all, organized. The fact that we have to "schedule in" prayer time or "make room" for quiet time is indicative that the fragmentation of time might be reflected in an unconscious and pernicious fragmentation of our souls.

Nestled at the heart of this way of conceiving time is a relatively simple piece of machinery: *the clock*. The development of clocks, and the creation of the mechanical clock in particular, has been one of the most powerful shapers of Western understandings of time. Clocks, in all of their different forms, capture, systemize, externalize, and display the movement of time. It is clocks that make time *feel* real. One of the reasons that time feels so real is because clocks enable us to think we can see it. The real power of clocks lies not so much in what they do—record the movement of temporal cycles lasting for twelve or twenty-four hours—but in what they represent: the impression that we can *control* time. When we look at a clock, we imagine that we can see time. When we see something, we are able to name it. When we can name something, we feel that we can control it. Whereas previous to the centrality of the clock in Western thinking about time, time would have been gauged by the seasons or the sun and the moon—that is, things that we can have no control over—with the coming of the clock, controlling time becomes not only possible but necessary.

Clocks concretize time and enable us to believe that we know what it is and that we can control it. They also give the impression that time is moving in a single direction: *forward*. As the hands of our clocks (or the digital equivalent), pass from one–two–three o'clock, so the feeling of unrelenting linear temporal advancement irresistibly seeps into our psyche. Clocks provide people with apparent empirical evidence that time exists, that it is moving, and that it has a forward and onward direction. The various changes that come to us with aging seem to provide further proof that the forward movement of time is relentless, unstoppable, uncontrollable. Clock time may have a fundamentally forward dynamic, but it has no inherent meaning. It relentlessly moves forward, toward no particular goal. The movement of time is assumed to be open and undetermined by anything other than human desire and temporal aspirations. By "open," I mean that there is no fixed end point or goal. A Christian understanding might see time as moving towards a time when God "will wipe every tear from their eyes. There will be no more death or mourning or crying or pain, for the old order of things has passed away" (Rev 21:4 NIV). "Open time" means that the outcome of time is determined by what people want. As such it is open to the whims of human desire. God's time is meaningful and directed; clock time is open and uncertain in terms of its outcome. Unbridled clock time demands that "we make the best of *our* time," because "we can't get it back." Time, however, has not always been perceived in such ways.

A TIME BEFORE THE SECOND HAND

Clocks in various forms have been around for a long time. However, Robert Levine points out that the clock and clock time as we currently understand it are relatively new developments. From early times astronomers were able to trace years and to some degree months. However, the idea of hours is a relatively modern creation. The creation of minutes and seconds is even more recent.[9] The first clocks were developed in the European medieval age by Benedictine monks. St. Benedict placed a great emphasis on activity and order. Each day was scheduled with various spiritual activities occurring at particular times during the day.[10] To ensure that everyone commenced each activity at the same time, a system of bells was conceived to help hold the shape of the day and the conformity of activities: "Bells pealed, jangled, and tinkled throughout the day, hurrying the monks along to their appointed rounds. The most important bells were those that announced the eight canonical hours when the monks celebrated the Divine Offices."[11] To ensure that everyone complied with the schedule of the day, the Benedictines "developed a tool that could provide them with greater accuracy and precision of time measurement than could be obtained by reliance on bells and bell ringers. They invented the mechanical clock."[12] These clocks were used by the Benedictines to ensure conformity to their daily spiritual practices. Neil Postman observes:

> The impetus behind the invention was to provide a more or less precise regularity to the routines of the monasteries, which required, among other things, seven periods of devotion during the course of the day. The bells of the monastery were to be rung to signal the canonical hours; the mechanical clock was the technology that could provide precision to these rituals of devotion.[13]

The original mechanical clocks therefore had a quite specific purpose: *to enable people to structure their lives in ways that were faithful to their beliefs and their spiritual way of life*. Levine informs us:

> Before this new invention [the mechanical clock], monks had mostly relied on hourglasses, which suffered from the inconvenience of needing to be turned regularly. In some monasteries, in fact, a designated monk had to stay up all night to keep the hourglass going until it was time for morning prayers or work. The first clocks were developed to simply sound bells at the appointed prayer hours. Most of these early clocks, which became community centerpieces, didn't even have hands or hours marked on their faces. They were designed not so much to show the time as to sound it. The Middle English word *clok* derived from Middle

> Dutch and German words for bell. The earliest mechanical timepieces were not technically considered clocks unless they sounded bells. It was several centuries before dials were placed on clocks, and the first dials used only hour hands.[14]

A clock that did not sound a bell was not considered to be a clock. Like the Muslim muezzin or the Christian church bell, these clocks had a particular meaning, purpose, and intention: *to call the religious to spend time with God*. Time had a purpose beyond the mundane and the instrumental. The chief end of time was to facilitate the glorification of God. Time's function and purpose was to ensure that humans remained faithful to their duty to worship God. The mechanical clock was a device brought into existence specifically in the service of God's people. It enabled people to spend their time faithfully.

CLOCKS WITH NO HANDS

These first mechanical clocks had no dials. All they did was sound a bell on the hour. This is not inconsequential in terms of the kind of time they created and visualized. Clocks without hands, and particularly clocks without second hands, create a world with no minutes and no seconds, a world in which the idea of *punctuality* had not yet been invented:

> Not until the late seventeenth century did the word "punctual," which formerly described a person who was a stickler for details of conduct, come to describe someone who arrived exactly at the appointed time. Only a century after that did the word "punctuality" first appear in the English language as it is used today.[15]

Monks were not expected to be punctual; they were expected to be *faithful*. Both punctuality and faithfulness require that the monk be on time, but the motivation for each is quite different. Punctuality relates simply to routine and order; one is punctual because the system requires one to be. Faithfulness relates to one's desire to please God through one's routine practices of worship. If a monk was late for the spiritual devotions, the abbot would not be waiting at the door pointing at his watch shouting, "You are five minutes late!" (not least because he would not have had a watch—time had not yet become a personal commodity). The problem would have been conceived as relating not to punctuality as we might conceive of it within SAET, but rather to such vices as sloth, spiritual weakness, a lack of discipline, and/or sinfulness. Not arriving on time would be perceived not in terms of bad timekeeping but as a spiritual error or weakness. The clock was intended to ensure the development of faithful habits, rather than good timekeeping. These early mechanical clocks created an understanding of time quite different from that of Standard Average European Time.

EVENT TIME

Benedictine time was not premised on promptness, punctuality, and productivity in the way that SAET would much later conceive of our relationship with time. Such ideas would not emerge until clocks were accurately able to measure small units of time. Only then "would the idea of being 'on time' or apologizing for being 'five minutes late' become meaningful."[16] The focus of this kind of time was on the meaning of the various *events* that occurred during the day. Benedictine time was *event* time.

Thomas Hylland Eriksen points out that traditional cultures are marked by event-driven time:

> Events regulate the passage of time, not the other way around. If a traveler, or an ethnographer, to an African village wonders when a certain event will take place, the answer may be: "When everything is ready." Not, in other words, "at a quarter to five."[17]

Within the monastery it would have been the *events* (daily and hourly spiritual practices) and their spiritual significance that were deemed important. The early Benedictine clocks were intended to capture time in terms of events and spiritual practices rather than to capture discrete, abstract units of time that could be extrapolated from the particularities of any given situation and used for the glory of human beings. Without minutes and seconds, time was seen to have a wholeness and a sense of purpose within which the events of the day served as constant reminders that time belongs to God.

It is certainly the case that the Benedictines scheduled their days and that this was seen as a revolutionary idea. The typical peasant serf in medieval Europe would not have understood the concept of scheduling: "A day then was roughly divided into three sectors, sunrise, high noon, and sunset. The only reminder, says Lawrence Wright, were 'the seeding and harvest bell that called them to work, the sermon bell and the curfew bell.'"[18]

Creating a day wherein tasks were done in a certain order at particular times of the day would have sounded more than a little unusual to such folks. However, Benedictine scheduling had nothing to do with productivity in the way that we understand such a term in postindustrial capitalist societies. The particular events that the clock scheduled had to do with holding and shaping the day in such a way that sacred values, spiritual concerns, and mundane issues could be seen as occurring within God's time and according to God's purpose. The development of these early mechanical clocks emerged in an attempt to bind the monks into the timefullness of God. Spiritual time was not scheduled into the day. Each aspect of every day was conceived as irresistibly and irrefutably spiritual. Each event was seen as participating in a timefull whole within which the clock was a reminder of and a call toward a higher power.

HANDS, MINUTES, AND SECONDS

These original clocks were meant to regulate spiritual practices within the monastery, a function that they performed effectively. However, Postman points out that

> what the monks did not foresee was that the clock is a means not merely of keeping track of the hours but also of synchronizing and controlling the actions of men. And thus, by the middle of the fourteenth century, the clock had moved outside the walls of the monastery, and brought a new and precise regularity to the life of the workman and the merchant.[19]

Within Europe Rifkin observes, "Giant clocks became the centerpiece of city life. Erected in the middle of the town square, they soon replaced the church bells as the rallying point and reference point for coordinating the complex interactions of urban existence."[20] In this way time was placed at the heart of community life. But time, it was a-changin':

> By the sixteenth century, clocks were chiming on the quarter hour and some were being constructed with dials to demarcate the passing of each hour. In the mid-1600s the pendulum was invented, providing a much more exacting and reliable timing mechanism.[21]

Around this time the minute hand came into existence, followed by the invention of the second hand, which emerged in the first decades of the eighteenth century as a way of enabling astronomers, navigators, and doctors to make more accurate measurements. The idea of minutes and seconds was quite a late development within the European history of time. While the idea of minutes, hours, and seconds had been talked about by mathematicians from the fourteenth century onward, clocks were not precise enough for it to be a concern to the general public until around the sixteenth century. When these ideas found themselves epitomized by the mechanical clock, which, as mentioned, had now gained a good deal of social power, the possibility of a revised temporal consciousness became inevitable.

Punctuality now became an option:

> To become "regular as clockwork" became the highest values of the new industrial age. Without the clock, industrial life would not have been possible. The clock conditioned the human mind to perceive time as external, autonomous, continuous, exacting, quantitative, and divisible. In so doing, it prepared the way for a production mode that operated by the same set of temporal standards.[22]

The emerging bourgeois class of merchants grasped the double-handed mechanical clock and ran with it with frantic economical urgency. Postman puts it thus: " 'The mechanical clock,' as Lewis Mumford wrote, 'made possible the idea of regular production, regular working hours and a standardized product.' In short, without the clock, capitalism would have been quite impossible."[23] Hauerwas draws on Jaques Le Goff's analysis of time, work, and culture in the Middle Ages[24] to make the observation that changes in time led to the eventual marginalization of the church:

> Only with the organization of commercial networks in the twelfth century did time become an object of exact measurement. First, the merchant communes acquired the right to have bells marking the day differently from the monastery. This development was the forerunner of the manufacture of more accurate clocks that signaled that the unit of labor would be the hour rather than the day. According to Le Goff, this change separated the time in which the merchant worked professionally from the time in which the merchant lived religiously. Le Goff suggests that the church, at least for a while, was able to keep the times together by prohibiting usury, just to the extent that the prohibition depended on the presumption that time could not be sold since time was a gift held in common. Increasingly, however, the clock undercut the presumption that time is a common good not to be bought or sold.[25]

In this way, time was put to work shaping, sustaining, and guiding the new economics. Gone were its spiritual roots and values. Now, time was perceived as fully in the service of human beings:

> The paradox, the surprise, and the wonder are that the clock was invented by men who wanted to devote themselves more rigorously to God; it ended as the technology of greatest use to men who wished to devote themselves to the accumulation of money. In the eternal struggle between God and Mammon, the clock quite unpredictably favored the latter.[26]

Time had become a commodity that was judged worthy according to its economic utility and commercial instrumentality rather than its ability to shape, hold, form, guide, and sustain human faithfulness to God: "Time was snatched away from its biological and environmental moorings and locked up inside the gears of an automated machine that now parceled it out in steady nondescript beats."[27] With these developments a new kind of time had emerged: *the time of the clock* or *o'clock* as we have come to know it.[28]

The timing of our lives

Jeremy Begbie observes that within the time of the two-handed clock, our lives have become strictly timed:

> Even a cursory glance at Western contemporary (especially urban) life indicates that the largest part of it is strictly timed . . . daily time-structuring through schedules and timetables is one of the features which distinguishes school, work and institutional life from the routine of those on holiday or the unemployed. But even those on vacation or at home are inescapably influenced by the opening hours of banks, shops and so on, by their own habits and those of people around them. . . . "Whether we are affected in primary or secondary ways, we cannot escape the clock time that structures our daily lives."[29]

Events no longer shape time; time shapes events. Even the nurturing of our souls is timed. The Christian organization the Navigators urges us to spend seven minutes each day with God:

1/2 Minute: Preparing Your Heart
4 Minutes: Listening to God (Scripture Reading)
2 1/2 Minutes: Talking to God (Prayer).[30]

We have become a people who think we have to fit God in rather than fit in with what God is doing. Time has ceased to be perceived as a gift in which we participate; now it seems to have a life of its own. Eriksen sums this up nicely when he notes that in the time of the clock we have turned time into

> an autonomous entity, something that exists independently of events. "An hour" may exist (in our minds) in an abstract way; it is an empty entity that can be filled with anything. Hence it is common to speak of clock time as "empty, quantified time." It is chopped up into accurately measured "pieces," like metres and decilitres. These entities are presupposed to be identical for everybody, anywhere and any time.[31]

The time of the clock as it worked itself out within the monastery was deeply meaningful. SAET is profoundly empty and meaningless. Charles Taylor suggests that such empty, homogenous time is typical of the way that time is perceived in modernity.[32] He is not wrong.

TIME AND OTHERNESS

All of this has significant implications for perceptions of and responses to disability. The time of the clock contains a worldview, a politics, and an economics. It also creates and sustains a quite particular anthropology. The desirable state for human beings living within SAET is to be able to handle the economics of time efficiently in a world that adores speed, loves intellectual prowess (quickness of mind), and worships comfortably at the altar of competitiveness, productivity, efficiency, and self-sufficiency (using *your* time well on your *own* behalf). The implication is that to live humanly is to learn to live one's life effectively according to a series of culturally constructed time tracks that are laid out according to the fixed and relentless rhythm of the two-handed clock (or the four-figured digital clock). Not to be able to move one's body or one's mind to such a temporal rhythm is to live in a way that pushes the boundaries of acceptable humanness. Time and its close corollary, speed, combined with an awareness of the nature of our linear, progressing temporal direction, are intricately woven into what we consider to be *normal* and *abnormal*. If time is money and money is the product of temporal dexterity, speed, competitiveness, and efficiency, then being quick and efficient inevitably becomes the norm. If our identity (who we think we are in the world) has to do with knowing who and where we are at any given temporal moment, then our autobiographical awareness becomes central to who we are. Thinking, speed, self-awareness, and autobiographical identity all become entangled in what personhood is assumed to be and what is presumed necessary to retain such a status. The problems that this raises for people with certain forms of disability are obvious.

Riyad A. Shahjahan observes that the time of the clock as it has developed within modernity encapsulated "an 'Other' notion of time."[33] Reflecting on the connection between perceptions of time and the activities of the European colonizers, he highlights the development of what he describes as a "chronology of difference" that he believes emerged from the logic of colonialism:

> Time became a trajectory against which to measure indigenous and other subaltern individuals and groups in terms of the degree to which they are out of sync, behind in development, anachronistic, and resistant

> to progress. Linear Eurocentric notions of time were used to sort individuals into opposing categories such as intelligent/slow, lazy/industrious, saved/unsaved, believer/heathen, developed/undeveloped, and civilized/primitive; in the process, most of the world's people and their knowledge came to stand outside of history.[34]

The worldview and assumptions created by Standard Average European Time functioned as an agent for the development of a polarizing dichotomy between the wanted and desirable and those groups of people who were not wanted and were considered undesirable. As we will see in the next chapter, people with disabilities were easily categorized and downgraded on the basis of their "faulty" engagement with this kind of time. Tuhiwai Smith, in her work on decolonizing methodologies, notes the ways in which colonizers sought justification for what they were doing by framing "the colonized" according to some kind of deficit model:

> The connection between time and work became more important after the arrival of missionaries in the development of more systematic colonization. The belief that natives did not value work or have a sense of time provided ideological justification for exclusionary practices which reached across such areas as education, land development and employment. . . . It was hard work to get to heaven and savages were expected to work extra hard to qualify to get into the queue.[35]

The imposition of clock-driven SAET as the temporal standard in opposition to more indigenous modes of time placed European clock time as *the* criterion for human value and worth. In so doing, the colonized were placed in a position of Otherness based on their perceived "temporal weaknesses."

This was so in terms of productivity, but it also appears to have been the case in terms of spirituality. Slow, nonproductive people were going to struggle to find their way into heaven. According to Shahjahan:

> Using this temporal logic, anything or anyone not aligned with history in forward motion must be converted, saved, developed, or improved. It is not the case that the reckoning of time was not present elsewhere, it is that this particular concept of time was tied to linear progress, which was then used to suggest that only Europe was progressing, while others were in a different period of time. . . . The colonizing impetus of temporal difference persists today . . . in the form of terminologies that classify regions and nations as either "developed/modern" or "developing/traditional."[36]

Ideas about time, normality, and personhood are deeply intertwined within such historical developments, the impact of which resonates down to the present day. It is important to note that the experience of time as linear and progressive is not an inevitable consequence of the development of the clock. "The clock actually records temporal cycles of 12 or 24 hours."[37] It is the clock, plus economics, plus science, plus ideas about evolution and progress that makes for the development of a particular form of linear time, a form of time that can, as we will see, be literally deadly for people with disabilities. It is to that complex history of linear progressive time and how it relates to understandings of disability that we now turn.

2

Time and Progress
Disability and the Wrong Kind of Time

> But Jesus said, "Let the children come to me. Don't stop them! For the Kingdom of Heaven belongs to those who are like these children."
>
> (Matt 19:14)

The connection between time and disability is not obvious, but when we come to see it, it becomes disturbing and yet deeply enlightening. Take, for example, the controversies that surround issues relating to euthanasia and prenatal testing for disabilities. At one level they look like standard ethical debates. At another level we can see that they emerge from conflicting understandings of time.

ON KILLING DISABLED PEOPLE IN THE NAME OF COMPASSION: A MATTER OF TIME?

It is interesting (and deeply disconcerting) to observe current development in people's thinking around the issue of euthanasia. In Belgium they have recently passed a law whereby children with certain forms of terminal illness can opt for euthanasia.[1] In Holland it is possible to apply for euthanasia on the basis of an initial diagnosis of dementia.[2] People have been euthanized because they are deaf, blind,[3] or even because they are old![4] Recently a prisoner convicted of murder and rape won the right to be euthanized on the basis that he was depressed and that his life in prison had no meaning.[5]

Along similar lines the conversation around prenatal testing for disabilities is concerning. In Denmark, for example, in 2015, 98 percent of Down syndrome pregnancies were aborted, leading one headline to proclaim:

"Down Syndrome heading for extinction in Denmark." Within thirty years Down syndrome could be a thing of the past in Denmark. With the introduction of a scan for Down syndrome—a nuchal scan—the number of abortions involving children with Down syndrome has dramatically increased. Lillian Bondo, the head of the midwife association Jordemoderforeningen, says, "When you can discover almost all the foetuses with Down Syndrome, then we are approaching a situation in which almost all of them will be aborted." The majority of Danes feel that such a drop in Down syndrome babies is a good thing. "An Epinion survey for DR revealed that 60 percent believed it was good there were considerably fewer kids with DS being born."[6]

In a world wherein we quite correctly wonder at the magnificent accomplishments that medical technology brings to us and are rightly proud of the rights that we ascribe to people with disabilities, one cannot help but wonder why many of us seem to think it is okay to develop tests and interventions that are designed to track down people with disabilities and destroy them before they get the chance to fulfill their vocation within God's creation.[7]

Oddly, this is often done in the name of compassion. As Stanley Hauerwas observes, "Humanism gone bad makes compassion something deadly. This sort of 'compassion' would 'cure' Down syndrome by eliminating people with Down syndrome before they are born."[8] The meaning of compassion and dignity is always contextual. For such ideas to be protective of people with disabilities requires a moral context that respects disability and values persons living with differences. Such a moral context is not always available. One has to question what it is about Western cultures that makes certain forms of vulnerability, dependence, and disability the targets of violence and fear. Perhaps, as Jean Vanier suggests, "tears and violence can be ways of protecting ourselves from what is unbearable, from our own vulnerability, from our own pain."[9] Within modernity the existence of vulnerable lives does not seem inevitably to draw out love and a desire to care. Rather, such lives act as reminders of the fragility of our cultural idols of reason, intellectual prowess, autonomy, freedom, and self-representation. Reminding people of such fragility challenges our taken-for-granted perceptions of human flourishing and draws out anxiety and fear. Violence is the inseparable companion of fear.

In what follows I will argue that the underlying fear that so frequently erupts into violence is the product of malignant cultural understandings of time. Our historical and cultural constructions of time have taught us to pay the wrong kind of attention to people living with certain forms of disabilities. The question we must begin with is this: *Why is it that we assume that certain ways of being in the world are a waste of time?*

PEOPLE WITH DEMENTIA ARE A WASTE OF TIME! LET'S JUST KILL THEM?

In a 2008 interview with the Presbyterian Church of Scotland's magazine *Life and Work*, the renowned British philosopher and ethicist Baroness Mary Warnock made some highly controversial comments about what she thought should happen to people with dementia: "If you're demented, you're wasting people's lives—your family's lives—and you're wasting the resources of the National Health Service."[10] She then moved on to suggest that people with dementia should be encouraged to take their own lives and that the state should license people to put people with dementia down since the *real* person is no longer there and what is left is "just a shell."[11] I will not explore the issue of the personhood of people with dementia here, as I have looked at this in some detail elsewhere.[12] There are, however, aspects of Warnock's perspective that are important for our present purposes. According to Warnock, people with dementia are nonproductive and therefore nonpersons. As such, they are without value or worth: a burden. Productivity, remembered autobiography, self-awareness, autonomy, cognitive acuity, and personhood are seen to be inextricably tied together. Not to be self-aware and productive is to cease being a person; to cease being a person is to cease being of worth; to cease being of worth is considered to be a justifiable rationale for killing people. People with advanced dementia are to be considered a burden on the state and on their families. Keeping them alive is professed to be a waste of time and resources. It is therefore not simply justifiable for the state to relieve society of such a burden; it is a moral duty.

Now, one might at first glance wish to reject Warnock's position as extreme. However, while her articulation of the issue may be quite sharp, as we have seen, the elimination of people with dementia and other forms of disability is already a reality in some parts of God's creation. A colleague from Belgium informs me that there are in fact dedicated teams within hospitals whose job it is to assess situations and make the decision as to who should or should not be allowed to participate in euthanasia. Warnock simply gives something that is already going on within different contexts a sharp public voice. What is useful to observe at this point is the way in which Warnock's view is clearly tied in with the economics of the time of the clock. Those deemed incapable of using their time productively are denied any inherent right to live. Why? Because they are an economic burden on the state, a social and relational burden on their families, and a burden on the time of lay and professional health-care workers. In this understanding our ultimate value and indeed our personhood relates very closely to the ways in which we are assumed to be able to inhabit and use time.

SHOULD THE BABY LIVE? RICHARD DAWKINS AND THE STRANGE INCIDENT OF THE TWEET IN THE NIGHTTIME

A second example will take us into yet another dimension of the complex relationship between time and perceptions of disability. The somewhat notorious scientist, "new atheist," and champion of biological and social evolution Richard Dawkins hit the headlines recently when he sent out a tweet indicating his position on the value of the lives of people with Down syndrome. In response to another Twitter user who said she would be faced with "a real ethical dilemma" if she became pregnant with a baby who had Down syndrome, Dawkins tweeted, "Abort it and try again. It would be immoral to bring it into the world if you have the choice." He claimed that he accidentally sent it to his more than one million followers:

> Dawkins claimed he had hoped that his million-plus followers would not see his comments, which would instead only be sent out to the people who follow both himself and the woman who posed the question. He also claimed there was not enough space in his Twitter reply to get his fuller argument across.[13]

It is quite difficult to see how meaning to send a controversial tweet to only a few people rather than to a large amount of people is much of an excuse. Putting that to one side for the moment, he went on to say:

> What I was saying simply follows logically from the ordinary pro-choice stance that most of us, I presume, espouse. My phraseology may have been tactlessly vulnerable to misunderstanding, but I can't help feeling that at least half the problem lies in a wanton eagerness to misunderstand.[14]

I am not sure why Dawkins assumes that most of us would be pro-choice in general, but more than that, it is not clear why we would be particularly "pro-choice" with regard to disabled children. The logic is not as obvious as he seems to assume. Bearing in mind his basic atheistic worldview, presumably he assumes that this is the "obvious" way for postreligious people, who value choice over external moral authority, to think. Likewise, it is quite difficult to see how "abort it and try again" could be significantly misunderstood even if one were wantonly eager to do so. Dawkins' defense of his tweet is revealing:

> If your morality is based, as mine is, on a desire to increase the sum of happiness and reduce suffering, the decision to deliberately give birth to a Down's baby, when you have the choice to abort it early in the pregnancy, might actually be immoral from the point of view of the child's own welfare.[15]

Well, at least he seems to acknowledge that prior to birth babies with Down syndrome are, well, *babies*, rather than "fetuses," "embryos," or "its." His "defense" seems to be to restate the message of the tweet a little more eloquently. Of more concern is the fact that his elaboration appears to suggest that the way in which we should ensure children's welfare is by killing them! I do not think you have to be a trained ethicist to see the flaw in such an argument. Now, the reader may be thinking, "That's all very interesting and evocative, but how does it relate to the issue of time?" The answer is that Dawkins' position, like Warnock's, finds its roots in quite specific perceptions of and assumptions about time and history (the passing of time). These perceptions are deeply tied in with the perspective on the time given to us by the clock.

TIME AND DISABILITY

Cultural historian Douglas Baynton, in his exploration of the relationship among disability, time, and eugenics, draws attention to the intricate historical connection between time and disability. In particular he highlights how perceptions of time are deeply enmeshed in the ways in which disability has been named and responded to within American social history and how such naming is deeply interconnected with concepts and perceptions of time.[16] Baynton's focus is on American history, but his argument applies across a broad range of Western cultures and perspectives on time. Reflecting on the question of why social attitudes toward the disabled in the United States became dramatically more negative around the turn of the century, Baynton suggests that one of the major causes of this shift was the changing understandings of time that accompanied the advent of evolutionary theory and the development of competitive industrial economies:

> As analogies of competition became culturally ubiquitous, new words to talk about disability such as "handicapped," "retarded," "abnormal," "degenerate," and "defective," came into everyday use, all of them explicitly or implicitly rooted in new ways of thinking about time. The intense fear of disability that characterised the eugenics movement grew, in good part, from this new and unsettling vision of time.[17]

As geological discoveries and evolutionary biology became popularized and industrialization accelerated and became widespread, perceptions of the nature of time began to shift and change accordingly. With these changes came new ideas about disability, its roots, origins, and meaning and, significantly, new ways to talk about people with disabilities that were "explicitly or implicitly rooted in new ways of thinking about time."[18] Previously, disability had been described in terms of "infirmity" or "affliction," designators that people with disabilities shared with the poor, the elderly, the sick, and widows and orphans. Such people were assumed in some way to be aliens or outcasts who were legitimate recipients of care and charity. At a metaphysical level, disability tended to be perceived by many as divine in origin and orientation, with sin and providence being among the primary guiding explanatory narratives. The general assumption was that, in the end, such "human imperfections would be done away with"[19] as this time ends and a new time comes to fruition: heaven. Disability was therefore assumed to be something that had meaning, purpose, and a place within God's overall plan.[20] Disability occurred in a world that was assumed to be consciously designed and full of meaningful, intentional, purposeful direction.[21] The point is not that people with disabilities were treated better in these times. That may or may not have been the case. The point Baynton wants to draw out is that disability (explicitly and implicitly), was explained according to a particular set of narratives that were driven by a specific understanding of time within which the Divine was perceived to pay a significant explanatory role.

Disability as a disorder of time

The emerging new language of disability placed people with disabilities in a quite different temporal space from the place they had inhabited previously. By the 1890s the terms "affliction" and "infirmity" were replaced by the term "handicap." This term originated in a seventeenth-century gambling game known as hand-in-cap, which had to do with drawing money or slips of paper from a hat. The rules dictated that, every time a player lost, his or her odds of winning improved in the next game. In the eighteenth century, the term migrated to horse racing, with the idea of a "handicap race" being one in which weights were attached to faster horses to even the odds for slower horses. In the nineteenth century, the term "handicap" became generalized to any context where the stronger player in a particular game or contest was disadvantaged in some way or other. In time the idea drifted out of sports and into society. The expression was and continues to be frequently used to express something that will disadvantage a person. So, for example, "Don't handicap your chances of finding a girlfriend by not taking a shower!" or "Don't handicap your family's happiness by caring for a person with dementia or carrying to term a child with Down syndrome."

LIFE IS A RAT RACE!

By the end of the nineteenth century, under the influence of metaphorical thinking emerging from evolutionary biology, life frequently came to be described as "a race" and later as a "rat race."[22] Those unlucky enough not to be able to compete effectively in the race were considered to be "handicapped in the race for life, handicapped in the battle of life, or handicapped in the struggle for existence";[23] that is, they found themselves in a position where they were burdened in such a way as to prevent them from competing effectively in the race of life. People's impairments handicapped them and slowed them down in ways that eliminated them from effectively participating in the rat race.

> It was in this context that *handicap* began to be used in connection with disabilities. An 1890 newspaper obituary, for example, described how the deceased had accomplished much "despite the handicap of physical infirmity." By the early 20th century *handicap* was commonly used as a stand-alone noun more or less synonymous with disability. Soon the phrase *the handicapped* emerged as a general label for persons with impairments.[24]

This way of framing impairments was carried over into a variety of disciplines and perspectives:

> Educators spoke of disabled people as "seriously handicapped in the race for life," or "by this defect handicapped in the struggle for existence," and needing help to "win the battle of life." . . . There was not one but two races in which disability was a handicap: the economic race for life in which the individual might succeed or fail, and the evolutionary competition by which races and nations would rise or fall.[25]

It is not difficult to find resonance here with Warnock's and Dawkins' views on the nature and form of valuable life. One of them seems to follow in the footsteps of the economic model of time we considered in the previous chapter, and the other appears to draw from the evolutionary worldview that Baynton finds so significant in his analysis of the connections between disability and time.

Evolution and time

It is within this latter aspect—the developing evolutionary perspective—that the issue of time begins to come sharply to the fore. Baynton argues that the prevalence of evolutionary explanations being applied to social issues was accompanied by a movement away from teleological understandings of the world. Gone was any sense of a fixed and stable direction provided by divine time and providence. In its place came an open history within which human beings could in principle, through evolution, evolve into many different possible futures through a combination of circumstances that occurred without any kind of an idea of a divine plan. The idea of God, providence, and eschatological hope no longer provided a plausible vision of the past, the present, or the future. Now people were viewed as the products of blind, random evolution, a way of coming into being that is simply the consequence of randomness and chance.

With this revised understanding of the world and the place of human beings within the world, people's sense of time and history began to encounter quite radical change. With the development of the theory of evolution, the past was expanded by billions of years and conceptions of history were shifted from a planned, divinely guided strategy toward a disorganized, meaningless, random movement with an undefined and indefinable goal. History was now perceived to be open, accidental, and defined by haphazard biological changes. Above all else history was now malleable, manipulable, open to construction by human beings for human purposes. The whims of biology and intelligent human endeavor and choice now became the primary drivers in the perception and management of historical change. Freed from the shackles of divine wisdom and prudence, choosing one's own personal future that one could fulfill with minimal assistance from others became not only an option but an expectation and ultimately a human right. The idea of human *progress* became the central guiding secular doctrine, supplanting providence as the means of understanding the direction and meaning of time.

Within such a context, time inevitably came to be perceived as morally neutral and instrumental, the uncaring arena for the working out of blind nature and the striving for human desire. Time became a blank sheet onto which human beings could inscribe their histories. Competition, strength, force, intellectual acuity, physical dexterity, and speed all emerged as aspects of the new worldview acquired for biological and social development. Within such a worldview, any perceived difference in capacities inevitably came to be seen as a form of suffering insofar as it prevented people from fully engaging in the forward, progressive movement of time and history that is required for the betterment of the species. If genes truly are selfish, as Richard Dawkins has argued, then there can be no space for genetic structures that produce the need for selfless altruism.[26]

Industrial time

This changing cosmological background combined with increasing human knowledge of science and technology provided the backdrop for the development of industrialization and its accompanying perspective on time: industrial time. Using time more efficiently became an assumed norm as the traditional work place was overpowered by the speed of the free market economy; the essential goal was to be faster, stronger, and more competitive than the next business or worker.[27] Understood from this perspective, the significance of time and speed for people with disability becomes obvious. If you cannot keep up and use your time productively, you will become an economic and social burden on the state, on your family, and on society; you will become a "handicap" to progress, a drag on the desired forward movement of society within which everyone is expected to strive to create their own personal history. *As "time became money," so the disabled became a burden and a handicap.*

MENTAL RETARDATION

A dynamic similar to that which underpins the idea of naming something or someone as "handicapped" can be traced in the history of the term "retarded." The original fifth-century meaning of the verb "to retard" was to slow down or to hinder:

> In the twentieth century . . . it followed the same path as "handicapped" from general multi-purpose adjective, to one applied frequently to disabled people in the sense of retarded development, to a stand-alone noun: "the mentally retarded." Like handicapped, its usage tracked the changing understanding of the significance of time, as the problem shifted from a mind that was "feeble" to one that could not compete.[28]

People with intellectual disabilities were considered to be "backward" (i.e., not progressing) and *atavistic*. The term "atavistic" relates to the idea that congenital disabilities such as Down syndrome were throwbacks to earlier stages of evolutionary development. So, for example, Langdon Down, after whom Down syndrome is named, assumed that the particular facial features of people with Down syndrome reflected a relation to the Mongol race. Down believed that people from Mongolia, along with all other non-European races, were subhuman in the sense that they had not developed to the same extent as Europeans. The implication was that people with Down syndrome belonged to a different time and place.

DARWIN AND "THE RETARDED"

A somewhat shocking example of atavism can be found in Charles Darwin's book *The Descent of Man*. In this text Darwin presents a powerful and somewhat depressing example of the ways in which atavism could be used not only to explain the existence of people with intellectual disabilities but also to help us understand the missing link between humans and the rest of the animals. Darwin was somewhat flummoxed by the fact that there was at that time a fossil gap between human beings and the higher primates. According to Steven Gelb,

> Darwin wished to convince readers that human beings and animals were of common descent and not the result of two separate creations as described in the Bible, however, the fossil evidence, at that time, was less than wholly convincing. No "ape/man" had yet been found that could conclusively prove the common descent of humans and higher primates.[29]

How then was he to bridge the gap? In the future the fossil gap may well be overcome, but for the time being people with intellectual disabilities provided Darwin with a solution. He purported that, "although no 'missing link' fossil had yet been discovered, actual living forms, intermediate between apes and the 'civilized races' existed."[30] In Darwin's thinking, people with intellectual disabilities were precisely such intermediate links. To make this point, Darwin had to place animals and humans in a particular relationship:

> To convince readers that evolution explained human as well as animal origins, Darwin needed to raise the public's estimation of animals' capacities while simultaneously lowering their regard for human beings. Variation lay at the heart of the theory of natural selection: vigorous organisms survived and propagated whilst the weak or "unfit" were eliminated. Darwin's strategy was to seek out the highest examples he could find of animal functioning and present these against the lowest of humans. In arguing that "Animals manifestly enjoy excitement and suffer from ennui . . . [and that] all animals feel Wonder, and many exhibit Curiosity" . . . he aimed to show that there existed an overlap between

> the most highly evolved animals, and the least developed human beings. Thus, Darwin found much to praise in animals and much to condemn in humans.[31]

Darwin's strategy was to make an argument that the evidence for evolution does not have to rest simply with fossils or the discovery of tribes of ape-men. People with profound intellectual disabilities made the case. In a sense they were the missing link. An extract from *The Descent of Man* will help to make this point:

> Idiots are strong and remarkably active, continually gambolling and jumping about, and making grimaces. They often ascend stairs on all fours; are curiously fond of climbing up furniture or trees. . . . Idiots also resemble the lower animals in some other respects; thus several cases are recorded of their carefully smelling every mouthful of food before eating it. One idiot is described as often using his mouth in aid of his hands while hunting for lice. They are often filthy in their habits, and have no sense of decency; and several cases have been published of their bodies being remarkably hairy.[32]

This was not a new strategy. As J. P. Lesley had put it three years before the publication of *The Descent of Man*:

> Individuals scattered all over the world, through all the human races, with low foreheads, small brains, long arms, thin legs, projecting, tusk-like teeth, suppressed noses, and other marks of arrested development; to say nothing of millions of idiots and cretins produced by the same arrest in every generation of mankind, sustain the argument.[33]

In attempting to use the existence of people with intellectual disability to support his theory of evolution, Darwin simply followed suit. "Idiots" were presented in four ways:

> (1) an intermediate rung on the evolutionary ladder connecting humans and primates; (2) exemplars of the inevitable waste and loss produced by natural selection acting upon variability; (3) the floor of a scale representing the "lowest," most unfit variety of any species when individuals were rank ordered by intelligence; and (4) atavistic reversions to extinct forms whose study would reveal the characteristics of earlier stages of human evolution.[34]

In this theory, the intellectually disabled were to be perceived as strange and savage creatures that bridged the gap between apes and humans: embodied, timefull reminders of what humans once were but are no more.

But what about Giddlums?

There was, however, a somewhat strange tension between the harsh caricaturing of people with intellectual disabilities that Darwin used in his professional life and the notable tenderness that he showed toward his own disabled son. When faced with intellectual disability within his own family, his descriptions differed quite drastically from those laid out in *The Descent of Man*. Darwin's last child, Charles Waring Darwin, was born on December 6, 1856. Darwin's wife, Emma, had conceived when she was forty-eight years old. It was a difficult pregnancy. Darwin's daughter Henrietta reflects on the life of Charles Waring Darwin in this way:

> I remember very well the weary months she [Henrietta's mother] passed, and reading aloud to her sometimes to help her bear her discomforts. The poor little baby was born without its full share of intelligence. Both my mother and father were infinitely tender towards him, but, when he died in the summer of 1858, after their first sorrow, they could only feel thankful. He had never learnt to walk or talk.[35]

There is much discussion around precisely what the condition of Charles Waring was. Based on certain photographic evidence and Emma's advanced age, it has been speculated that the baby may have had Down syndrome, but it is not completely clear.[36] Irrespective of the diagnostic issues, what is fascinating is the contrast between the way that Darwin talks about his son and the way he talks about people with intellectual disabilities in *The Descent of Man*. This entry in Darwin's diary helps to draw out the tension:

> When crawling naked on the floor he [Charles Jr.] looked very elegant. He had never been ill and cried less than any of our babies. He was of a remarkably sweet, placid and joyful disposition; but had not high spirits, and did not laugh much. He often made strange grimaces and shivered, when excited; but did so also, for a joke and his little eyes used to glisten, after pouting out or stretching widely his little lips. He used sometimes to move his mouth as if talking loudly, but making no noise, and this he did when very happy. He was particularly fond of standing on one of my hands and being tossed in the air; and then he always smiled, and made a little pleased noise. I had just taught him to kiss me with open mouth, when I told him. He would lie for a long time placidly on my lap looking

> with a steady and pleased expression at my face; sometimes trying to poke his poor little fingers into my mouth, or making nice little bubbling noises as I moved his chin. I had taught him not to scratch, but when I said, "Giddlums never scratches now" he could not always resist a little grab, and then he would look at me with a wicked little smile. He would play for any length of time on the sofa, letting himself fall suddenly, and looking over his shoulder to see that I was ready. He was very affectionate and had a passion for Parslow [the Darwins' butler] and it was very pretty to see his extreme eagerness with outstretched arms, to get to him. Our poor little darling's short life has been placid, innocent and joyful. I think and trust he did not suffer so much at last, as he appeared to do; but the last 36 hours were miserable beyond expression. In the sleep of Death he resumed his placid looks.[37]

Love changes things

It is not my intention to make a polemical point out of Darwin's love and grief. Nor do I seek to use the dissonance in his perspective on disability as any kind of argument against evolution. I am sure that in a professional capacity Darwin thought his strategy was sensible, logical, and useful. I do not imagine that his overall position changed much because of his encounter with his son's disability. I am not trying to place experience as a counter for scientific endeavor. I simply want to draw attention to the fact that—even within the perception of time that is evoked by a worldview focused on evolution and that names certain people "retarded" and "atavistic" because they remind us of times past—close, personal encounter with those experiencing such profound disabilities can draw people into a different mode of time and experience, a mode of time that is personal, present, deep, loving, caring, and timefull. Darwin clearly enjoyed spending time with Charles: they had quality time together. Even if Darwin's arguments had proven to be correct, the way in which he went about creating the argument inevitably served to alienate, distance, and exclude people with profound intellectual disabilities from the realm of humanness, or at least full humanness. Science is never neutral; it always contains and produces a social theory. Darwin's personal life is indicative of a clash between the social theory constructed by his professional scientific arguments that he deemed necessary for bridging the gap, and the social theory that emerged from his personal experience with young Charles that touched and moved time in a quite different direction. One pushes people with disabilities back into history to a time that is no more; the other embraces those with disabilities in the present time. When Darwin was drawn forward into his love for Giddlums, when that love caused him to pay attention to his son in new ways, things looked quite different. Young Charles may have been damaged, but clearly he remained loveable. He does not simply bridge a gap between animals and human beings; he is clearly human and unmistakably perceived as human by Darwin.

From concepts to persons

I am not normally a fan of the American politician Sarah Palin. However, I was struck and moved by her response to Richard Dawkins' tweet and her follow-up comments on Down syndrome.[38] Palin has a son, Trig, who has Down syndrome. Many people responded with anger and outrage to Dawkins' comments, but Palin's response was different: simple, thoughtful, and powerful. Palin's response was not to criticize or ridicule but rather to offer an invitation:

> Mr. Dawkins,
>
> I'd let you meet my son if you promised to open your mind, your eyes, and your heart to a unique kind of absolute beauty. But, in my request for you to be tolerant, I'd have to warn Trig he must be tolerant, too, because he may superficially look at you as kind of awkward. I'll make sure he's polite, though!
>
> Love,
>
> *Sarah Palin & family*[39]

As far as I am aware, Dawkins has yet to reply. Politeness is not his greatest gift, so maybe it is just as well. Perhaps if, like Darwin, Dawkins took the time—or, better, was gifted the time by Trig—to open himself to the possibility of loving people with Down syndrome, he would come to realize that issues of life and death require more than 140 characters to do them justice.

THE TYRANNY OF NORMALITY

Before we move on to offer a counter-story of time, there is one final issue that needs to be thought through, and that is *the question of normality*. Both Warnock and Dawkins seem to be working from quite particular understandings of time and how time is implicated in our responses to disability. Running alongside such perceptions of time is an accompanying implicit and explicit model of normality and abnormality. We might presume that they understand that normality is described or understood in terms of biological, statistical, social, intellectual, and economic terms. Something that may not be quite as obvious is the fact that the question of what is normal and what is abnormal is essentially related to perceptions of time.

What is normal?

The use of the term "normal" to describe someone or something as being without defect or conforming to a statistical average is a relatively new phenomenon, which emerged in the second half of the nineteenth century. Prior to this the term "normal denoted the 'normal' or 'right' angle for the corner of a structure."[40] The philosopher Ian Hacking notes that the "Latin root of the term 'normal' refers to a builder's T-square, which is a device for measuring right angles, and the Greek root refers to a surveyor's rod."[41] He traces the first usages of the understanding of "normal" in English back to the 1820s, when it was borrowed to describe French advances in physiology and medicine:

> As a word, "normal" . . . acquired its present most common meaning only in the 1820s. . . . The normal was one of a pair. Its opposite was the pathological and for a short time its domain was chiefly medical. Then it moved into the sphere of—almost everything. People, behavior, states of affairs, diplomatic relations, molecules: all these may be normal or abnormal. The word became indispensable because it created a way to be "objective" about human beings.[42]

The term "normal" enabled scientists, doctors, mathematicians, educators, and sociologists to stand back from the particularities of human beings and measure them according to a unified and agreed-upon, neutral and generalizable standard.

Baynton notes that early in the nineteenth century medics began to use the term "normal" to describe healthy (as opposed to unhealthy) organs. The term then migrated, first into sociology via Auguste Comte's idea of the "healthy state of society," and from there, on into wider society through politics and the idea of "the normal nation" and through education with the development of the "normal" school (as opposed to the "special" schools within which the disabled were later placed).[43] Soon the term "normal" was being used across a wide range of contexts. Hacking notices that

> by the end of the century . . . normality had "displaced the Enlightenment idea of human nature as a central organizing concept" in western societies; rather than inquire into human nature, the modern question was what was normal for people to do.[44]

The downward push of normality

The term "normal" was inevitably loaded. "A normal angle for the builder was both a *type* of angle and *the desirable* angle."[45] There is therefore an inbuilt ambiguity in the term "normal." Mason points out, "Function or dysfunction depends on context. Normal and abnormal cannot be defined without understanding the beliefs, values, and power structures of a cultural group."[46] We have already seen some of the ways in which the temporal context within which disability is experienced and perceived draws out judgments of normal and abnormal. On the one hand, talk of normality is *descriptive*. It simply describes the state of something. It can, however, be somewhat difficult to know precisely what it is descriptive of. Take, for example, statistical norms. At one level statistics appears objectively to describe a set of numbers that indicates similarities across groups of people or things. "Surely," one might think, "numbers cannot lie. A statistical average is a statistical average, is it not?" However, J. N. Reichmann points out that statistics can be deceptive:

> The average man does not exist. The average applies to a set of data and not to an individual and if the average man could exist he would be such an odd specimen that by his very uniqueness he would deny his own title.[47]

So, for example, we might say that normal has to do with averages. People with disabilities are "abnormal" because they do not meet the benchmark of the average human person. However, Reichmann's point is that *no one does!* The "average person" is a fictional character. If anyone ever did meet the criterion, he or she would be a most odd-looking person. Mason also notes an ethnocentric bias in certain research strands:

> An ethnocentric bias means that human groups tend to think of themselves as the rule and not the exception. However, contemporary statistical notions of normal are undermined by the discovery that most behavioral science theory is built upon research that examines an intensely narrow sample of human variation. In an empirical review of the top psychology journals, Henrich et al. found that most studies disproportionately sample US university undergraduates who are Western, Educated, Industrialized, Rich, and Democratic (WEIRD). Henrich et al. uncovered that in the context of global populations, these WEIRD subjects tend to be outliers on a range of diverse culturally variable traits including visual perception, sense of fairness, cooperation, analytic reasoning, spatial cognition, and memory, among other basic psychological traits.[48]

It would appear, somewhat oddly, that the WEIRD are assumed to be the criterion for the norm!

THE MORALITY OF NORMALITY

Normality also has a significant moral dimension. If the descriptive criteria for normality are questionable, its moral dimensions are equally open to challenge. Hacking notes the moral tone that underpins talk around that which is normal and that which is considered abnormal:

> A line may be orthogonal or normal (at right angles to the tangent of a circle, say) or not. This is a description of a line. But the evaluative "right" lurks in the background of right angles. It is just a fact that an angle is a right angle, but it is also a "right" angle, a good one. Orthodontists straighten the teeth of children; they make the crooked straight. But they also put the teeth right, make them better. Orthopedic surgeons straighten bones. Orthopsychiatry is the study of mental disorders chiefly of children. It aims at making the child normal. The orthodox conform to certain standards, which used to be a good thing.[49]

The word "normal" thus has the power to suggest that what is normal is also what is right, desirable, and true. The "normal" is the desirable. Abnormality is not just neutral difference; it is an undesirable deviation from the "norm." To ask whether a child is normal or whether a particular human experience such as aging or disability is "normal" rarely expresses a concern about *above*-average abilities. There is always a downward push that accompanies ideas about normality. People with disabilities have historically and contemporarily experienced the brunt of this push. With evolutionary theories positing such concepts as change, process, and struggle as central to human progress, and economic theories pushing people to think of competitiveness, strength, productivity, and success as desirable norms, it is not difficult to see the ways in which ideas about normality came to place disabled lives within a particularly difficult frame. Baynton is no doubt correct when he states that

> in the context of an assumption that the normal tendency of the human race was to improve steadily, to advance ever further from its animal origins, normality was implicitly defined as progressive. Normality on the individual and social level contributed to forward motion. Abnormality was a retarding or atavistic force that could potentially slow down or reverse progress.[50]

Understood in this way, we can see that normality does not simply have to do with statistics and averages. In fact, it is a deeply social, cultural, and timefull concept that reflects specific historical and cultural shifts and understandings about what time is and how time should best be used. To be normal is not simply to have a statistical similarity and connection with other people. Normality has to do with locating one's self in the flow of evolutionary, economic, and political time, which occurs in what we might call "empty" or "plastic" history. To be normal is to have the ability to participate in the movement of one's own personal history, to progress toward one's own goals, and to achieve both individual goals and those that are expected of a person by society. Not to achieve such milestones—to be abnormal—is to retard the progress of evolution (cultural and biological), to fail to participate in the economics of society, and, as such, to become not only handicapped but ultimately a lesser human being: a burden.

RECOGNIZING THE FALLENNESS OF TIME

Read against such a backdrop of culture, history, politics, economics, science, statistics, and time, it becomes easier to understand why certain types of disability attract the sort of violence that was highlighted at the beginning of this chapter. In a world where productivity and a particular understanding of happiness determine whether someone is deemed worthy of living or dying, people whose lives challenge such ways of being in the world inevitably become vulnerable. The "easiest" and "most economically sensible" way to deal with them is to get rid of them. The idea that we are defined by productivity, independence, intellect, and reason and the suggestion that we should not be a burden or a handicap on others (we must not retard the progress of others) is quite typical of people who accept the worldview of industrial, commodified evolutionary time. How could you possibly enjoy your time on earth and be enjoyable to others if you cannot produce anything? How could you possibly be the person you used to be if you cannot do or think in the way you used to think? How could you possibly enjoy life when you move so slowly and cannot think quickly? The suggestion that we are a burden on others because we cannot contribute is simply another way of saying that the way in which persons with profound disabilities use their time is incompatible with current temporal assumptions and expectations.

Someone like Dawkins, whose life is profoundly shaped and formed by belief in biological and social evolution and who is convinced that humans are nothing more than selfish gene carriers, would quite naturally choose a morality that is based on personal productivity and happiness. Someone who holds to the idea that you should prevent the birth of a baby who does not bring maximal happiness, someone who assumes the experience of Down syndrome can be perceived only as a form of suffering caused by a flaw or weakness in the gene pool, would see no real problem with counseling a million-plus people that it is immoral to try to live well with people who have Down syndrome. The idea that you can kill one child "for its own good" and then create another who will make you happier requires an understanding of time and history that makes apparent sense in a world of clocks, speed, power, blind evolution, progress, and efficiency, but it makes much less sense—indeed no sense at all—in a world that sees time as a divine gift that is meant for the glory of God and the edification of all God's creatures. In the strange new world within the Bible—a world wherein grace is found in weakness—life in all of its fullness is discovered in the broken body of Jesus, and time is found to have a beginning and an end with a journey in between that is both meaningful and determinative of what occurs when time ends. In such a world, things will inevitably look different. Why? Because a very different mode of time exists within the world as perceived as God's timefull creation. Within such time the lives of those living with disabilities play a rather different role.

II

LEARNING TO LIVE IN GOD'S TIME

3

Time and Christ
A Brief Theology of Time

> But when the fullness of time had come, God sent forth his Son, born of a woman, born under the law, to redeem those who were under the law, so that we might receive adoption as sons.
>
> (Gal 4:4-5 NKJV)

> The ways we experience, name, and interpret time contribute to the kinds of communities we imagine and inhabit.
>
> (Scott Bader-Saye)[1]

> Prolonged busyness is a state of violence.
>
> (Simon Carey Holt)[2]

The time of the clock has taught us to pay attention to the realm of time in ways that are grasping, utilitarian, instrumental, focused, selfish, and ultimately idolatrous. The time of the clock may be deeply influential and formative, but it is not the only kind of time or even the best kind of time that is available.

WHAT, THEN, IS TIME . . . ?

In book 11 of his *Confessions*, Augustine wrestles with the nature and purpose of God's involvement in time. How could God, who is timeless and eternal, be involved with time without ceasing to be both of these things and thus ceasing to be God? For Augustine it is crucial that God be timeless and unchanging. If God were involved with time, God would be mutable and changeable rather than timeless. If God can change, God is not timeless, and if God is not timeless, eternal, and unchangeable, then God cannot be God. The stakes are high.

The Christian tradition clearly asserts that God is the creator of all things: "In the beginning, God created the heavens and the earth" (Gen 1:1). These opening words of Genesis indicate that there was a time when there was nothing and then there was a time when there was something. The question Augustine's peers asked was, "Where was God before time began?" The problem for Augustine is in the underlying premise of such a question, a premise that he believed makes the question foolish. If God and the world were separate things within the same temporal continuum, then asking what God was doing before God made the world would make some sense. However, in Augustine's thinking they are not. There was *no* time before creation. The question is therefore foolish. In temporal terms God was not doing anything with God's time before God created the world, because there was no time for God to do anything with. There was no time before time began. Timothy George puts it thus:

> Eternity is the dimension of God's own life. It has no beginning and no end, no parameters or margins or boundaries outside of God himself. . . . [T]ime was willed and created by God as a reality distinct from himself.[3]

Time and the world were created by God simultaneously: "They were cocreated, for time is coextensive with the world."[4] For Augustine, "God created the world not *in* time but *with* time."[5] *Time is a creature*.[6]

Such an understanding of time has important implications. Time is not simply something that has always been there and into which God slips creation like a foot into a slipper. There was a time when time was not and a time when time was. Time is something that came into existence simultaneously with creation. It is a dimension of creation. This is an important perspective to grasp fully. Time is not an impersonal, free-floating commodity intended for the satiation of human desire. It is an aspect of God's relationship with the world, a gift from a loving Creator. Time is best conceived as an aspect of God's love for the world. As an aspect of God's love, *the purpose of time is to facilitate and sustain love*. God is therefore not subject to time, even if, in Christ, God did subject himself to time. Time is a creature born out of God's love, intended as the arena for the revelation of that love. In this way Augustine is able to hold on to the timelessness, eternality, and immutability of God while at the same time leaving space for God to be involved in time without becoming the subject of time.

THE ISSUE OF TIMELESSNESS

We need, however, to be careful as to what precisely is meant by the claim that God is eternal and timeless. A criticism of Augustine might be that his position is overly close to Neoplatonism. The Neoplatonists set up a direct opposition between God's eternality and the world of human existence. Timelessness and human temporality were perceived as incompatible opposites. Such a polarity makes the incarnation incomprehensible. While Augustine does not seek to deny the incarnation, his thinking on time, timelessness, and the eternality of God leaves room for the accusation of Neoplatonism.

In his book *Preface to Theology: Christology and Theological Method*, John Howard Yoder offers an important corrective that steers us away from the difficulties implicit in Augustine's position:

> In biblical thought, the eternal is not atemporal. It is not less like time, but more like time. It is like time to a higher degree. The kingdom is not immaterial, but it is more like reality than reality is. If real events are the center of history—certainly the cross was a real event, certainly the resurrection is testified to as in some sense a real event—then the fulfilment and culmination of God's purposes must also be really historic. The God of the Bible is not timeless.[7]

For Yoder, God is not timeless but deeply time-full, temporal, and involved in the ordinary lives of God's creatures. God's involvement with time should not be seen as somehow apart from God's involvement in human history. Indeed, as Stanley Hauerwas notes, it is within human history that God ultimately reveals God's self:

> Christians believe that the ordinary processes of history constitute a straight line of time through which God reveals himself as the Lord of history and nature. . . . Few phrases are more significant than "in the beginning."[8]

God creates the world and seeks to redeem it through the death and resurrection of Jesus. These are historical, timefull events wherein we discover more precisely who God is. God is not atemporal. If God is indeed timeless, it cannot mean that God is without involvement in human time. Drawing on the work of Oscar Cullmann,[9] Hauerwas calls attention to the fact that "Christians believe that salvation is bound to a continuous time process that has a past, present, and future."[10]

The historical fact of the life, death, and resurrection of Jesus is the midpoint of history, an unrepeatable act that leaves a mark on the whole of history.[11] In Genesis, time is initiated and is considered to be good. In the fall, time, like all of creation, begins to lose its goodness. In the resurrection of Jesus and his initiation of the sanctification of creation, time is being redeemed and put to its proper purposes. The eternal has become present in Jesus. The complete bifurcation of God and human time is unsustainable. If God is timeless, then it is a mode of timelessness that is quite different from the Neoplatonic resonances that emerge from a certain reading of Augustine's thinking on time. How then might we understand more precisely how the eternal and the timeless might be present in the ordinary and the temporal?

IN TIME BUT NOT OF TIME: DIVINE SIMULTANEITY

Theologian Jonathan Tran, in his impressive work on time, memory, and the Vietnam War, offers a perspective that helps ease the apparent tension.[12] Tran suggests that the idea of eternality as normally understood designates life without limit, something that exists all at once, without succession. Such an understanding tends to separate God completely from human temporality, which is limited and successive; that is, it has a beginning and an end. The danger here is one of projection. Human time has a beginning and an end; God has no beginning and no end; therefore, God is timeless. Timelessness here means simply a modification and an expansion of our understanding of human timefullness. We are bound by time, God is not; we do not go on forever, God does. Tran urges us to move beyond such projection toward a quite different understanding of time and our perceptions of what it might mean for God to be in time but not of time.

There is, of course, a sense in which God is without limit or succession. Augustine's formulation of the nature of time draws that out quite helpfully. However, that does not inevitably necessitate distance or a lack of God's involvement in creaturely time. Rather, to return to Yoder's perspective, God is immersed in "time to a higher degree." In Tran's view:

> God is time*less* in that time does not determine God; God does not occur *in* time. Still, one can say that God is time*ful* in that whatever time is, time occurs *in* God. The life that is God's eternality, as eternal, abides amidst time as its all-at-once simultaneity. . . . It is exactly this simultaneity that names temporal existence as ordinary in the creaturely sense, for in relation to the eternal, time is seen as changing, and existence in time ensues relative to time's continuous change. Rather than eternity denoting a transcendent space beyond the flux of time, such that ascending the

> eternal achieves a type of pure gaze, eternity relativizes all such pretensions while allocating time productive of genuine difference.[13]

Time occurs in God; God does not occur in time. In making this move, Tran is able to retain time's creatureliness alongside God's eternality while at the same time helping overcome the Neoplatonic dualism that is inherent within Augustine's perception of time. Time does not determine God; God determines time. God is thus able to participate within time (because time occurs within God), without God being determined by time. Sequential time as human beings experience it is therefore quite real for God, but it is not definitive of God's eternal location. God can be very much with us in our joys and in our pain without being confined to the temporal locality of the experience or the temporal limits of any response to both sadness and joy.

God is not apart from sequential time as we understand and experience it. Nonetheless, as George Hunsinger points out:

> God's apprehension of time . . . is not limited to these sequences. There's a sense in which—and this is mysterious and there's no way to really see how this can be the case, but that it is the case is affirmed—these sequences are seen by God somehow also as being simultaneous.[14]

This is why "a day is like a thousand years to the Lord, and a thousand years is like a day" (2 Pet 3:8). Peter's point is not that a thousand years *feels* like a day. A thousand years *is* like a day. God's time is not linear in the way that we are used to understanding linearity. It contains linearity, but once again it is not defined or constrained by linearity. God's time is neither progressive nor static. Paradoxically, it is both. God's time mediates the fullness of God's kingdom in-the-now and yet contains within it the knowledge that the fullness of that kingdom is still to come. " 'I am the Alpha and the Omega," says the Lord God, "who is, and who was, and who is to come, the Almighty' " (Rev 1:8 NIV). God's time is uncontrollable; unmanageable; simultaneously past, present, transient, and in the future; an enigmatic container; and a bridge that emerges from and leads us into God's unchanging, loving heart.

One time: God's time

The fact that God inhabits creaturely time and yet remains eternal is not to suggest that there are two types of time. Quite the opposite. God's time is "a quality of time that is the internal basis of human time."[15] As Karl Barth has put it:

> The history of salvation attested in the Bible cannot be considered or understood simply in and for itself. It is related to world history as a whole. It is the centre and key to all events. But again, world history cannot be considered or understood simply in and for itself. It is related to the history of salvation. It is the circumference around the Centre, the lock to which that key belongs and is necessary.[16]

God's relationship with time is thus seen to be simultaneously outside of creaturely time and within creaturely time. God is able to participate in time without being determined by time. We might conceive of this point in Trinitarian terms: God the Father participates in time through God the incarnated Son in the power of the Holy Spirit. God is both time*full* and time*less*. God is a full inhabitant of creaturely time and a being whose timelessness is of another order that has overspilled to create the time we know. Such an understanding recognizes the presence of God in every moment without any moment being definitive of who God is. Jonathan Tran moves in a similar direction:

> According to Aquinas, God as eternal is present to each moment of time, and as such can bequeath goodness on the ordinariness of time, as something declared "good." The self in time then names not a timeless sovereign subject but rather a creature coming to be as creature, a condition which when understood in light of the eternal becomes the occasion for alterity and the self's inexhaustible contingency. The creature at all times remains affixed to and in time (she is not eternal), and yet such temporality does not curse but rather sacramentally references the before and after in movement.[17]

This understanding elaborates Augustine's account of God's eternality as God's presentness within each and every creaturely temporality:

> Time comes to God as the present of the past, the present of the present, and the present of the future. Because God exists without succession all at once, all things are present to God all at once; just as God is not absent to time so time is not the totality of God, meaning that God can be present to but not dependent on time.[18]

"Immanuel (which means 'God with us')" (Matt 1:23 NIV) is a description of Jesus, but it is also a statement about God's presence in time. The simultaneity of God's time will become crucial as we move on in this book. As we begin to explore such issues as traumatic brain injury, personality change, and advanced dementia, the suggestion that God is in time but exceeds time will prove to be vital. The fact that God can be equally present to the past, the present, and the future while remaining undetermined by them opens up powerful vistas of hope for people with the types of disabilities that we will focus on later in this book.[19]

REDEEMING TIME: LEARNING TO TELL THE TIME PROPERLY

The simultaneity of God's time is revealed paradigmatically in the incarnation of Jesus. God's timefull simultaneity finds its transformative locus in the body of Jesus. With the coming of Jesus, time has been radically reoriented. In Galatians 4:4 (NKJV) the apostle Paul writes, "But when the fullness of time had come, God sent forth his son, born of a woman, born under the law." Such an observation leads Judith Shulevitz to reflect:

> The time is full, Paul explains, because it is the moment when God "sent forth his Son." Kierkegaard called the fullness of time "the pivotal concept in Christianity, that which made all things new." Paul endows this over plenitude with an aching sensuality. The fullness of time is the moment when God (through Christ and the Holy Spirit) invades the present and fills it with his presence.[20]

Jesus is the Lord of all time. "He is the one who redeems time and who redeems us *in* time and so makes us ready for eternity."[21] In Jesus, fallen time begins to encounter its redemption. In Jesus the time*fullness* of God is revealed. In Jesus, as Timothy George puts it, time has become "the arena of redemption and hope."[22] Time matters eternally because Jesus opens its fullness up to the world and draws creation into the heart of God. In Jesus we have the opportunity truly to become timefull people.

In his reflections on time and providence, Scott Bader-Saye points out that "the ways we experience, name, and interpret time contribute to the kinds of communities we imagine and inhabit."[23] We have already gained some insight into how this might work itself out negatively in relation to the connection among clock time, disability, and Western culture. Positively, in the light of the time revealed in and through Jesus, Christians are called to learn to inhabit the world in quite particular ways and come to engage with time in ways that are distinctively different from those of people who have bought into different narratives that produce different kinds of time. As Bader-Saye puts it, "God's work in history indelibly marks time so that the time framed by incarnation and consummation needs to be lived in a way that recognizes God's intervention in history."[24] We need to be careful here with what we mean by "intervention" lest we drift into deism. God does not intervene from outside of human history for the reasons that are argued within this chapter. What Bader-Saye means by the term "intervention" is the coming of Jesus. Jesus is the one who intervenes in history at a particular moment in time, but God is not outside of human history prior to the arrival of Jesus. Jesus is the ultimate marker of God's presence *within* human history. God's time needs to be lived in a way that recognizes the breaking down of *our* time in light of God's intervention in Jesus. Living in God's time requires that we shape and form our lives and our communities in ways that will enable God's people to participate faithfully in Jesus' redemptive work in time. As Paul states in Philippians 2:5-8:

> You must have the same attitude that Christ Jesus had. Though he was God, he did not think of equality with God as something to cling to. Instead, he gave up his divine privileges; he took the humble position of a slave and was born as a human being. When he appeared in human form, he humbled himself in obedience to God and died a criminal's death on a cross. (NLT)

If we are to have the same attitude as Christ, we need to allow God's time to come upon us; we cannot assist it; all we can do is receive it. As it is received, we are allowed to enter into a quite different relationship with time. To be humble, contingent, obedient, and faithful requires that we inhabit God's time in ways that match the nature of the time within which we live.[25] If time is indeed a gift, this inevitably and absolutely changes our relationship to it. The giftedness of time means that we cannot and indeed should not attempt to master time. To try to master time is to try to master Jesus, and that can never end well. When we try to master time, violence becomes inevitable. That is why Simon Carey Holt can make the rather startling statement that "prolonged busyness is a state of violence":

> According to the Macquarie Dictionary, violence is 'an unjust and unwarranted exertion of force or power.' Such is unchecked busyness, for it is an unwarranted, unjust state destructive to the human soul, to the community, and even to the earth itself.[26]

Misunderstanding time leads to violence, and violence inevitably alienates us from one another and from God who *is* peace: "And Gideon built an altar to the LORD there and named it Yahweh-Shalom (which means 'the LORD is peace')" (Judges 6:24 NLT).

Recognizing time properly is a movement away from idolatry and violence toward faithful timefullness. Those who are made in God's image have time for one another. To give generously of one's time—to care, notice, value, and appreciate time—is to adopt the attitude of Jesus and to begin to tune one's body into the cadence of God's time and the redemption of all time. To live into God's image is, at least in part, to learn what it means to live within the Creator's time. When the world is looked at in this way, those things that we name "disability" begin to look very different.

4

Becoming Friends of Time
Love Has a Speed

> The Lord is not slow in keeping his promise, as some understand slowness. Instead he is patient with you, not wanting anyone to perish, but everyone to come to repentance.
>
> (2 Pet 3:9 NIV)

The previous discussion has indicated that everything that needs to be done has been done for us in the life, death, and resurrection of Jesus Christ.[1] If everything that has to be done has been done for us in Jesus, human beings have no real need to race along trying to do everything on their own, in their own time, and by their own strength. We are freed to slow down and learn what it looks like to accept that everything that is important for the redemption of the world has actually been achieved and, paradoxically, continues to be achieved by, in, and through Jesus.[2] As we have seen, culture informs us that our lives are intended to be lived at speed and that time is of use only if we use it up quickly and efficiently. "If this is the only time you have, do not waste it!" However, if in Jesus the fullness of time is upon us, the Christian calling will be to live out a different understanding of time and to learn how to dwell peaceably within God's time. The beginning point for living out and living within God's time is really quite simple. God is love and God calls us to love. *Such love takes time.*

THE THREE-MILE-AN-HOUR GOD

One of the fascinating things about the extended history offered to us by the theory of evolution is that it emphasizes that God moves very slowly. The slowness of God should not be mistaken for sloth or lack of interest. God is not slow in keeping his promises, as the apostle Peter highlights in the epigraph to this chapter. Rather, God's slowness redefines our understanding of the nature of slow. God is a God who takes time to do things. This observation may be a source of frustration for modern speed-oriented people. It clearly was for the psalmist:

> How long, O LORD?
> Will you forget me forever?
> How long will you hide your face from me?
> How long must I take counsel in my soul and have sorrow in my heart all the day? How long shall my enemy be exalted over me?
> (Ps 13:1-2 ESV)

The answer to the psalmist's cries is, of course, just as long as it takes. God is a God who moves slowly. This may be frustrating, but it is nonetheless important to acknowledge if we are truly to understand what living within God's time means.

In a wonderful book entitled *Three Mile an Hour God*, theologian Kosuke Koyama makes a startling observation about the speed at which God moves and the way in which God uses time. "Forty years in the wilderness points to [God's] basic educational philosophy."[3] Koyama points to the fact that the average speed at which a human being walks is three miles per hour. Jesus walked at three miles per hour. Jesus walked slowly; *Love has a speed*:

> God walks "slowly" because he is love. If he is not love he would have gone much faster. Love has its speed. It is a spiritual speed. It is a different kind of speed from the technological speed to which we are accustomed. It is "slow" yet it is Lord over all other speeds since it is the speed of love. It goes on in the depth of our life, whether we notice it or not, at three miles an hour. It is the speed we walk and therefore the speed the love of God walks.[4]

Koyama's point is that love takes time and love moves slowly. The average speed that a human being walks at is three miles per hour. In his earthly experience, Jesus, who is God, who *is* love, walked at three miles per hour. There is nothing to suggest that he has speeded up following the ascension. We may choose to live our lives very quickly. "When time is money, speed equals more of it."[5] We may choose to stigmatize, alienate, downgrade, and exclude people for taking up too much of our time—for being slow in pace, speech, wit, or intellect—but in the face of the three-mile-an-hour God, such ways of being in the world become revelatory of what it means to love and to be fully human. The reality is that, when time is love, speed equals *less* of it. The love of God is inexorably slow. Jesus walked slowly: Love takes time.

I spoke to a colleague a few weeks ago who is a doctor at a major research hospital in the United States. We were talking about Koyama's book, and he said, "Well, I reckon in my job I have to walk at around six miles per hour!" I said to him, "Who are you following?" If Jesus is walking at three miles per hour and we are walking at six miles per hour, who are we following? God's love is slow; it takes time. Faithful discipleship is slow and attentive to the things that pass us by when we insist on traveling at high speed. There is a great power in slowness.

ON SLOWING DOWN

> Many forms of disability mean that many things in life have to be done more slowly.
>
> (John Hull)[6]

John Hull, a British practical theologian who in his fifties lost his sight because of progressive disease, notes the ways in which his perception of time changed:

> Michael [his work colleague] tells me that he thinks my perception of time has undergone a change since I lost my sight. He thinks that of all the people in the faculty I am the only one who always seems to have plenty of time. Everyone else is rushing around, chasing their tails, trying to cram every minute with necessary tasks and to squeeze the last drop out of time. I alone seem to have all the time in the world. Michael remarked that in my work I don't cut corners; I just go on, doing what has to be done, until it's finished. It does not matter how much time it takes. In his own work he has to cut corners all day long, in order to get his work finished.[7]

Hull's encounter with blindness changed his perception of time. From being a highly busy person who, like many of us, found his life profoundly driven by the clock, he now discovered himself having to engage in a totally different relationship with time. He could no longer *see* the clock and simply could not move at the speed he used to be able to move. Time had become experiential, embodied, less demanding. As the visualization of minutes and seconds disappeared, time slowed down. Somewhat strangely, now he found himself able to get things done, often more things than his sighted colleagues. Time remained the master of those around him, but for Hull time had become different: slow, useful, controlled, bounded. Hull goes on to relate a story about one of his friends who had a mobility issue:

> I had a disabled friend whose restriction of mobility was such that he could only travel about one mile from his home. That, for him, was a day's journey, there and back. He once told me that it took him three-quarters of an hour to tie up his shoe-laces. "Heavens!" I said. "That's a long time!" My friend replied that he did not think of it as a long time; that was just how long it took to tie shoe-laces.[8]

What an interesting way to think about time. Instead of being locked into a master–slave relationship with time, in different ways, Hull and his friend seemed to have come to terms with time and had begun to engage with it in ways that were quite different from those of people who are bound and determined by clock time. Hull continues:

> Most forms of disability mean that many things in life must be done slower. Things take more time. But it is not the things that take the time; it is our bodies that take the time, and the time that takes our bodies. Thus time for the disabled person is neither long nor short; doing this particular job takes me longer than it takes you. However, if I do not compare myself with you, but just concentrate on the task, I am not impatient because I know that this is just how long the task takes.[9]

The way in which Hull articulates his experience of the changes in the feeling, shape, speed, and purpose of time is quite startling. It is not things that take time; bodies take time and time takes our bodies. The key issue seems to be one of *comparison*. To whom should we compare our bodies? If our comparator is the high-speed, progressive, efficient, and self-sufficient body that Standard Average European Time demands, the disabled body can look only inadequate, deficient, slow, handicapped, abnormal (in the senses described in chapter 2). However, if the benchmark is the three-mile-an-hour God—a God who moves slowly and for whom the transformation of creation is a long and timefull process—things look quite different. Viewed in this way, the slowness of disability is seen to be much closer to the slowness of God than is the speed that is demanded from modern societies. The apparent abnormality may well *not* lie in those who are forced to slow down. The great cultural mistake that certain forms of disability draw to our attention is the assumption that speed and its equation with the effective use of time is in any way "normal" for those who perceive themselves as God's creatures. As we begin to notice the dangers of false comparison between the processes of slowing down that disability brings with it and the speedy demands of the clock, we are given the opportunity to notice how far modern perceptions of time are from the ways of God. For Hull to suggest that the point is not how long something takes but that it gets done is indicative of a quite different temporal movement, one in which each body holds its own time and each task moves to its own rhythm. Every task completed is the product of steady, purposeful, timefull action rather than frenzied, time-deprived drives for efficiency.

SLOWNESS IS NOT SLOTH

One objection to my emphasizing slowness in this way might be that the term "slow" has a history of pejorative usage in relation to people with disabilities. This is, of course, an issue; we have previously explored some of the reasons why, in a world of speed, the term "slow" can be highly problematic. Nevertheless, the slowness of God is a different kind of slowness. It is a form of slowness that we can be proud of. The apostle Peter's words are helpful here: "The Lord is not slow in keeping his promise, *as some understand slowness*" (2 Pet 3:9 NIV). If slow is potentially good, godly, loving, and beautiful (as Jesus is), the negative power of the term is significantly reframed. If slowness is in fact the speed of love, then there may well be a deeply revealing beauty in the slowness of disability and a profound challenge to the whole idea of stigmatizing slowing down. God does not understand slowness in the way that many within our own culture might do. The ways in which the slowness of disability reminds us of the slowness of the Divine provides an opportunity to reflect critically on the model of time that guides our lives and to seriously rethink with whom we choose to compare ourselves.

Another objection to the suggestion that slow is both good and divinely valued might be with regard to concerns about the relationship between slowness and sloth. The slowness that disability draws to our attention should not be mistaken for slothfulness. To slow down is not to become lazy, uninterested, or disengaged. It was the slothfulness of the wicked servant that caused him to be cast out into the outer darkness (Matt 25:26). In the book of Proverbs, we find stinging criticism of slothful people:

> I passed by the field of a sluggard, by the vineyard of a man lacking sense, and behold, it was all overgrown with thorns; the ground was covered with nettles, and its stone wall was broken down. Then I saw and considered it; I looked and received instruction. A little sleep, a little slumber, a little folding of the hands to rest, and poverty will come upon you like a robber, and want like an armed man. (24:30-34 ESV)

Sloth is the deliberate attempt by human beings both to own and to waste time. Sloth is a mode of indolence that leads to a willful cessation of faithful participation in God's plans for redemption. Sloth leads to poverty, both material and psychological as well as in terms of our effective usage of time. This is quite unlike the type of slowness we discover as we look toward God's time. Slowness that reflects the slowness of God is not an avoidance of speed or a desire not to do the things that God desires us to do. There is a world of difference between valuing the slowness of our bodies and our minds and living lives that deliberately waste the gift of time.

THE GIFT OF SLOWNESS

In the type of social context we have been exploring in previous chapters, the gifts that slowness brings can easily be misinterpreted and misunderstood. The late and much-missed advocate for inclusion Judith Snow who, since she was seven months of age, lived with spinal muscular atrophy, one of the muscular dystrophies, makes an interesting observation on what she describes as the "gifts" that disability can bring:

> Anyway, some of the other gifts: grounding. Slowing people down. Making them aware of actually where they are or what they're actually doing, and who they're actually doing it with. A lot of people say that when they're with someone who's been labeled something they're forced to get out of their daily rhythm. It takes longer to eat. It takes longer to get into the car and get out of the car. It takes a little bit more time to get communication across and understand what the person is saying. And that in that process of simply slowing down they become much more present to what is going on. Now we do that sometimes in our society but we don't call it helping people so much. Like if I create a spa, and I make people pay big money to lie down and relax, you know, everybody thinks it's great. But if you hire somebody to be with somebody who takes three times as long to walk to the store, somehow there's something wrong with that person, and the other person is really nice for helping me out. And that's the whole conversation of disability.[10]

To be with persons experiencing certain forms of disabilities, people need to slow down. Snow suggests that this slowing down is actually a gift that people with disabilities bring to the table of life: to help others become grounded, to slow down and realize the importance of being present in the moment rather than always rushing on to the next moment. People pay good money to experience this, be that through spas or mindfulness training. However, instead of receiving slowness as a gift from those with disabilities, people are tempted to transpose the gift into acts of charity and in so doing turn the receiver of the gift into an object of charity and the gift giver into an object for the outworking of a slightly paradoxical form of self-centered altruism. Becoming friends of the three-mile-an-hour God means learning how to recognize and to receive gifts that do not always look like gifts. It requires that we readjust our understanding and relation to time. It calls us to become *friends of time*.

BECOMING FRIENDS OF TIME

In the summer of 1995 the British newspaper editor Robert McCrum suddenly and distressingly encountered a radical change in time:

> With no warning, he suffered a stroke that has left him seriously physically impaired. In an essay entitled "My Old and New Lives," he described his initial frustration with the slowing it caused in his life: In the past, I was noted for the impressionistic speed with which I could accomplish things. At first, the contrast was a source of great frustration. I had to learn to be patient. In English, the adjectival and nominal meanings of "patient" come from the Latin for "suffering" or "endurance"—*patientia*. A patient is by definition "long-suffering." When preparing McCrum for the post-crisis stage of recovery, one of his doctors warned him how fast the world was going to feel in his new restricted body, offering the prognosis: "You are about to go through the rapids." But one year after the stroke, McCrum had come to appreciate his temporal life change. "I have," he declared, "become friends with slowness, both as a concept and as a way of life."[11]

"Become friends with slowness." What a striking idea. Once we learn to slow down and realize that, as Stanley Hauerwas has put it, "God *became* time with Christ, which means that we have all the time in the world to do what's necessary,"[12] things begin to look different. Being a friend *of* time means being a friend of Jesus. As we learn to live in God's time, we discover that we are living into Jesus. When we learn to slow down, we begin to see the world as God sees it. When we learn to see the world as God sees it, we begin to understand what it means to be a friend of time.

Jean Vanier, reflecting on the nature of community, talks about the shape and form of becoming time's friend:

> An individual's growth towards love and wisdom is slow. A community's growth is slower. Members of a community need to be great friends of time. They have to learn that many things will resolve themselves

> if they are given enough time. It can be a great mistake to want, in the name of clarity and truth, to push things too quickly to a resolution. Each member of a community who grows in love and wisdom helps the growth of the whole community. Each person who refuses to grow, or is afraid to go forward, inhibits the community's growth. All the members of a community are responsible for their own growth and that of the community as a whole. Perhaps the most essential quality for anyone who lives in community is patience: a recognition that we, others and the whole community, take time to grow. If we are to live in community, *we have to be friends of time*.[13]

Patience, love, wisdom, slowness, and time. Such ways of being in the world are radically different from the clock time–driven, anxiety-ridden ways of living that we have looked at previously. And yet, when understood within the context of God's time, such ways of being can be seen as the core practices that mark faithful living within time that is being redeemed. God's time is slow, patient, and kind and welcomes friendship; it is a way of being in the fullness of time that is not determined by productivity, success, or linear movements toward personal goals. It is a way of love, a way of the heart.

TIME AND GENTLENESS

So, three miles per hour is the speed of love. When we (whether by choice, circumstance, or necessity) slow down and walk with Jesus in God's meaning-filled simultaneous time, we find ourselves noticing new aspects of the world and acting differently in response. Slowing down and paying attention to God's time moves us toward the possibility of gentleness. Jesus is restful, slow, timefull. He holds our burdens (Matt 11:28). But, Jesus is also *gentle*. Timefullness and gentleness are deeply interconnected. In Matthew 11:29 Jesus says, "I am gentle." David Ford notes that

> Jesus' statement, "I am gentle" (Matt. 11:29, my translation), follows on from this beatitude: "Blessed are the gentle, for they shall inherit the earth" (Matt. 5:5). In the rest of the New Testament gentleness appears as one of a small family of interested qualities. The list in Galatians 5:22-3 is: "Love, joy, peace, patience, kindness, goodness, faithfulness, gentleness and self-control." Ephesians urges leading a life "with all lowliness and gentleness, with patience, forbearing one another in love, eager to maintain the unity of the Spirit in the bond of peace" (4:2-3).[14]

There is something quite magnificent about this observation. God, the creator and maker of all that we know, is gentle. It is not that God acts gently or happens to prefer gentleness: God *is* gentle. Scripture is quite clear that God's time contains the shape and form of Jesus: the Alpha and the Omega, the beginning and the end (Rev 22:13). The ethos and movement of time and history is Christ shaped. Jesus *is* time in the sense that in Christ human beings can see clearly what time looks like and what time is for. If this is so, then God's time not only contains gentleness, it *is* gentleness. Gentleness is written into the heart of the universe. God's time is gentle time. The gifts of time and the practices of timefullness that I am suggesting accompany the experience of certain forms of disability reveal different facets of living in God's time, because they are all facets of God. All of these gifts coalesce within the practices of gentle timefullness. God's time is gentle time because God is gentle; God's time is imbued with trust because God *is* trust; God's time is slow, loving time because God *is* love and the coming of the kingdom takes time. When we slow down and pay attention to the slowness of God's time, we encounter one another differently.

TAPPING INTO GENTLENESS

Early in 2014 I spent a few days with Jean Vanier at a L'Arche community in France. Vanier formed the first of the L'Arche communities in 1964: he responded to a call from God and took two men with profound intellectual disabilities out of an institution in Paris and lived with them in the spirit of the Beatitudes and the friendships of Jesus. They lived not as carer and cared for but as friends who shared their lives in mutuality and vulnerability. From that small gesture emerged a movement that now comprises 149 communities, within which people with intellectual disabilities are welcomed and in turn welcome one another as friends—not as carer and cared for but as friends in the Spirit. They live together in an ethos of mutual hospitality, inhabiting a dynamic space within which disability exists but in a way that is quite different from that of the alienating, stigmatizing, clock-oriented society to whom these communities are called to bear witness. Within the L'Arche communities, disability is perceived not as sometimes tragic but more often as a way of being in the world within which gifts are given and received. Disability is seen as a particular way of being human that holds much potential for understanding and practicing love. One of those gifts freely given and received is the gift of time.

Vanier and the L'Arche communities bear witness to a different kind of time. They urge us (all of us together) to become friends of time. In Vanier's words, "The friend of time doesn't spend all day saying: 'I haven't got time.' He doesn't fight with time. He accepts it and cherishes it."[15] Vanier reminds us that in God's good time those people whom the world refuses to spend time with become the very focus of God's attention. God takes time for those things that the world considers to be trivial. Those who follow Jesus—God incarnate—are expected to do the same. There are no lesser lives in the kingdom of God. Spending time doing what the world assumes to be trivial is the essence of the way of the heart and the spirituality of L'Arche.

During my visit to L'Arche, Jean and I spent some time in one of the facilities, La Forestière, which was designed for people with profound intellectual disabilities who have high support needs and communication difficulties that present major challenges to getting their views and preferences heard and understood.[16] After our meal people left the table to do their chores. I was left at the table with Jean and a middle-aged woman Christine, who had no words and apparently, although who knows, little cognitive or intellectual ability. She also had quite significant cerebral palsy. I watched Jean. He looked at her intently, trying to catch her gaze. Eventually she looked at him. He began to tap the table gently. Their eyes met and they looked deeply into one another. Eventually, without looking away from Jean, Christine began to tap her hand in rhythm to Jean's gentle, perseverant tapping. They moved together in a remarkable, gentle, and deeply engaging rhythm. Vanier had nothing to say, and even if he had, what words could he use? There was nothing that needed to be said. In that silent, tender, rhythmic embrace, they were truly together, learning from one another, creating new patterns of knowing that transcended words. Josef Pieper describes love as saying to the other: "It's good that you are here; I am glad that you exist."[17] As I watched Jean and Christine, I could *see* their love. Christine needed Jean to be patient, timefull, slow, and gentle in order that he could see her properly and, in seeing her properly, engage with her in ways that were trusting and evocative of trust. Jean needed Christine to trust him and to show him that he was worthy of trust. Both needed trust, gentleness, and the gift of time in order that the deep cadences of love that were captured in the movement of their rhythmic relationship could flourish. Both engaged and moved with the cadence of the words of the writer to the Hebrews who beseeches us to be sure of what we hope for and certain of what we cannot see (11:1). Jean seemed sure of what he hoped for and certain of what he could not see. And so did Christine. Both exchanged gifts in a form of timefull embodiment that meant that each made time for the other and received time from the other. Time, slowness, gentleness, perseverance, and love: these are the qualities of people who have become friends of time. Time should not be our enemy; it should be our friend. The redemption of time has to do with turning time from an overbearing ruler into a gentle friend.

GOD IS A GOD WHO RESTS

One final observation on the nature of redeemed time will help us further understand the difference and the strangeness of God's time. *In God's time people are commanded to slow down and to rest*. Anxiety is a scourge of our age. Time and our use and perceptions of it are deeply linked with anxiety. The ethos of busyness, competition, and the desire for a certain kind of success inevitably generates anxious people who are constantly concerned that they will fail to achieve their goals or satiate their desires. Even if we are "successful," often we become even *more* anxious, constantly worrying and fretting about how we might lose it all. So we feel that we have to try harder, spend *more* time at work, generate *more* income to buy *more* things that can assure us of the veracity of our success and the wisdom of the ways in which we utilize our time. We can find no time to rest. Even if we do rest, we seem to believe that we really should be "doing something" more productive. It is not difficult to validate such claims. Imagine for a moment being able to answer the question "What are you doing today?" with "Nothing much!" and being proud of that fact. For many of us that is a hard thing to conceive. The fear of failure and the danger of being accused of slothfulness make faithful timefullness difficult. The problem is that when many of us choose to live in such ways we forget that we are Sabbath people who are commanded to *rest*:

> Remember the Sabbath day, to keep it holy. Six days shalt thou labour, and do all thy work: But the seventh day is the Sabbath of the LORD thy God: in it thou shalt not do any work, thou, nor thy son, nor thy daughter, thy manservant, nor thy maidservant, nor thy cattle, nor thy stranger that is within thy gates: For in six days the LORD made heaven and earth, the sea, and all that in them is, and rested the seventh day: wherefore the LORD blessed the Sabbath day, and hallowed it. (Exod 20:8-11 AV)

In the midst of our busyness, it is easy to overlook the fact that God does not just *ask* the people of Israel to rest. God *commands* them to rest. Michael Fishbane draws our attention to the deep dissonance between the time that is embedded in the command to take Sabbath and the time demanded by the clock:

> The Sabbath and its observance may cultivate a theological mindfulness. . . . How so? The Sabbath sanctifies time through sanctioned forms of rest and inaction. On this day certain workaday activities and ordinary busyness are suspended and brought to a halt. In their stead, a whole host of ways of resting the body and mind are cultivated.[18]

Time is sanctified through the Sabbath. What a warm statement. Time is dignified and made holy as it is brought under the command of God. The Sabbath is, as Walter Brueggemann puts it, "a sphere of sanctified inaction."[19] It is a time when God rests and commands human being to rest. "By the seventh day God had finished the work he had been doing; so on the seventh day he rested from all his work" (Gen 2:2 NIV). Such rest does not simply have to do with the cessation of work: "Thank God it's Friday!" Rather, the rest that God commands is "a gift of divine creativity, given to humankind in sacred trust."[20] It is a way of being in the world without anxiety.

> This Sabbath space is sanctified space, a space that restores and renews; one that reintegrates what has become fragmented and strained. In a sense, it's about moving from one experience of time to another; from time that is linear and sequential, purposeful and progressive, directed toward a goal, to a time that is not directional in shape, but a spherical whole that draws the pieces of yesterday, today and tomorrow together. As such, Sabbath is about much more than ceasing work. It's about reconnecting with our origins, living fully the present moment, and anticipating the freedom for which we are ultimately destined. It is time given to "being" and "stillness" over "production" and "movement." It is time for the soul.[21]

This is a very different kind of time.

PHARAOH'S PROBLEM

In his book *Sabbath as Resistance: Saying No to the Culture of Now*, Brueggemann urges us to understand Sabbath rest in the context of the story of the Exodus and in particular the specific nature of Israel's slavery. Pharaoh's main problem, Brueggemann suggests, is that he was driven by profound anxiety. He demanded that the people of Israel work without reward in the toughest of conditions in order that he could overcome his anxiety that there may be another famine. The slave's toil was Pharaoh's Valium! He turned people into commodities to ensure that his heart's desire could be achieved. Time was all about production and the satiation of human desire and angst. There could be no Sabbath under Pharaoh and indeed no Sabbath for Pharaoh.

But with YHWH things are very different. YHWH is not anxious. He has no need to be chasing the next deadline or building empires on the backs of others to alleviate the fear of not achieving YHWH's desires. Rather, as Brueggemann puts it, the conclusion that the Exodus narrative offers to us is

> that wherever YHWH governs as an alternative to Pharaoh, there the restfulness of YHWH effectively counters the restless anxiety of Pharaoh. In our own contemporary context of the rat race of anxiety, the celebration of Sabbath is an act of both resistance and alternative. It is resistance because it is a visible insistence that our lives are not defined by the production and consumption of commodity goods.[22]

YHWH's time is quite different from that of Pharaoh and of contemporary standardized European time: o'clock time. The radical beauty and peacefulness of the ways of God is that this mode of resistance to Pharaoh and all who might think like him is restful, caring, and rehumanizing:

> The Sabbath rest of God is the acknowledgment that God and God's people in the world are not commodities to be dispatched for endless production and so dispatched, as we used to say, as "hands" in the service of a command economy. Rather they are subjects situated in an economy of neighborliness. All of that is implicit in the reality and exhibit of divine rest.[23]

An economy of neighborliness. Now, that is a quite different way of looking at the world and what we should be doing with our time. Work, activity, movement, even speed may well remain important as long as such activities find their proper direction. But now, in YHWH's good time, restfulness—the process of slowing down and taking time for God and self—becomes not only possible and valuable but an irrevocable dimension of faithfulness. The well-being of creation does not depend on endless work and action.[24] Our God is a resting God. "Restfulness and not restlessness is at the center of life."[25] Such an economy of neighborliness "does not produce so much; but it creates an environment of security and respect and dignity that redefines the human project."[26]

Sabbath, then, is a subversive action and a spiritual practice or, perhaps better, a timefull practice. It is a way of being in the world that is restful, timefull, slow, relational, and nonanxious. Some tasks may well require speed and the economic usage of time. But they should be the exception rather than the rule and always focused on glorifying God rather than pleasing humans. Time should never be a burden; it is always a gift. As Jesus says:

> Come to me, all you that are weary and are carrying heavy burdens, and I will give you rest. Take my yoke upon you, and learn from me; for I am gentle and humble in heart, and you will find rest for your souls. For my yoke is easy, and my burden is light. (Matt 11:28-30 NIV)

Jesus embodies the gentleness and the peacefulness of the Sabbath. We are all called to rest in Jesus. As we rest in Jesus, so we learn to be restful people: not simply people who rest but people who can do nothing other than rest in the presence of the Lord.

JESUS RESTS WITHIN US

A story that was given to me by one of the members of the L'Arche community in Trosly, France, will help to consolidate and embody something of the conversation thus far. Danny was a man who lived with Down syndrome. He also had a serious heart condition. One day Danny returned to his community after visiting the cardiologist in Paris. One of his friends asked him where he had been. "To see the doctor," replied Danny. "And what did the doctor do?" his friend asked. Danny replied, "He looked into my heart." His friend smiled. "And what did he see there, Danny?" Danny paused and looked intently at his friend. "He saw Jesus," replied Danny. "And what was Jesus doing?" Danny paused, smiled and looked away. Then he said, "He was resting." Danny smiled and looked away. For Danny, having Jesus in his heart was not simply a useful way of describing and illustrating the pneumatological indwelling of the Holy Spirit, as those of us who interpret the presence of Jesus according to the machinations of our left brains might tend to do. For Danny, Jesus was literally in his heart and he was resting. I ask the readers of this book, is Jesus resting in your heart? I wonder whether when God looks into our heart he finds Sabbath peace or whether all that can be found is Pharaoh's anxiety. Sabbath is not only a day; it is a way of being within creation, a way of living time*fully* and faith*fully* with God. Danny, a man with Down syndrome who has a heart problem, someone whom some would want not to exist and others might consider a waste of time and resources, turns out to be the gentle bearer of deep revelation: *Jesus desires to rest in our hearts*. If Jesus rests in our hearts, then we are surely living in God's time.

IS GOD WITH US WHEN WE RUN?

Not everyone will be comfortable with the idea of slowing down or the suggestion that God moves slowly. What about speed? Are we to somehow reject speed? What kind of society would we be if we were all wandering around at three miles per hour!? The answer is that we should both reject *and* accept speed. I had an interesting conversation with my good friend Lydia Dugdale, who is a doctor at Yale School of Medicine. She had heard me give a lecture on the idea of the three-mile-an-hour God and the importance of slowing down. She was not convinced:

> I listened to your first lecture tonight with great interest. With the exception of your opening comments about God not being fast but slow, I agreed with everything else. God is not slow (he does not walk at 3mph), because as you go on to point out, God created time and is thus outside of time. Since God is outside of time, I am convinced he can run with me when I am running (how else did I make it through residency training with a faith more robust than when I started?) and he can walk with me when I am walking. Sure, sometimes he calls me to sit when I am running or to run when I am stagnant, but I do not think he is a 3mph God. And yet, he is unchanging. But by "unchanging" he can be one who is always outside of time yet always capable of entering into time.[27]

Lydia's point is fair, and we have previously in this book looked in some depth at the "God outside" versus "God inside" time conundrum. It is certainly the case that God is not confined to any form of time and speed. Of course, God can run with us when we run and walk with us when we walk. God sits with us when we sit and stands with us when rise and move on. God is omnipresent, always with us and always for us. Nonetheless, Koyama's point is that three miles an hour is the *average* speed that Jesus walked at. Moving faster is not the norm. Jesus probably did not wander slowly into the temple and slowly overturn the moneychanger's tables! Jesus had his faster times. Slow time does not necessarily rule out or stand opposed to fast time. It is, however, in the slow times of Jesus' life and death that we discover the shape and meaning of love. Whether he is slowing down and taking time with children, stopping and calling Zacchaeus down from the tree, reaching out and bringing healing to the leper, sitting down with crowds on the mountaintop, slowly turning around to see who had taken power from him when the woman with the issue of blood touched his cloak, wandering into the wilderness to listen to the voice of God, or slowly living out the agonizing last few moments on the cross—moments that just dragged on and on—Jesus reveals his love slowly. Jesus takes time because love takes a certain kind of time.

Most of us love our families. However, we do not express that love by running around the living room at twenty-five miles per hour shouting commands and informing them of how much we care for them (although it may sometimes feel that way!). To reveal the depth of our love for our children, our partners, our friends, we need to slow right down, take time, and pay the right kind of attention to them. True, we might run together or do any number of mutually beneficial tasks quickly. But it is in the slow times—when we sit down together, talk, share our innermost secrets—that we learn the timing of love. Slow time is the place where we develop the inner core of love.

Perhaps one way in which we can encapsulate this is by suggesting that the call of the Christian is to develop a slowness in our hearts. We will explore something of what the heart means as we move on. For now, we need to dwell with the suggestion that to walk with the three-mile-an-hour God is to create space within our hearts that is always available to look slowly at our brothers and sisters, to look slowly at God's creation, to look slowly at God, and in looking slowly come to grasp the fullness of what it means to love. Speedy people need to begin their movement from a place of slowness and rest. Busy people need to learn how to work from a place of rest, instead of resting from a place of work.

SLOW AND TIMEFULL FRIENDS

My point in raising the issue of slow time in this chapter has been twofold. First, I have tried to highlight the dissonance between God's time and the types of time that we examined in some of the previous chapters. Commodified clock time is harsh, linear, grasping, and fast, and it pays attention to the world in ways that are reflective of these core tendencies. God's time is slow, gentle, and personal, and it is focused not on human desire but on the divine aspiration for love, redemption, and faithful resting.

Second, a focus on slowness offers a radical counter to some key assumptions that inhabit and seek to colonize both the language of disability and the assumptions that emerge when we name one another incorrectly from within a flawed perspective on time. In God's time we do not compare ourselves to the strongest, the fittest, the fastest, the cleverest, or the most competitive among us. The only comparison that we make is with the God who walks at three miles per hour, a God who waits for us if we cannot keep up and sits with us if we cannot walk. A God who always has time for us. Slowness is a spiritual blessing rather than a negativizing label. Temporally driven name-calling that stigmatizes and alienates people with disabilities as slow either bodily or intellectually is crushed, transformed, and reoriented by the revelation born within the presence of the three-mile-an-hour God.

REDEEMING TIME

We began this chapter by asking what it might look like to live within God's redeemed time. Our reflections on people experiencing a variety of disabilities have begun to open up some fascinating possibilities for answering, or perhaps better, for living out the answers to such a question. Redeemed time, that is, time that is wholly determined by and focused on what God has done and continues to do in Christ, reveals a very different way of encountering the world and a radically changed way of using and experiencing time. In

God's time, the idea of killing people with dementia because they are a drain on our resources and cannot contribute to the so-called good of society seems to come crashing in from another world and another time. Likewise, the suggestion that the world would somehow be a better place without people with Down syndrome is revealed for what it is: a mistake. The intention in this chapter has not been to raise up people with disabilities as somehow ideal exemplars of living within redeemed time. What we have tried to do is to highlight the way in which different bodily experiences reveal different modalities of time and in so doing offer a challenge to our (everyone's) general understandings of what "normal time" might look like and how the experience of disability can help us to see the world and all of us within God's creation differently.

The ideas of slowing down; taking Sabbath, finding Sabbath moments; learning to be gentle, patient, and perseverant; coming to know what it means to become friends with slowness; and becoming friends of time (the practices of timefullness) are not easy to understand or to value in a world filled with clocks and meaningless evolutionary history. However, if in God's coming kingdom "slow is the new fast" and if gentleness and vulnerability are the new modes of transformative power, we find ourselves in a quite different world that holds to a different perception of time. This in turn leads to a different understanding of what the "problem" of disability actually is and who it is that the problem belongs to. In this "upside-down world," which I would argue is the beginning point for understanding the gospel—"These who have turned the world upside down have come here too" (Acts 17:6)—time seems to run in exactly the opposite direction from the ways in which many of us suppose it should: from fast to slow, from idolizing speed to settling into slowness, from clock time to God's time. I will allow Koyama to have the penultimate word:

> The people of God were taught the truth of bread and the word of God in the wilderness as they walked at three miles an hour by the three mile an hour God. The Canaanite woman believed in Jesus Christ against all her own speeds by trusting the speed of the promise of God.[28]

Love takes time. So also does redemption.

III

FROM INCLUSION TO DISCIPLESHIP

5

Time and Discipleship
Inclusion, Discipleship, and Profound Intellectual Disability

> By this everyone will know that you are my disciples, if you love one another.
>
> (John 13:35 NIV)

> For he will be great in the sight of the Lord. He is never to take wine or other fermented drink, and he will be filled with the Holy Spirit even before he is born.
>
> (Luke 1:15 NIV)

> Don't you realize that all of you together are the temple of God and that the Spirit of God lives in you?
>
> (1 Cor 3:16 NLT)

Timefullness, slowness, gentleness, love, patience, nonanxious presence, Sabbath. What a beautiful world we would live in if, in the power of the Holy Spirit, we could truly learn to live in such ways within God's time. When we concentrate on moving our lives to the cadence of such divine timing, we begin to see the world, God, and those who reside within it quite differently. In particular, in God's good time we (all of us together) can learn to see disability differently. Viewed from within God's time, disability is not perceived in terms of abnormality or tragedy. Rather, if we time it properly, disability plays powerfully into our understanding of the beauty of human diversity and opens up fresh conduits for receiving God's revelation. That is not to suggest that there is no tragedy or pain or lament within the experience of disability. As we will see later in the book, there is a dimension of horror even within God's time. Journeying within the movements of God's time forces us to recognize that one dimension of the experience of being-in-time has to do with loss, brokenness, suffering, and death. Time inevitably has a shadow side. Once something has happened, you cannot "unhappen" it. Nevertheless, even within the darkest regions of time, hope remains if we learn to pay attention to time in fresh ways.

The powerful tension between the expectations of clock time and the practices of slow time is brought into particularly sharp focus within the lives of those people whom society has chosen to name "profoundly intellectually disabled," those people whose intellectual capacities and communicational challenges mean that words and concepts are not the primary ways in which they communicate and make sense of the world. These are people who historically have been considered "weak" and dis-abled in body and mind, those for whom the term "slow" has been used as a damaging polemic. The ways in which such people inhabit the world are deeply countercultural and very often negatively construed. To be slow in body and mind in a hyperactive and hypercognitive society is to risk becoming subject to the type of deadly attitude that we discussed previously in our conversation around Richard Dawkins' comments on Down syndrome.

Within church communities it is often unclear as to precisely what position people living with this form of disability are deemed to hold within the body of Christ. These are people who have no access to the gospel, if access is assumed to require a certain level of intellectual awareness and knowledge. These are persons who reside within Christian communities and who are, I am sure, loved by many within their communities. Nevertheless, precisely what their identity and role is within the Body is often quite unclear. The presence of such lives raises significant practical theological questions: Are these people really disciples? If they are disciples, then what does it mean for them to know Jesus and to follow Jesus when they can never intellectually know anything about Jesus? How can they proclaim the name of Jesus and be saved (Rom 10:9) if they have no words or concepts that could facilitate such an action? Perhaps most importantly, what kind of vocation could they have? How could God call such apparently helpless people to do anything?

In spite of the fact that, as we have seen, the lives of people with profound intellectual disabilities seem to mirror central aspects of what it means to reside within God's time—slowness, gentleness, dependence, vulnerability, noncompetitiveness, trustfulness, restfulness, and so forth—they frequently find themselves rejected, stigmatized, and discarded precisely *because* their lives comprise such things. Even among the followers of the three-mile-an-hour God, there can be an implicit or explicit uncertainty as to the status of those with this kind of life experience. A critical theological reflection on the experiences of people who live within God's creation in such ways will not only help the church to practice time more faithfully; it will also bring some surprising blessings that may transform our understanding of what it means to live well as Jesus' body.

PROFOUND AND COMPLEX INTELLECTUAL DISABILITIES

It is important that we are clear with regard to precisely what type of disability we are focusing on in this chapter. We are not talking about disability in general or even intellectual disability as a broad concept. The people who are the focus of this chapter live with what is formally classified as "profound and complex intellectual disabilities." Put simply, the term relates to a group of human beings who are deemed to have limited communicational skills, restricted or sometimes no self-care skills, and significant intellectual or cognitive difficulties, or both. Such people reside in the world without the language and concepts that many people use and that are often assumed, by some, to be necessary to understand the fundamentals of the Christian faith. Those living out their lives in such ways are people to whom the modern category of free, autonomous individual—someone whose life is marked by individual choice—could never be applied. They have limited or no autonomy, power, freedom, or choice, and as such are essentially both vulnerable and dependent. People with such life experiences are perceived to be slow insofar as many have mobility impairments that slow them down and force those who are with them to do the same. They are also presumed slow because of the fact that their intellectual capacities simply cannot keep up with the expectations of highly intellectualized, hypercognitive Western societies and as we shall see, sadly, many of the demands of the church. They are precisely the people who Richard Dawkins suggests live lives that are inevitably marked by suffering and therefore should not be allowed to come into the world.

THE PARABLE OF THE WICKED SERVANT

In teasing out and exploring the nature of the vocation of people who live such lives within God's time, an interesting place to begin is with Matthew's rendition of the parable of the wicked servant (25:14-30). In this parable we encounter a powerful lesson about what God wants us to do with the time that God gives to us. In the parable a rich man decides to go on a journey. In his absence he entrusts his property to his servants. He gives five talents to one, two to another, and one to a third. The story tells of how those with the most talents took them into the marketplace and made more money for the master. But the man who had received the least talents simply dug a hole and hid his master's money. When the master returned, he was greatly pleased with the servants who had invested his money well. He was, however, less than happy with the servant who had simply hidden his talent, accusing him of wickedness and slothfulness. The master takes his talent from him and casts the wicked servant into the outer darkness, where there is much weeping and gnashing of teeth. It would seem that making proper use of one's time and talents pleases God and wasting one's time and talent brings on an encounter with God's wrath.

I imagine that most Christians have no real desire to identify themselves with the wicked and lazy servant! Many of us are keen to discover the nature of our vocation and to strive to do that which God has called us to. We have a desire to maximize the talents that have been given to us. All of us desire to hear the words, "Well done, good and faithful servant. You have been faithful over a little; I will set you over much. Enter into the joy of your master" (Matt 25:21 ESV). However, what if we look at this parable from another angle? What if our primary hermeneutic of the passage is the life experience of people with profound and complex intellectual disabilities? Reflecting on the parable with such lives as our lens, it could be argued that we (and in this case the term "we" refers to the whole church, all of those who claim to be followers of Jesus) were in danger—explicitly or implicitly—of behaving in precisely the way that the wicked servant behaved. The only difference being that, instead of burying our own talents, we may wittingly or unwittingly be party to an attitudinal and theological process that serves to bury the talents of others. Think of it in this way: Imagine that the church is the servant and the "talents" are the various vocations of all of its members. If we fail to recognize some persons' vocations, do we not force them to bury their talent? If that is so, then the church may well be functioning in a way not dissimilar to that of the wicked servant. The argument of this chapter and the next will propose that the church needs to move away from framing the lives of people with profound and complex intellectual disabilities in terms of charity and pastoral care and begin to attend to issues of theology, discipleship, and vocation. What might the church look like if people with profound and complex intellectual disabilities were conceived of as *disciples* with a distinct *vocation—a calling given to them by Jesus*?

THE PROBLEM WITH MEMBERSHIP AND INCLUSION

A few years ago as part of a research project that was run out of the Centre for Spirituality, Health and Disability at the University of Aberdeen in

Scotland,[1] my colleague Elaine Powrie (now Carnegie) and I spent eighteen months exploring the spiritual lives of people with intellectual disabilities.[2] During the course of the project, we met Loraine. Loraine was a middle-aged woman who loved Jesus very much. She also happened to have an intellectual disability. She lived quite a full life and loved going to her local chapel. But she struggled to find friends. This abstract from our interview with her is enlightening:

> INTERVIEWER: You said that friends are important and people spending time with you?
>
> LORAINE: Well that's my opinion.
>
> INTERVIEWER: Is there anything else we all need to get through life?
>
> LORAINE: I can't think of anything.

Loraine longed for friendship but struggled to find any faithful, long-term friends. She was a warm and affable woman, but she just could not find anyone who was prepared to give her time. Loraine felt very lonely sometimes. She loved going to chapel and attended regularly. But there was a problem:

> INTERVIEWER: Where do you feel you belong?
>
> LORAINE: Well I sort of feel I'm trying to help in the community. I'm participating . . . I'm trying to build up a friendship.
>
> INTERVIEWER: You're trying to build up friendship. Where is that?
>
> LORAINE: At the church.
>
> INTERVIEWER: At the church, and how are you getting on there?
>
> LORAINE: OK.
>
> INTERVIEWER: Is that by meeting people or by them inviting you into their homes . . . or?
>
> LORAINE: By meeting people at the church.
>
> INTERVIEWER: And how do you find that? Do you find it easy or difficult?
>
> LORAINE: Easy.

INTERVIEWER: Quite easy. So do you go to meetings during the week or do you go to people's houses or do you just see them at Mass?

LORAINE: Just see them at Mass.

And herein lay the problem. Loraine attended church, participated in the worship, and loved having tea with her friends after the service. It looked as though she was included within that congregation, and in one sense she was. The people there certainly did not reject her, but when I asked her how often she saw her church friends during the week, the situation began to look a little different. She *never* saw them. Within the boundaries of the Sunday morning religious service of worship, she seems to have found acceptance, inclusion, and a certain level of friendship. However, that acceptance and friendship stopped at the door of the chapel. Loraine was *included* within the fellowship of the church, but she did not *belong*. No one visited her, no one *missed* her, because no one, I suspect, really loved her. Loraine's loneliness points toward a subtle, hidden brokenness within Jesus' body as it revealed itself within her experience of church. Even though God's people may have thought they were doing a good job of including her, I imagine that Jesus wept for her loneliness.

INCLUSION AND THE NEED FOR LOVE

Loraine's story raises critical questions around the veracity of the idea of inclusion. To date, a primary focus within the field of disability theology has been on issues of justice, equality, self-representation, and, in particular, *inclusion*. The driving need has been to ensure that people with disabilities can find a place of inclusion within church communities, and more broadly within society, where they can be treated fairly and equally. This is, of course, a most important conversation that has had some success in opening up spaces of inclusion for people with a variety of disabilities. There is no question that inclusion is important, but so also is the *reason* that one might desire people with disabilities to be included. Often the term "inclusion" has been framed as a *political* concept grafted in to ensure that certain rights and expectations are safeguarded for people with disabilities. In line with the politics of inclusion, particular sets of social policies and accompanying practices have emerged that are designed to ensure justice and equality. In terms of legislation, the Americans with Disabilities Act in the United States and the Disability Discrimination Act in the United Kingdom encapsulate something of this political dimension. From this angle, the arguments around inclusion tend to be framed in terms of equality, access, freedom, autonomy, justice, and fairness.

The problem with the inclusion agenda is that there is no innate moral mechanism within the contemporary political discourse that might obligate or even encourage people to *love* those whom society considers to be different. Politics, law, and civil rights can certainly force people to include other people at a certain level. It can open up private and public spaces that have previously been closed to people with disabilities and make sure that these spaces are safe places where personhood is respected and new possibilities for acceptance, equality, and creative growth become real and transformative. This can only be a good thing. There is, however, a problem. To be included, a person just needs to have access and the authority to be in the room. There is no necessity for anyone to think what it might mean to love that person. This was Loraine's problem. She was included, but she did not belong and she was not necessarily loved.

The idea of inclusion therefore works well at the level of politics and social justice in that it enables people with disabilities to achieve certain goals and at least a minimal level of acceptance. It is, however, much less successful in opening up spaces wherein "mere encounters" can lead to meaningful friendship, belonging, and love. This observation is not a by-the-way for Christian communities. *It is the ability to love, not the ability to include or tolerate, that is a primary mark of discipleship*:

> A new commandment I give to you, that you love one another; as I have loved you, that you also love one another. By this all will know that you are my disciples, if you have love for one another. (John 13:34-35 NKJV)

Christian communities are not called simply to include people with disabilities; they may be obligated by law to do so, but this is not the nature or texture of their vocation. *The vocation of the Christian community is to learn to love God, and in coming to love God, learn what it means to love and to receive love from all of its members.* That is what disciples do, and that is what disciples *expect* other disciples to do. The failure to create spaces of belonging for people like Loraine, spaces wherein people can experience, participate in, and have the opportunity to share the love of God, is a failure of theology and discipleship, not just politics. If Loraine were to be truly conceived of as a disciple—someone called to love and share God's love—people would visit her, they would learn what it means to love her, and they would miss her when she was not there. My sense is that Loraine was conceived of as a member, but not necessarily as a disciple.[3]

FROM INCLUSION TO DISCIPLESHIP: CAN A PERSON WITH A PROFOUND INTELLECTUAL DISABILITY BE A DISCIPLE?

If it is difficult for Loraine—someone who loves Jesus and can articulate her love fairly well—how much more difficult will it be for people with profound and complex intellectual disabilities to be accepted as disciples who are called to love and to be loved? A number of years ago, John Hull wrote a short paper entitled "Could a Blind Person Have Been a Disciple of Jesus?" In it he tried to make the case that it would have been impossible for one of the disciples to have been blind, as Jesus would have considered himself obliged to heal him! Not to do so would have been a bad witness to Jesus' healing ministry. Hull's underlying and important point is the apparent incompatibility between disability (in this case blindness) and discipleship within certain readings of the Gospels. This incompatibility is compounded by the general scriptural tendency to associate blindness with darkness and to juxtapose it to a lack of divine enlightenment. Hull argues that there is negative dissonance within Scripture around disability and discipleship that raises significant difficulties for people who are blind and who desire to be acknowledged as disciples without being healed.[4]

The significance of Hull's point stretches beyond the world of blindness. A similar question could be raised in relation to the spiritual lives of people with profound and complex intellectual disabilities: *Could a person with such a form of disability be a disciple?* The answer to the question pivots around another question: *What exactly is it that one has to know, do, or be to become a disciple?* One apparently obvious answer is that disciples are people who believe in Jesus. However, the idea of believing in Jesus is not straightforward. Stanley Hauerwas draws attention to the fact that often within Christian communities

> a great emphasis is placed on the importance of "belief." In attempts to respond to critiques of Christian theology in modernity, the importance of intellectual commitments often is taken to be the hallmark of participation in the church. . . . Yet the more emphasis that is placed on belief, particularly for individuals, the more the mentally handicapped are marginalised.[5]

"Belief" here refers to intellectual awareness of and adherence to a set of rationally verifiable propositions. Hauerwas points out that this way of formulating belief emerges from a particular kind of apologetic carried out by the church in its attempts to find epistemological credibility within modernity. A cognitively oriented understanding of the relationship between belief and discipleship, unsurprisingly, appeals to the rational sensibilities of many modern Christians.[6] If this is what belief means, then those living with profound and complex intellectual disabilities can never believe in Jesus. This sounds rather disturbing. But then again, John the Baptist was filled with the Holy Spirit while he was still in the womb (Luke 1:15); before he could know God intellectually, God was with him. Perhaps there is another way of looking at the issue of what it means to know God?

WHAT DO DISCIPLES DO?

As one reads through the vast literature on discipleship, one limitation quickly becomes very clear. Most of it is not written with people who are profoundly intellectually challenged in mind. A good example is found in Kathryn Tanner's book *Theories of Culture*.[7] In her discussion of Christian identity and discipleship, Tanner concludes that

> Christians are identified by the importance they give to distinctive slogans or formulae (like the ones found in liturgical use and often summarized in early doctrinal statements), by the prominence in their way of life of certain patterns of speech or ritualized actions (say, the motif of dying and rising; baptismal and communion rituals), by their penchant for an unusual vocabulary (for instance, Jesus as "the Christ"). They gain their identity in virtue of the way their lives revolve around such things, in virtue of the central significance of these things for determining the course of their lives.[8]

If this is what identifies Christian disciples, then people with profound and complex intellectual disabilities can never be disciples. Indeed, I suspect many others would be excluded if this were the only criterion for being a Christian. Tanner seems to have in mind a distinctly modern anthropology that clearly prioritizes the intellect or at least assumes it to have a deep significance. For Tanner, Christians should be able to interpret a wide array of cultural materials and to use them as they develop their identity as faithful disciples. Being a disciple is a highly intellectualized activity that requires something akin to a mode of Kantian rationality that sits at the core of all human beings and enables them to make sensible, impartial judgments.[9] Part of the problem with Tanner's formulation of the issues is that, as Medi Volpe rightly points out, Tanner's understanding of discipleship is not christological enough:

> Tanner's insistence that we are disciples of *God* undermines discipleship entirely. . . . [T]he idea that we are "disciples" only arrives with *Jesus*. We

> are disciples of God, yes, disciples of God, the Incarnate Word. It is the master whose example we follow that makes us disciples. We may consider discipleship at least in part as the task of developing our capacity to reflect properly the God in whose image we are made . . . but as we do so we are always conscious that the perfection of that reflective activity has a face, a human form: Jesus is "the image of the invisible God" (Colossians 1:15).[10]

Volpe calls on us to pay attention to the significance of the christological nature of discipleship. Christians are disciples of *Jesus*, the one in whom the Word became flesh. Tanner seems to be trying to turn the flesh of Jesus back into words.

In formulations such as this, disciples have to think in quite complex ways and to use their intellect and knowledge as a means of coming to know and to follow Jesus (prayer and spiritual formation). Disciples need to actively and intentionally come to know and trust in Jesus with their minds (scriptural knowledge) as well as with their bodies (the practices of worship), to understand complex concepts and ideas about God, Jesus, and the Holy Spirit, the nature of Christian life, and the criteria for salvation (basic theology). Disciples need to engage and interact socially with other disciples within God's community in ways that enhance their sense of community and their love for God (fellowship, community, sharing, confession, friendship, *koinonia*, and so forth). They have to be able to articulate what they believe about God in a persuasive manner in the hope that those who do not share their beliefs can understand them and be enticed to accept them (evangelism, apologetics, proclamation). Being a disciple, it would seem, is a pretty complex business! Viewed in this way, it is not difficult to see why some might question whether those who can do none of these activities can really be called disciples. Members, yes, maybe; cared for yes, of course; included, yes; but disciples?

Now, one might counter, "What difference does such an observation make? As long as people are included, cared for, and allowed to participate at whatever level they can, surely that is enough? Why do they need to be perceived as disciples?" There are two answers to such questions, one obvious and one not so obvious. The obvious answer is that within many perspectives on the nature of Christianity, being a Christian is equal to being a disciple. There is no such thing as being a member and then being a disciple. Discipleship and membership in the body of Christ are the same thing, an integral part of the same dynamic. If people with profound and complex intellectual disabilities are not considered true disciples, even though they may be people whose inclusion is desirable, their status as part of the Body becomes at best tenuous and ambiguous and at worst untenable.

The second reason discipleship may be an important way of naming people living with this form of disability relates to the implicit assumptions that emerge if we *do not* use the language of discipleship. An example from a slightly different context will begin to illustrate and draw out why the language of discipleship may be important. In a project aimed at understanding the spiritual needs of people with profound and complex intellectual disabilities, my colleague Susannah Baines and I worked alongside a number of families, with the intention of developing an approach that would enable families and religious communities to work with people with intellectual disabilities in order to understand the spiritual needs and create communities where people truly belong. The story of one young man with whom we spent time will be helpful at this point.

JOHN'S STORY

John was fourteen years old when we met him. He had a profound intellectual disability and cerebral palsy, which meant that he required a polystyrene shell to hold his spine at a particular angle when he was sitting down. He spent most of his day in a wheelchair. John loved church, and in particular he loved the music in the worship service. He would sing without words and shout joyously as the worship band played. Within the congregation he was accepted and included, and he and his family were quite well embedded within the community. On the surface all seemed to be well, until the church decided to begin a healing ministry. The problem was not the healing ministry per se. John's family were of the opinion that if God wants to heal something, even disability, then God is completely free to do so. They did not seek healing for John, but they appreciated it is as a potential option. The problem that emerged had to do with the way in which the focus on healing within the congregation revealed people's implicit attitudes toward disabilities in general and the origins of disability in particular. Those heading up the healing ministry held the view that illness and disability were the result of transgenerational sin. Disabilities were perceived as a direct result of someone or some group of people being at odds with God's will at some point in a family's history, down through the generations. According to the theology that underpinned this community (and it turned out that this was a shared view within the community), such sins may have taken the form of membership in the Masons or Roman Catholic secret societies. These transgenerational sins evoked curses that then took the form of disease or disability, which the healing ministry hoped to relieve by prayer. All of this was news to John's family! Bad news . . .

The development of the healing ministry had two effects. First, it evoked fear. Even though John's disabilities clearly stemmed from physical damage he received at birth, John's mother believed that the leaders of the Healing Ministry would try to explain his disabilities according to the narrative of transgenerational sin. She was fearful that they would expect her to take John for healing. This never happened, but the fear remained.

Second, such a framing of disability revealed the fact that although John was included within the congregation, he clearly did not *belong* to it. Within the communal narrative that perceived his life experiences as the product of sin, it was very difficult to see how he could truly belong to the community even though he was included within it. In our research notes we jotted down:

> *Attempts to foster an inclusive environment for people with intellectual disabilities within a church holding such ideas is going to continue to be difficult for John's family.*

To put it mildly, that was an understatement! How could he or his family truly be a part of the community if the community believed that John was the product of sin and needed to be changed, healed, and cleansed? The community continued to welcome John and his family. They may well have cared for them. But their perception of his disability and its implications for his status within that community resonated with a deep and awkward dissonance. John was *in* the Body but not truly *of* it.

RETHINKING DISCIPLESHIP: EMBODYING THE CALL

John's story is helpful in that it illustrates some of the ways in which people can be in communities but not of them, included but not belonging. The underlying, previously unarticulated views of the community presented a difficult and perhaps ultimately impermeable barrier for John's family's sense of belonging. To be implicitly or explicitly perceived as a nondisciple within the "community of disciples," as Avery Dulles names the church,[11] is a difficult and uncertain space to inhabit, even if on the surface people are nice to you. Had that congregation considered John to be a disciple with a vocation and calling just as he was, then at a minimum the community's theological connection between sin and disability would have encountered a significant challenge and corrective.

Moving beyond "you and me, Jesus . . ."

How then might we proceed in rethinking discipleship in a way that takes seriously the suggestion that people with intellectual disabilities are disciples who have a calling and a vocation? Medi Volpe offers a useful beginning point for such reimagining:

> I wonder if part of the problem [with certain understandings of discipleship] is our tendency to make the practice of Christianity the activity of individuals in a common pursuit. We might pray and worship together, even envision ourselves to be on a journey together, but at the end of the day, we have a "Jesus and me" mentality. My hunch . . . is that being disciples of Jesus is only ever about Jesus and *us*, which gives us some more options for thinking about the way of discipleship for folks who are intellectually disabled. Scripture and tradition (broadly speaking) attest to the not-alone-ness of following Jesus. The episode of the paralytic whose friends lower him through the roof suggests . . . that getting to Jesus doesn't have to be something we do by our own ability or initiative.[12]

When we find ourselves paying attention to discipleship in ways that reduce it to an intellectual task with communal consequences, it becomes *individual* rather than *corporate*, something that we *are* as individuals rather than something we *do* and *become* together. Salvation is considered to be *mine*, not ours; vocation is inescapably *mine*, not God's gift to the community; my choices are *my* choices. "It's you and me, Jesus. . . ." If Volpe is correct, the problem of what we might call "the intellectualization of discipleship" is one that emerges from modern understandings of what it means to be a human being. Discipleship has been framed primarily as a *personal choice* that we make as individuals wherein we decide to follow or not to follow Jesus. Like the six-mile-an-hour doctor following the three-mile-an-hour God, many assume that in our self-made freedom we *choose* Jesus, often after a process of intellectual reflection wherein we discern the rational basis for making such a personal choice. This seems strangely opposed with what we encounter in the gospels wherein *the disciples are always called and told what to do*. The pattern of the gospel is not that we choose Jesus but that Jesus chooses us. The disciples are called and respond, not first and foremost because they know who Jesus is; as we will see, at least in the early days, they did not know who he was. They responded to his call because they trusted Jesus even though they did not truly understand him or know the fullness of his identity. They were called to *him*, not to knowledge about him, and their response was based not on propositional belief but on relational trust.

FAITH AS TRUST: WHAT DOES IT MEAN TO BE A DISCIPLE?

This critical tension between knowing things about God and knowing God is a central dimension of what the Gospels have to say about discipleship. Dietrich Bonhoeffer in his book *Discipleship* reflects on the call of Matthew and makes a somewhat surprising observation: *Matthew did not know anything about Jesus when he was called.* Bonhoeffer observes that in Matthew's account of the disciple's call

> the call goes out, and without any further ado the obedient deed of the one called follows. The disciple's answer is not a spoken confession of faith in Jesus. Instead, it is the obedient deed. How is this direct relation between call and obedience possible? It is quite offensive to natural reason. Reason is impelled to reject the abruptness of the response. It seeks something to mediate it; it seeks an explanation. No matter what, some sort of mediation has to be found, psychological or historical.[13]

One could infer that Matthew had heard the rumors and that he was prepared to answer the call according to previous knowledge of who Jesus was. However, the text simply does not say that. To make such interpretation you have to move to another place and another discipline. Bonhoeffer notes, "The text is not interested in psychological explanations for the faithful decisions of a person. Why not? Because there is only one good reason for the proximity of call and deed: Jesus Christ himself."[14] Matthew was not called to be a disciple because of what he knew about Jesus. His was not an act of intellectually driven choice, personal preference, or well-researched decision making. The actions of Matthew were simply manifestations of obedience and trust: Jesus called, Matthew followed.

Likewise, Jesus did not call Matthew because he recognized in Matthew a deep knowledge of who Jesus was, knowledge that was sustained by a profound and well-thought-through intellectual belief system. Matthew was called by Jesus simply because Jesus desired his company and had something for him to do. Jesus chose to walk with him and enable him to use his talents wisely and faithfully:

> It is he [Jesus] who calls. That is why the tax collector follows. This encounter gives witness to Jesus' unconditional, immediate, and inexplicable authority. Nothing precedes it, and nothing follows except the

> obedience of the called. Because Jesus is the Christ, he has authority to call and to demand obedience to his word. Jesus calls to discipleship, not as a teacher and a role model, but as the Christ, the Son of God.[15]

It is interesting to notice that throughout the Gospels the disciples were constantly confused about who Jesus was. They were clearly, in some senses, cognitively disabled! That being so, it seems that propositional knowledge of Jesus was not the main criterion for receiving the call to discipleship. The only content of the call was Jesus. As Bonhoeffer again observes:

> No further content is possible because Jesus is the only content. There is no other content besides Jesus. He himself is it. So the call to discipleship is a commitment solely to the person of Jesus Christ, a breaking through of all legalisms by the grace of him who calls. It is a gracious call, a gracious commandment. It is beyond enmity between law and gospel. Christ calls; the disciple follows. That is grace and commandment in one. "I walk joyfully, for I seek your commands" (Ps. 119:45).[16]

Jesus called the disciples to himself, not to an idea, a creed, or an ideal but to himself. Over time they learned what it meant to know things about him. However, that was not the *criterion* for their discipleship; it was the *consequence* of their discipleship. Coming to know things about Jesus—who he was, what his mission was and so forth—came about as a consequence of being with Jesus, not as a prerequisite for discipleship. It is true that over time and particularly after the resurrection, their intellectual knowledge of Jesus increased, at least in accuracy . . . eventually. But, to repeat, such knowledge was not the criterion for discipleship; it was only one aspect of the consequence of following Jesus. Knowledge about Jesus can thus be seen as a secondary consequence of being called by Jesus. It appears that the essence of discipleship has first and foremost to do with being with Jesus and learning to trust him.

God with us; us with God?

Part of the reason for the dissonance around knowing about and being with Jesus has to do with the ways in which we frame the nature of what it means to be in relationship with God. Human beings do have relationships with God. However, the nature of divine human relationality is easily misunderstood. Any interconnectivity that exists between God and human beings should not be mistaken for a relationship of *mutuality*. David Kelsey points out, "What Christians claim about humankind that nobody else does is that the triune God relates to humankind, and to all else, to create it, to draw it to eschatological consummation, and, when it is estranged, to reconcile it."[17] He asserts that the key issue for Christians is not that *they* relate to God but that *God relates to them*. Scripture consistently tells a story of God relating to that which is not God, to a "reality other than God."[18] The relationship between God and creatures is not like other relationships that human beings engage in. It is not static or mutual. This inequality between human and divine relationships is very important. Not only is there a difference between God relating to humans and humans relating to God, Kelsey also observes:

> The Christian claim is that humankind's relating to God is generally not congruent with, nor an appropriate response to, God's relating to humankind. That is, human relating to God is generally sinful. To declare abstractly that human creatures have the property of "God-relatedness" simply obscures the distinction between God relating to us and our relating to God. What makes Christian anthropology *theological* is that it is ruled by claims about God relating to us. More exactly, it is ruled by claims about the *triune* God relating to us. Such anthropology must be theocentric. Only in and from that context should we derive claims about our relating to God. Speaking of "God relating" rather than about "the God relation" brings that out.[19]

Kelsey's point is important for two reasons. First, to suggest that human beings have some kind of inherent property that constitutes their "God-relatedness" is an *anthropological* statement, not a *theological* statement; that is, it is a statement about human beings rather than a statement about God. Importantly, it is a statement about human beings that misses the point of the biblical narrative that is always about God's relational movement toward human beings and creation. It is this godly movement that should be perceived as the primary theological dynamic. Humans can certainly relate to God but only as a secondary act carried out within the context of God's primary relational activity toward God's creatures and within the boundaries that are placed upon all human relating by the reality of the presence of sin. Discipleship perceived as "you and me, Jesus . . ." is more of a projection than a reality. It is always "Jesus calling me" and me responding in obedience (or disobedience). Discipleship is the receiving of a call from Jesus rather than an outcome of human knowledge and sin-filled attempts at creating God-oriented relationality.

Second, if human understandings of what it means to relate to God were to provide the primary relational dynamic within which human and divine interactions are presumed to occur, our understandings of what it means to relate to God will be bound up in *human* expectations and *human* sinfulness.

Put slightly differently, if our understanding of what it means to relate to God emerges from and is bound by a human point of view, it will be similarly bound by what such limited human perspectives think relating to God means and what it looks like. If humans think that propositional knowledge is important, they will affirm that it is important in the ways in which they expect other human beings to relate to God. If they think that knowing God requires knowing things about God, they will affirm that as an important aspect of what faith in God is, what it looks like, and how that relates to what discipleship is and what it should look like.

However, if our understanding of what it means to relate to God is perceived as coming from a divine point of view, a whole new range of options emerge. Not noticing this tension between God relating to us and us relating to God sits at the heart of controversies over whether people with profound intellectual disabilities or people with advanced dementia can relate to God or should be allowed to participate in the rituals and practices of faith such as baptism and sacraments. If the presumption is that we need to know something or do something in order that *we* can relate to God, relating becomes primarily a human enterprise. However, framing the issue in the way that Kelsey does leaves conceptual room for "stressing that: 'God actively relating' is said in several senses, not one."[20] In other words, the active relating love of God is not univocal; it does not have a single voice. Nor does it function only through a single aspect of human beings: because the initiative is always God's and because God relational activities are multivocal (have many voices and cadences), all of the members of God's body can be seen to be open to God's call in a variety of different ways. In this way God can be seen to relate to all members of the body in ways that are simultaneously unified and diverse.[21]

If this is so, then discipleship is not about what *we* have and what *we* know. It has all to do with who Jesus is, who Jesus calls, what Jesus gifts to us, and what Jesus knows that we do not know. Discipleship in this frame is in a real sense a process of *unknowing*, learning to recognize the inadequacies of what we think we already know. Hauerwas puts it in this way:

> Discipleship is quite simply extended training in being dispossessed. To become followers of Jesus means that we must, like him, be dispossessed of all that we think gives us power over our own lives and the lives of others. Unless we learn to relinquish our presumption that we can ensure the significance of our lives, we are not capable of the peace of God's kingdom.[22]

The key insight from all of this in relation to people with profound and complex intellectual disabilities is that if discipleship is predicated not on human knowledge, wisdom, or choice but on the call of Jesus, their position can be interpreted in a quite different way. If a *lack* of a certain attitude toward propositional knowledge is in some senses important for becoming a disciple, it may be that our brothers and sisters living with profound intellectual disabilities are in a stronger position before God than are those of us who are in many ways held back by our intellect and the desire for life to be reasonable. The apparent "foolishness" of the lives of people with intellectual disabilities may be wiser than human wisdom, and the perceived "weakness" of such lives stronger than human strength.

If what has been argued thus far is accurate, faith seems more like *trust* than like propositional knowledge. Not that propositional knowledge is not important. It is simply that, for the original disciples at least, propositional knowledge was something that emerged from the experience of trusting in Jesus rather than the other way around.

SAVING KNOWLEDGE? RE-MEMBERING THE INTELLECT

None of what has been argued thus far should be mistaken for anti-intellectualism. Bonhoeffer is not saying that the disciples' knowledge of God was ultimately unimportant, only that it was not what they knew that drew them to become disciples. Likewise, Kelsey is not saying that human beings cannot relate to God and can know nothing about God. Rather, he points us toward the place that such relating has within the dynamic relationality that stems from God and into which human relations seek to participate faithfully. Neither Bonhoeffer nor Kelsey is advocating apophasis or blissful ignorance. Equally, my point in developing the argument in the way that I have done is not intended to downgrade intellectual knowledge but rather to put it in its proper place. Rather, it is my intention to re-member discipleship. If to take something apart is to dismember it, then re-membering something is to bring it back together again. The intellectual dimensions of discipleship are important. The problem is that they have become dis-membered from the fullness of discipleship. Our focus on the lives of people with profound and complex intellectual disabilities draws us toward the fullness of discipleship within which intellect has a role but is not definitive of what it means to be called by Jesus. So how best can we place the intellect as an aspect of our discipleship?

THE SAVING ROLE OF DOCTRINE?

Medi Volpe, in her paper "Saving Knowledge: Doctrine and Intellectual Disability,"[23] lays out a perspective that helps to hold the tension between the importance of intellectual knowing, discipleship, and Christian doctrine. Volpe recalls being challenged in the classroom by one of her students as to the relevance of the Arian controversy for most people's walk with Jesus. Volpe admits that it probably does not have much obvious relevance to the average Christian in the pew. Nevertheless, she argues, that does not mean that doctrine is irrelevant or superfluous for the church and for Christians. She draws out the implications of this conversation with the backdrop of her own experience as a mother of a child who has Down syndrome.

At the heart of her argument is the suggestion that doctrine should not be conceived of as saving knowledge, although it does participate in the revelatory and redemptive movement of God toward and within creation. The work that doctrine does, Volpe argues, differs according to the cognitive faculties that one has been given. Drawing on the thinking of Gregory of Nyssa, Volpe emphasizes that what we believe as Christians requires a degree of "epistemological reserve."[24] The parameters of what we believe cannot be allowed to run amok. Such epistemological reserve safeguards Christians against heretical ideas that distract us from truly loving God. Gregory points out how the human imagination is central to the ways in which we come to think about God. Imagination is necessarily creative and potentially good. There are, however, always boundaries across which the human imagination should not pass. The essence of sin is the human tendency to imagine a world without God. Volpe grasps the apostle Paul's phrase "taking every thought captive to the obedience of Christ" (2 Cor 10:5 NASB) and uses it as a way of explaining the function of doctrine and the nature of discipleship:

> Taking every thought captive to the obedience of Christ points to an intellectual dimension to discipleship. "Thought" encompasses the whole person: reason, imagination, desire. To be wholly obedient to Christ includes holding to the knowledge of God as Christ reveals God. Doctrine is the churches' unfolding of that knowledge through the interpretation of Scripture. Each move forward in interpretation answers some questions and raises others. Thus the Church is constantly involved in meditation on the Scriptures in the light of past interpretation and in the face of new questions to which Jesus is the answer, and new situations in which the Spirit's power is desperately needed.[25]

Doctrine is thus perceived to be a function and a gift of the church. Over time those called to be theologians enable the church to move toward a clearer and more authentic understanding of who God is in Christ. Doctrine feeds, shapes, forms, and informs our imagination and enables us to see Jesus more clearly. Such knowledge is not personal knowledge for the gratification of the individual knower. Rather, it is knowledge that is for the edification, guidance, and teaching of the whole of God's church over time.

Such knowledge places limits on our speculations and anathematizes those aspects of our knowing that stand against God. As such, doctrine is vital in that it "helps us as a community to remember Jesus faithfully, and remain true to his gospel."[26] Doctrine holds us in place as God's creatures, while at the same time drawing attention to the fact that, although there is much to know about God, there is much that can never be known:

> Doctrine helps us to know what we can and ought to see about God, how we should express our faith in God, and at the same time keeps us cognisant of the limitations: God is beyond all we can ask or imagine.[27]

In this way, doctrine helps the church to take every thought captive to the obedience of Christ.

However, the ability to comprehend doctrine with one's intellect is not a gift that is given to all of God's people. The average man or woman in the street does not need to know about the Arian controversy or the history of the doctrine of the Trinity in order to live well with Jesus. For those called to explore such matters and to communicate their importance to the body of Christ, doctrine is an important intellectual practice. However, Volpe argues, *doctrine in and of itself is not saving knowledge*. Only God can bring about salvation, and God is not bound by the limitations of human knowledge. Doctrinal knowledge remains important, because we need it in order that the body of Christ can imagine God faithfully. But it does not save us:

> Not being able to imagine God does not hinder anyone from approaching God, because God is the one doing the approaching! God gives the gift of doctrine to those who require it; God does not demand understanding of doctrine from those who do not need its discipline.[28]

Like Kelsey, Volpe emphasizes that salvation comes to us as God comes to us. Those Christians who are cognitively able (and I use this expression with some reserve) learn to use doctrine to train their imaginations to contemplate God's mystery and enable the church to imagine faithfully. We do not, however, use such knowledge to try to circumvent the mystery of God's approach to human beings. Volpe concludes:

> So doctrine is a tool for us, to remain in the "imagination of our heart" when it has gone, or is at risk of going astray. The limitation of imagination by cognitive infirmity or intellectual disability prevents that

> imagination going astray. This is not to say that someone with a profound intellectual disability cannot know God. It is, rather, to say that such an intellectual disability generally prevents one presuming to know God by reason of her own intelligence or capacity for abstraction. People whose understanding (and especially the communication of that understanding) is feeble remind us that we are always dependent on God to reveal God to us: we are equally incapable of reaching up to heaven even with our minds, to grasp the nature of the Divine. Knowledge of God comes from God; we who are talented with words and ideas and imagination share with one another our conceptions of God, trying to explain to each other what it is we're talking about when we say "God." And our words and ideas and concepts and pictures all fail us. Not that we shouldn't try. We must, actually, speak of what we have heard and seen and experienced. But we must remember that all we can conceive or imagine cannot hold God.[29]

God is mysterious and unable to be fully captured by human words and intellect. What knowledge we have of God is revealed and functional not in a salvific way (i.e., knowledge about God brings about salvation in and of itself) but in a way that expands our imaginations and helps the church (all of us together) to imagine God more clearly and accurately and in so doing facilitate practices and ways of being in the world that are in line with God's intentions and Jesus' calling. Doctrine (knowing things about God), then, has a specific task within God's redemptive movement toward creation, but it is not in and of itself salvific. That being so, for those whose imaginations are not likely to go astray, doctrine is not the way in which they come to know God. Knowledge about God is just one aspect of our life with God, important as that aspect might be. Those who cannot know certain things in certain ways are held and sustained by those who can. This works both ways between those who can use words and concepts and those who do not; both are necessary, and both are called to learn from one another. It is in the mutuality of different modes of knowing as they are manifested through the different bodies that comprise the one Body that we come to understand the fullness of God's love. *There are different ways in which people can come to know Jesus and different ways in which people can hear the call to become his disciples.*

BEARING WITNESS: EMBODIED DISCIPLESHIP

Maurice Merleau-Ponty has pointed out that the intellect is not the only source of human knowledge. Our bodies are an important source of knowledge.[30] It is as we engage with the world in and through our bodies (an engagement that involves but is not defined by our minds) that we come to know things. This mode of knowing prefigures any kind of intellectual conceptualization of knowledge. Our bodies are places through which we come to know the world. The shape, texture, and spatial location of our bodies mean that each of us encounters the world in quite different ways and therefore comes to know the world in quite different ways. We might think of it in this way: if you are blind you will never *see* the Scriptures; if you are deaf, you will never *hear* the word; if you have no arms, you will never *feel* what it is like to embrace someone even though you are embraced. To be embraced by the love of God will have a totally different meaning. If you cannot name Jesus, you will never know what it means to proclaim him with your lips. Such embodied ways of being in the world do not provide better or worse experiences of being with God. They are just different: if you *can* see, you will never know what it is like to encounter God without sight; if you *can* hear, you will never know what it is like to sign the word and to use your body in ways which a hearing person simply cannot grasp; if you *can* remember everything well, you will never know what it is like to encounter God without remembering God. Likewise, if you *can* grasp the concept of Jesus with your mind (and, of course, no one fully can), you will never know what it means to encounter him without words and concepts and, like John the Baptist, be dependent on the Holy Spirit and others to reveal what it *feels* like to be with God. Such embodied ways of being in the world do not provide better or worse experiences. They are just different. They may *seem* better or worse if one resides in a culture that prioritizes certain ways of being in the world, but they are not. It is only when all of these experiences as they are manifested within the body of Christ are recognized, re-membered, explored, respected, and shared that the fullness of what it means to know Jesus can begin to come to the fore. The discipleship of people living with profound and complex intellectual disabilities is not a poor approximation of the discipleship of others within the Body. Quite the opposite, it is a revelation of the fullness and the diversity of the God who calls each one of us within Christ's body and gives us a vocation. The body of Christ is a place of embodied learning wherein the presence of profoundly intellectually impaired people reminds the Body of the necessity and responsibility of revealing the love of God through the practices of love, practices that are not exhausted by the world that the intellect reveals. As we love one another, so we learn what love is and what it *feels* like. As the bodies of disciples relate, so, over time, all of us together learn what it means to be with Jesus and to trust Jesus. As together we engage in loving gestures—taking time for one another; patiently sharing experiences; dwelling faithfully within difficult silences; recognizing the power of passing touches, brief meaningful glances, and moments of eye contact—so we learn to trust and to feel loved. As our autistic brothers and sisters teach us the times and situations when we *should not* use our bodies in such ways, as we share a common history together in a multitude of different ways, so we encounter powerful moments of love within which Jesus comes to be known even if, for some, he is never named.

If we are to take seriously the fleshy nature of learning to be a disciple and as, together, we come to learn the practical and literal wisdom of Paul's statement that our bodies are the temple of the Holy Spirit (1 Cor 6:19), we can begin to see the significance of embodied love as a mode of knowledge and as a way of transmitting practical knowledge about Jesus. As the Spirit within us encounters the Spirit within the other, so in the power of the Holy Spirit we are drawn into the mystery of God and come to learn what it means to *experience* knowledge of God. *Faith is trust.*

BAPTIZED INTO JESUS' BODY

The context that lies behind the conversation that has been laid out in this chapter is the body of Christ, the church. The arguments presented thus far should not be read as necessarily applying to every person with a profound and complex intellectual ability anywhere, anytime, and in any context. In other words, it is not intended to be an argument for some form of universalism or some form of universal love. The arguments presented here relate specifically to those people with profound and complex intellectual disabilities who are part of the Christian community, those who have been baptized into and have become a part of the body of Christ and have therefore found a place of belonging.[31] Baptism, as Jason Whitt nicely puts it, is "a person's initiation into the Church where the gospel narrative—the way of living according to the life, death, and resurrection of Christ—is the identity-forming account of the community."[32] Baptism is a ritual wherein the beginning of our identity as Christian disciples is brought into public view. Bonhoeffer points out:

> What the Synoptics describe as hearing and following the call to discipleship, Paul expresses with the concept of baptism. Baptism is not something we offer to God. It is, rather, something Jesus Christ offers to us. It is grounded solely in the will of Jesus Christ, as expressed in his gracious call. Baptism is essentially a paradoxically passive action; it means being baptized, suffering Christ's call. In baptism we become Christ's possession. The name of Jesus Christ is spoken over baptismal candidates, they gain a share in that name; they are baptized "into Jesus Christ" (, [10] Rom. 6:3; Gal. 3:27; Matt. 28:19). They now belong to

> Jesus Christ. Having been rescued from the rule of this world, they now have become Christ's own.[33]

Baptism is deeply timefull insofar as it implies a *break*.[34] It symbolizes that in Christ "past and present are thus torn asunder. The old has passed away, everything has become new."[35] Baptism is a timefull event wherein we are enabled to participate in the fruits of Jesus' sacrifice historically wrought out on the cross but now available in all of their fullness in and through the sacrament. Baptism is a break with the past that occurs in the present and points toward a new future.

Baptism is a ritual of belonging. As we are baptized into the body of Christ, we are not simply included in what Jesus has done; we *belong* to his new creation. Baptism opens up a liturgical space wherein people with profound intellectual disabilities can be publicly welcomed into Jesus' body and provided with a unique place of discipleship and belonging that is carved out within God's hospitable community. As people are accepted into the body of Christ, as they come to know and experience the love of God as it is mediated by their brothers and sisters in Christ, through the Holy Spirit, so people living with this kind of disability come to know and experience Jesus. Baptism is appropriated by faith, but faith (knowing and trusting God) is learned and shared through the faithful loving presence of Spirit-filled fellow disciples. When people are baptized, welcomed, and enabled to come to know and experience Jesus, so the body of Christ comes to recognize and understand the meaning of slow, gentle, and sometimes wordless discipleship. When this happens the servant can be seen to be acting faithfully.

THE PROBLEM OF SIN

Viewed from the perspective that has been developed thus far, both the nature of discipleship and the process of discipling people with profound intellectual disabilities is relational and embodied. Discipleship has crucial intellectual dimensions for those whose vocation is to communicate those intellectual dimensions of belief to the whole body of Christ. However, those whose imagination does not require to be renewed in this way bring a powerful reminder of the embodied nature of Christian discipleship and the significance of our bodies for understanding who Jesus is and what it means to love and be loved by him.

"But what about sin?" one might ask. Does a vital dimension of discipleship not relate to realizing that one is a sinful, fallen human being who needs to repent past sins and accept the forgiveness of God in a way that at least minimizes sin in the future? Is not making a conscious decision to turn from one's sins and acknowledging the centrality of worshipping God central to discipleship? How can those with profound intellectual disabilities repent and find forgiveness for their sins if they have no concept of what sin is?

These are fair questions. The intention in making a case for faith as trust and love as embodied presence is not to attempt to make people living with profound intellectual disabilities into some kind of holy innocents, somehow to be perceived as above or beyond the fall. It is clear that all of us share in the consequences of human beings' fall from grace. As Paul puts it: "For all have sinned and fall short of the glory of God, and are justified freely by his grace through the redemption that came by Christ Jesus" (Rom 3:23-24 NIV). Nevertheless, it is quite difficult to envisage precisely what sin might look like in the lives of people with the kinds of disabilities we have been reflecting on in this chapter. My good friend and colleague Brian Brock neatly sums up something of the heart of the difficulty:

> If you don't have enough brainpower to name Jesus, you also don't have enough brainpower to be worshipping any false gods, and therefore could only be following the always accessible idols of self or of opening one's self in trust to the other. And as Christians we know there is only one Other in the final analysis. This is not "anonymous Christianity," but an inflection of the theme that God sends rain on the just and the unjust—to receive the rain, and human care, in gratitude and trust is, it seems to me, to be moving toward the Trinitarian God (and this *movement* is what discipleship names), however much one can rationally articulate about the God toward whom one is moving (and we all fall short on being able to articulate this).[36]

Unless we take the Augustinian line that sin is somehow passed on seminally down through the ages, a position that is somewhat difficult to justify from the biblical text, it is difficult to see with any kind of precision what sin might look like in the lives of the people who are the focus of this chapter.[37]

At root, sin is disobedience. One thing that seems perfectly clear from the Genesis accounts of creation is that Adam's primal sin was basically not doing what he was told. God told him to do one thing and Adam chose to do another. God asked Adam to trust him and not to eat from the tree of knowledge. Adam chose not to trust God and decided to do his own thing. Sin is not so much a refusal to believe in God (Adam was not a doubter), as it is a refusal to obey and to trust God. If it is the case, as Brock suggests, that a person with a profound intellectual disability "does not have enough brainpower to name Jesus," the idea of disobeying God seems unlikely. Worshipping false gods is also highly debatable, and at a minimum egoism would have to be quite radically redefined if it were to be applied to people living with this kind of disability.

It is, however, possible for people with profound intellectual disabilities not to trust in the goodness of God and in this sense to have their faith taken from them. If, as has been suggested, people living with such disabilities come to know Jesus through learning to trust in the embodied love of the members that comprise Jesus' body and if that love does not induce faithful trust, people with profound intellectual disabilities will in a real sense come not to trust God's goodness. However, the sin here does not lie with the individual with the disability. Rather, the blame sits firmly with the members of the body of Christ. Any lack of trust (lack of faith in the sense that I have outlined it above) emerges from a failure of the community to reflect and embody the love of God. If this happens, then it is the Body that needs to repent in response to the recognition of such a failure. Repentance means turning from one's sins. It also means turning toward the one you have sinned against. Is that not the essence of forgiveness that leads to reconciliation with God and humans? It may be that people with profound intellectual disabilities are deeply implicated in and influenced by sin, but that the sin may well be located within their communities' inability to share embodied love, rather than in their own deliberate acts of disobedience. If people with profound intellectual disabilities can sin, their sinning is much more corporate and external than many modern perceptions of sin as the act of an individual.[38]

Recontextualizing repentance

It is, of course, the case that in one sense all human beings do share in the primal sin of Adam. We clearly live in a world that is fallen and broken. All of us experience the consequences of sin. There is, however, a difference between sin as a human reality and sin as a particular act or set of actions for which one is morally culpable. For those with the cognitive capacity to recognize sin as a way in which humans have come to inhabit the postlapsarian world and who can understand particular human actions as deliberately, consequentially, or implicitly disobedient, the conscious act of repentance makes perfect sense. Turning away from such actions and learning what it means to walk faithfully with Jesus is desirable and necessary. However, the *point* of repentance is to walk well with Jesus. We should be careful not to confuse the *process* of repentance with its *outcome*. For those who have no way of recognizing and making sense of the nature of primal sin and for whom individual sinful acts not only make no sense but are probably not realistic potentials (willful disobedience, worshipping false gods, failing to name the name of Jesus with accuracy are not options or choices for the people we have been focusing on in this chapter, at least not if such sins are conceived as being cognitive and intellectual in origin and practice), repentance will take on a different form and meaning. If the process of repentance has to do with ridding ourselves of what separates us from God and from others and if the outcome is to walk well with Jesus, then repentance for people with profound intellectual disability—if it relates at all—will relate to the body of Christ finding ways to enable them to trust in God and to live well with Jesus. In this sense repentance will relate to overcoming the effects of sin (separation, alienation, loneliness, and self-sovereignty) and in so doing enable people to trust in God and experience God's love even if that love cannot be directly named. Repentance, in this sense, has to do with overcoming the effects of sin and learning what it means to change sin into something beautiful. Repentance in this way of thinking is not simply an individual choice. Rather, it is something that we do together. Such repentance is a work of the Body.

The reader may at this stage be asking, "What does all of this have to do with time?" The answer is that time sits at the very heart of discipleship, vocation, and call. It is only within a vison that is driven by God's time and God's purposes that any of what has been argued thus far makes sense. In God's time people with profound and complex intellectual disabilities are called by Jesus and have a vocation that is both beautiful and challenging. Such a vocation is also deeply timefull.

6

Time and Vocation
Slow and Gentle Disciples

> But now, this is what the LORD says—he who created you, Jacob, he who formed you, Israel: "Do not fear, for I have redeemed you; I have summoned you by name; you are mine."
>
> (Isa 43:1 NIV)

> Being human means one is drawn towards a destiny—and not simply as a worker or as a religionist, but as a soul that properly belongs to that which is yet dimly seen, but which already lays claim to one's very existence.
>
> (A. J. Conyers)[1]

> What really makes us human is the capacity to ask for help . . .
>
> (Frances Young)[2]

Moving the conversation from inclusion to discipleship opens up new possibilities for genuine participation not only for people with profound intellectual disabilities but for the whole body of Christ. As we move from membership to belonging and from inclusion to discipleship, so we are freed to discover and come to value the wonderful diversity that *is* the body of Christ. We have seen that central to our understanding of what discipleship is is the notion that we are called by Jesus and given a calling. This calling is our vocation: that which Jesus calls us to do as our way of participating in God's coming kingdom. Vocation is never simply for personal edification; it is always participation in something bigger than one's self. God's time sits at the heart of vocation. Vocation has to do with being called out of perceptions of ordinary time, wherein our future is a matter of personal choice, into God's time, a mode of time where our vocation can be seen as participation in God's redemption of time. When Jesus called Matthew, he opened up his conceptions of time, moving him to recognize the limitations of simple ordinary time and calling him to join with God within the wonderful complexity of God's time.

PROVIDENCE AND VOCATION

The call that *is* our vocation is an aspect of God's providence. Providence has to do with learning to live within God's time and coming to know what it means to live meaningfully and faithfully within the temporal rhythms of God's unfathomable timefullness. The understanding of providence that I have in mind here resonates with Scott Bader-Saye's suggestion that providence should be seen not as God predetermining every human movement as if life occurred on some kind of giant, transcendent chessboard. Rather, says Bader-Saye, providence is best viewed as "a way of narrating our lives in light of God's larger purpose rather than as a way of explaining every event as caused by God."[3] Providence is the way in which God places a hopeful story on the happenings of the world. Bader-Saye wants to redirect the idea of providence away from the idea that it means that God is in charge of every moment, every second, every action, as, for example, John Calvin might suggest,[4] toward a different narratively reoriented understanding. Rather than being a way of describing God's involvement in every incident that occurs in the world—a perspective that makes God directly responsible for the most terrible events—Bader-Saye proposes providence is the way that we come to "name our conviction that our futures can be trusted to God's care, even when we cannot believe that God is the direct cause of all that happens."[5] Providence provides a narrative that we can trust:

> Providence, at its heart, has to do with the conviction that our lives and our world constitute a coherent story, a drama in which God and humankind, together, drive the stories towards its proper conclusion.[6]

Providence provides a powerful narrative that ensures that in the midst of the fallenness, brokenness, and confusion of God's creation, God's story is not lost. If God's story is not lost, then there is hope for the human story. Providence is a way of mapping out God's time.

Within this narrative perspective on providence, vocation is perceived as a way of placing ourselves and the events of the world within a narrative that is bigger than ourselves. Providence provides a narrative that allows us to reorient ourselves within God's time and, in so doing, create the context for effective, faithful participation in the providential movement of God as time moves inexorably toward God's conclusion. Our vocation occurs in God's time and is intended to fulfill God's purposes. Within such a context, vocation is never perceived as a personal achievement or goal; it is not an individual search for the fulfillment of our own destiny. Rather, it is an opening up of our hearts to the callings of the Spirit in order that we can be enabled to participate faithfully within God's timefull redemption of the world. Put slightly differently, vocation enables us to use our time authentically, not for personal gain but as a mode of worship that we express as we encounter God in the day-to-dayness of our ordinary lives.

While all humans have a vocation, not all human beings hear or fulfill their calling. Those who have not yet encountered Jesus have not yet heard or have chosen not to respond to their call. The task of the church is to ensure that those who are called to be disciples not only hear their calling but also fulfill their vocation. If that is so for all of God's disciples, it can be no less so for those disciples who live with the experience of profound intellectual disability. The question is: *What might such a vocation look like?*

The vocation of profoundly disabled people

The obvious place to begin to think through these issues is by working through more precisely what vocation means. A. J. Conyers informs us:

> The familiar term "vocation," whether used in religious or secular contexts, is rooted in the Latin *vocatio*, meaning a "call," a "summons," or an "invitation," and is related to Latin-based words such as "voice" and "invoke." The Greek word is *klesis* and is found in our words "cleric" and "ecclesiastical." It is the root of the New Testament word for the Church, *ekklesia*, a point that can be over-stressed since assemblies of all kinds were referred to with the same term. However, to say that the church consists of those "called out" is significant for more reasons than can be traced through linguistic usage: it is the reality of being called by God to which the church has always attested.[7]

Vocation has to do with being called out of the world by Jesus and at precisely the same time being sent back into it with something to do or to be. Vocation is countercultural in the sense that it is not based on individual human choice or desire. Rather, it is based on God's command. The idea of vocation is the opposite of a reasonable choice:

> The specific way in which the enlightenment used reason was as a replacement for the idea of vocation. One could then make reasoned choices. The true locus of personal decisions was to be found in the individual who "thinks for himself," as Kant would put it, and who declines to depend upon the "guidance of another."[8]

Within a secularizing culture that was gradually beginning to allow science and reason to usurp ideas about God, reason came to replace the idea of vocation. Vocation contradicts the will of the person who is called. To have a vocation is to receive something from outside of yourself, to have your life profoundly shaped and directed by forces beyond your own control and comprehension. To be reasonable is to be able to think clearly, make good choices about yourself, and run and plan your own life. Reason assumes that time is for us to spend on whatever we desire. Vocation assumes that time is a gift that is designed to fulfill the wishes of the giver. Reason asks us to personalize our talent and use it for whatever we desire.[9] Vocation asks us to obey the Master's command and use our talents in the way that God desires. There is a world of difference between receiving a vocation and trying to figure out what you can do with the rest of your life.

Luther on vocation

One theologian who has written quite influentially on the issue of vocation is the Protestant reformer Martin Luther. Luther was concerned at the way the Catholic Church had grasped the power to define and confine the nature of vocation. Vocation had been taken out of the hands of the whole people of God and handed over to a spiritual elite: those who were ordained priests. Gary Badcock points out that a

> doctrine of priesthood . . . developed in medieval theology in which the sacrament of ordination rendered the priest qualitatively different from ordinary Christians: an "indelible character" imprinted on the soul placed him in a new relationship with Christ, a relationship that differed qualitatively from the one opened up in baptism.[10]

In this way the Catholic Church created a two-tiered spiritual structure within which those who were formally ordained were perceived as specially blessed by God in a way that other members of the church were not. Luther considered the creation of such a spiritual hierarchy an abomination.

He argued that among believers there is only one state and that is the status of being in Christ by virtue of a person's baptism. The idea of a spiritual elite was anathema to Luther. In contradistinction he posited that the church should be understood as containing a common priesthood: *the priesthood of all believers*. Only Jesus is the true High Priest. Our place within the church and the promises of our salvation come not from the emissaries of the high priest but only from the High Priest himself: Jesus. As Luther puts it:

> There is no true, basic difference between lay men and priests, princes and bishops, between religious and secular, except for the sake of office and work, but not for the sake of status. They are all of the spiritual estates, all are truly priests, bishops, and popes. But they do not all have the same work to do.[11]

This is the key point for Luther's understanding of the priesthood of all believers and the nature of vocation. We all share a common priesthood that emerges from our initiation into the Christian community through baptism. God does not choose special people to stand before him in the place of others. Only Jesus stands before the Father and pleads our cause. Church congregations are communities of priests. To think otherwise is, according to Luther, like "ten brothers all king's sons and equal heirs, choosing one of themselves to rule the inheritance in the interests of all."[12] For Luther, vocation is central for a proper understanding of who God is, who human beings are before God, and what it means to live faithfully within God's time.

Such a shift does not mean that the role of the minister or the priest has been surpassed or replaced by the laity. People are still called to be ministers and priests. The difference is that such a calling is not prioritized over other callings. The particular vocation of minister or priest is no longer considered to be the only or even the primary place where God's work is done. The role of the minister or the priest remains a distinct vocation. However, so also are the roles of shoemakers, nurses, husbands and wives, parents, and shop assistants. All of these vocations come together to form a network of neighborly love wherein God's providential work is carried out. All people have been given a place, a station, as Luther puts it, within God's providential narrative, and each vocation is intended as a locus for the dissemination of God's providential and graceful love.

Luther's intention inter alia, was to move the spiritual power of vocation away from the monastery, the priest, and the minister and to relocate it within the everydayness of human life. The picture he offers is of a highly complex matrix of interacting human vocations, all focused on glorifying God and manifesting God's neighborly love toward the world. It is important to note that "vocation" is a *theological* word; that is, it applies primarily to believers. Unbelievers also have work to do, but without faith, Luther argues, this does not constitute their true calling. It is the presence of faith that prevents a person's vocation from becoming mere works. Believers realize that as creatures they are in the world only through the gift of God's sustaining providential grace. Unbelievers use works to try to persuade God of their goodness. Believers recognize their vocation as an aspect of God's sovereign love, not as a way of grasping toward salvation. Only God saves. Vocation thus facilitates participation in something beyond the immediate and the obvious.

It is important to be clear that this doctrine—the priesthood of all believers—*does not* mean that each member of the church is a free autonomous being who can interpret Scripture or practice church in whatever way he or she wants, free from mutual responsibility apart from the general connection with the Body.[13] The idea that underpins the priesthood of all believers is that each member of Jesus' body is called to participate in certain aspects at certain times and that there should be no hierarchy or prioritizing of any particular calling. The key is, to repeat, that vocation is *participation*, not personal fulfillment. Vocations are not about personal desire or ambition or individual striving for salvation. They have to do with faithful participation in the body of Jesus and the mission of God. Each vocation is necessary for the upbuilding of the Body, but none of them are definitive of the Body.

The multiplicity of vocations

Importantly, vocations are not single but multiple, each of us having a variety of different vocations. Gene Edward Veith observes that

> God is graciously at work, caring for the human race through the work of other human beings. Behind the care we have received from our parents, the education we received from our teachers, the benefits we receive from our spouse, our employers, and our government stands God himself, bestowing his blessings.[14]

This multiplicity of vocations gives one's individual and corporate life a sense of meaningful direction within which common purpose is carved out through a shared focus on the ongoing sanctifying work of God. We are called by God to work together for the good of humanity, our goal that is inevitably bound up within the worship and graciousness of God.

> The purpose of one's vocation, whatever it might be, is serving others. It has to do with fulfilling Christ's injunction to love one's neighbor.

> Though justification has nothing to do with good works, vocation does involve good works. The Christian's relationship to God is based on sheer grace and forgiveness on God's part; the Christian's relationship to other people, however, is to be based on love. As Wingren puts it, "God does not need our good works, but our neighbor does."[15]

Vocation then, is one of the physical locations for Brueggemann's Sabbath-based "economy of neighborly love" that we touched on in chapter 4. As we love our neighbor, so we are brought into the presence of God's gracious, enduring love.

SLOW AND GENTLE DISCIPLESHIP: THE VOCATION OF THE PROFOUNDLY DISABLED

With these provisional thoughts about discipleship and vocation in mind, we can begin to tease out what all of this might actually look like within the lives of people with profound and complex intellectual disabilities. In her book *Arthur's Call*, Frances Young tells the story of her experience with her son Arthur, who has a profound intellectual disability. Young is a Methodist minister and former Edward Cadbury Professor of Theology at the University of Birmingham. Arthur was born in 1967 with a serious brain injury. As a consequence, Arthur was profoundly intellectually disabled. He has been unable to do anything for himself for the whole of his life. Arthur lived with his mother and father for forty-five years until in the summer of 2012 he moved out into a care-home facility. After narrating the complexities, pain, and beauty of her life with Arthur, Young concludes with a deep and poignant reflection on Arthur's vocation and, by inference, the vocation of many other people who share Arthur's disability. Young suggests that Arthur is a disciple, baptized into the body of disciples:

> It has always been of the greatest importance to me that Arthur was baptised as a baby—even though he cannot receive the sacrament or make a profession of faith, he is held in God's grace and belongs to the body of Christ.[16]

Sitting at the heart of Young's reflection on Arthur's vocation is the way in which Arthur has taught people, implicitly and explicitly, not only what love means but what such love *looks like*. She points out that St. Paul informs us that the fruits of the Spirit are love, joy, peace, patience, kindness, generosity, faithfulness, gentleness, and self-control (Gal 5:22). These, she suggests, are precisely the gifts that Arthur has brought to her and to those whom he has touched during his life. Arthur has not directed Young and her family toward the cultural norms of competence, efficiency, productivity, competition, or any other qualities that clock time and the values of modernity indicate are central to being human. Rather, he has revealed a different way of being in the world and valuing one human life:

> Basically it's about appreciation, fascination, vaguely seeing yet not seeing, cheerfully being, just existing with a never-ending capacity for wonder at the simple things. That in itself may be the most significant message: a contemplative simplicity made infinitely problematic for most of us by our overactive consciousness and need for novel stimulation.[17]

To be with Arthur, it is necessary to become uncomplicated. One cannot be with Arthur if one is traveling at speed, be that physical or intellectual speed. To truly be with Arthur, one needs to be slow, kind, generous, gentle, timefull, and self-controlled. None of these things are easy for "fast people" to achieve. Disciples who are impatient, frenetic, anxious, or easily frustrated will struggle to be with Arthur. But in that struggle they will discover new aspects of themselves. Some of this newness will be a blessing, but some of it will be deeply disturbing.

Young meditates on the ways in which the desert fathers and mothers used to head out into the desert to seek a space of displacement within which they were moved out of the comfort zone and enabled to discover new depths within themselves and new depths within their relationship to God. She sees Arthur as functioning in a not dissimilar way. As her life has been displaced by the power of the presence of Arthur's disability, so Young has discovered new depths to herself and new depths to God. Some of these new discoveries have been joyful, but some have been deeply dissonant and traumatic:

> I recall those long, bitter nights when he'd not slept, so neither had I, and that occasion when in sheer frustration I had given vent to my feelings by hurling a pillow on to the foot of his bed with force (well away from doing any actual harm). The inner demons were exposed: self-pity, anxiety about not sleeping with a heavy day of commitments ahead, the helplessness that comes from lack of control over the situation and not knowing what to do—yes, there was concern for him and his discomfort, desire to put things right for him if only I knew how, but it was overlaid by so many self-oriented passions. I discovered to my shame that I understood how some parents could batter their babies.[18]

Being with Arthur sometimes functioned as a wilderness experience wherein Young discovered destructive anxiety, self-oriented passions, and the potential for violence. The gentleness and vulnerability of Arthur's life was a place of revelation wherein passion and love as well as inner demons crept into the light.

It is hard to resist reflecting on this powerful vignette in the light of the passion of Jesus. Jesus who is gentle, Jesus who commands love, Jesus who walks slowly at the speed of love evoked anxiety, violence, and dissonance. Young points out that for Arthur to draw out such inner demons means that he is at risk even from those who love him.[19] Jesus' abandonment by those who loved him and his exposure to violence from those who feared him opens up Arthur's experience in a way that is both profound and revelatory of the difficult tension between God's gentle, slow time and the anxiety-driven time that forms the backdrop to many of our lives. Arthur's vocation was simply to be Arthur; to live out a life of vulnerability and gentleness; to teach and share the blessings, the dangers, and the power of slow and gentle discipleship. Previously, I suggested that the people of God are called to help those with experiences similar to Arthur's to discover what God's love feels like. Young's narrative reminds us of the mutuality of such a task. It is not simply that "we" teach Arthur about God. It seems fairly clear that Arthur has a role as teacher as well as student, giver as well as recipient of God's love, guest as well as host. In order that God's people can become gentle disciples, we will need to learn to accept the gifts that Arthur's vocation brings to us ("us" being the whole body of Christ). We will need to learn what it means to become slow disciples. Frenetic disciples may get a lot of things done, but in doing a lot of things they may miss the very things that God is doing.

THE POWER OF DOING NOTHING: THE SACRAMENT DOES ITS OWN TRAVELING

What is striking about Arthur's story is that his vocation was not to *do* something but rather to *be* something. There is a great power in doing nothing. I recently spoke with a member of the Trosly L'Arche community. His name was Michael, and he was working as an assistant. He told me that he used to be an atheist. Every week he was obliged to take David, a middle-aged man with profound intellectual disabilities, to the chapel, and every week Michael seemed to hate it more and more. He recognized that David enjoyed it and realized that he had to carry out his duty. So every week Michael plodded off to chapel, disliking the experience more with every step. Then, unexpectedly, David died. Michael was heartbroken. But something rather remarkable happened. Michael told me, "It was the strangest thing, but I *missed* the chapel and I missed the sacrament! I guess the sacrament does its own traveling." All of his time with David, Michael had presumed that he was going to the chapel for David's sake. It turned out it was for Michael's sake. Even though he hated the experience of going to chapel, it had become a place of belonging for him; he missed it. As day by day, week by week, Michael had accompanied David to the chapel, he was being transformed not by what David knew, said, or did, but simply by accompanying David on his spiritual journey. David loved the sacrament. Michael had no interest in the sacrament. But the sacrament did its own traveling. Michael was changed and his own desires reshaped into the form of Jesus because of the gentle and faithful presence of David. David's heartfelt desire became Michael's salvation. There is a blessing and a power in the vocation of doing nothing, in simply being who you are.

It is a vital and most beautiful fact that some members of Jesus' body may simply be called to bear witness to the powerful truth of *being*. In a world that has been seduced by the idolatrous power of speed, clocks, and busyness, bearing witness to the divine significance of simply being is indeed a noble vocation. Being, properly conceived, is a deep and powerful vocation. It is, of course, a vocation that we can only really begin to make sense of as we come to realize the implications of living in God's time.

KATIE'S PRAYERS: TALKING TO GOD WITHOUT ANY WORDS

My point is not that the only thing people with profound intellectual disabilities can do is nothing other than be themselves, crucial as that may be. My point is that if we slow down, think differently, and open ourselves to the gentle power of God's time as it works out in the calling of people with profound intellectual disabilities, we can be enabled to see wonderful new truths. Katie's story will help to enforce and embody this point.

Susannah Baines and I met Katie during the work on spirituality and profound intellectual disabilities that was mentioned previously. Katie was a very sociable, lively, thirteen-year-old girl who had an active social life that was encouraged and facilitated primarily by her mother. Katie was the elder of two children. Even though she had no words, and no obvious comprehension of what words might mean, Katie loved to sing . . . without words. As she moved rhythmically to the music of the worship in her church, one could not help being caught up in witnessing something wonderful and slightly mysterious. Who knows what worshipping Jesus without words feels like? It certainly looked like fun! Katie and her family were regular attenders at their local Anglican church where Katie was baptized as a baby. Katie used a wheelchair for many years and although she still needed her chair for longer distances, she was now able to walk. This was a really big achievement for Katie and for her family.

Shortly after Katie was born, she was diagnosed with Sturge-Weber syndrome, which is characterized by port-wine birthmarks and varying degrees of intellectual disabilities. In Sturge-Weber syndrome the facial birthmarks usually extend over the brain, which can cause various problems including restrictions in movement and seizures. The difficulties experienced by people with Sturge-Weber syndrome vary widely,[20] so when Katie was first diagnosed there was no indication of what problems she might experience. When Katie was five years old, she had a series of nose bleeds. The blood flow would not clot, leaving Katie very unwell, weak, and hospitalized. The exact cause was never established, but it was thought to be related to her birthmarks. Katie was put on medication, and her nosebleeds stopped. As the cause was never fully established, the threat of it reoccurring did remain a worry for her parents. This was a very difficult time for the family, but her church rallied, and various people within the congregation helped with child care for her brother, David, as well as offering other forms of practical support.

Although their neighborhood was close to major urban centers, their community was small and kept a village ethos with its own small shops and community events. The Anglican church the family attended was housed in a modern building close to their home. Katie's parents attended their church before having children and had brought their children up there. Their vicar had been the vicar at their church for over fifteen years. He described the church as having a community ethos that was very inclusive. The church had been remarkably supportive to Katie and her family. Katie was clearly included in all the church groups and events for her age group and the family, and, despite certain issues around Katie being unable to develop close friendships, she seemed to feel that she was well embedded within the community. Katie and her family felt they had found a community within which they truly belonged.

Katie started secondary school in September 2009 and at the time we met her, was attending mainstream school one morning per week, including lunchtime, and a special school the rest of the time. She attended several after-school clubs and three youth evening activities including Girls' Brigade (an international and interdenominational Christian youth organization). Katie was recently honored with a medal for endurance by the Girls' Brigade.

Praying without words

Katie's communication was extremely limited, she had few words and used Makaton symbols[21] to communicate. Katie loved to pray. The leader of the Girl's Brigade wrote about how she tried to support Katie to pray:

> During Youth group I try to get Katie involved in prayers by either saying thank you for mum, dad and David and she sometimes will try her best to say these, I also get her to stand up and get her to do the prayer drill. It is sometimes hard to get her to stay quiet but I have seen a massive improvement in how she is communicating. Some of the songs have actions that Katie can do well; she loves to sign Jesus whenever it is mentioned.[22]

Whenever prayer was undertaken either at church, at home, or at one of her clubs, Katie put her palms together and urged others around her to do the same. An interesting link Katie had made is between saying thank you and praying. Often when asked to say thank you, for example, after being given a biscuit, Katie put her hands together in prayer. This was different from the Makaton sign for "thank you," which involves touching the fingers to the chin and then moving the hand away from the face. Katie was not necessarily confusing the two Makaton signs. She seemed to have somehow linked the idea of saying thank you with the idea that prayer can be used to say thank you to God.

Katie's mother remarked in her diary on an incident that took place at one of the girls' clubs that Katie attends at her local church. One of the leaders had fallen over and broken her foot. The break was a bad one, and she was totally incapacitated. The children were asked who would like to lead the prayers for healing the woman's foot. Katie indicated that she would like to. The group closed their eyes and Katie said . . . nothing; she simply put her hands together. When she had finished, she raised her head, opened her eyes, and everything carried on as before. Or so it seemed. . . . The next day the leader who had broken her foot went to the hospital to have her break rechecked. The doctor told her that her foot had healed unusually well and that she was now able to stop using crutches. The leader believed that it was Katie's prayer that made the difference. This is intriguing. The mechanics of how Katie might pray are unusual because private reflective prayer often utilizes an individual's internal monologue. Katie had no words.

It would, of course, be easy to be skeptical of such a narrative. How do we know what or whether Katie prayed? How do we know that the healing was not just natural? These things happen, do they not? Of course, the obvious response to such questions is: How do we know whether anyone prays? Certainly we can hear people using words, words that are often rich, deep, and pious. But we cannot see into people's hearts. We have no idea whether what we are hearing is prayer or simply people trying to persuade us that they are praying. Recent scandals within the church would indicate that simply knowing the right words in the context of liturgy, worship, and ministry does not really tell us very much about whether someone really has been praying to Jesus. The assumption that anyone prays is always an act of faith: being sure of what we hope for and certain of what we cannot see. If we begin by assuming that someone can pray, then we will interpret the outcome of that encounter accordingly. One might suspect that the more charismatic among us would have no problem in accepting that a self-proclaimed healer had mended the leader's foot. However, the suggestion that an almost wordless child could have a vocation to the ministry of healing prayer is less obvious.

And yet none of us should really be surprised. The apostle Paul seems to be quite clear that prayer is not a human work but a work of the Spirit, a work that is not bound by words. In Romans 8:26, Paul informs us, "And the Holy Spirit helps us in our weakness. For example, we don't know what God wants us to pray for. But the Holy Spirit prays for us with groanings that cannot be expressed in words." Perhaps the community of disciples needs to think seriously about what a prayer ministry might look like when it includes, recognizes, and listens to what may seem to be the weakest members of the Body who may in fact have the strongest "voices."

One of my colleagues recently told me of the time she spent with a woman living with advanced dementia. For much of her current life the woman, Janet, was quite unresponsive. She would sit for hours, apparently unaware of what was going on. But when my colleague prayed with her, everything changed. Last week she sat with Janet for ten minutes while she prayed incessantly. All around her was noise, music, television, and distraction. But in the midst of the hustle and bustle of her ward, she prayed. My colleague joined her, but it was Janet's time.

In God's time the vocation of prayer takes on many shapes and forms. Janet did not have an intellectual disability, but she did have a firm vocation in the midst of intellectual and cognitive change. It just needed to be noticed and facilitated. The writer to the Hebrews informs us that faith is being sure of what we hope for and certain of what we cannot see (11:1). This is true of our faith in God. Perhaps we (all of us together) should reflect on how this might apply to the ways in which we understand one another's vocations. Approaching someone with a profound intellectual disability and being sure of what you hope for and certain of what you cannot see is the beginning point for enabling slow and gentle discipleship.

PRACTICING THE WAYS OF THE HEART: LIVING HOSPITABLY IN GOD'S TIME

There is a beautiful painting of Cardinal Bergoglio (who became Pope Francis) kneeling at the feet of a child in a wheelchair.[23] It is clear that the child is dying of AIDS. In the picture we are provided with a vision of one of the most powerful religious leaders in the world prostrating himself before one of the most vulnerable people in the world, "the least of them." The cardinal takes time to be with the boy. In humility he bows down and kisses the boy's feet. As he kneels down and looks up, two things become clear. First, the cardinal has to adopt the postures of worship in order to be with someone who is deeply broken, tragically vulnerable, and utterly helpless. He has to take exactly the same posture that he would take if he were worshipping Jesus. Second, as he adopts this posture, he inevitably sees things very differently than he would if he were standing up and towering over the boy. The cardinal appears to be giving us a sense that he is a *guest* in the life of the dying child. Like Jesus, he does not simply try to host the child, to draw the boy into his world in order to try to get him to "be like him." Rather, he accepts the boy's hospitality, and in accepting that hospitality he receives the gift of knowledge of what it is like to look at life from a different angle. When he kneels down, he sees things in a different way, feels things differently. He is open to the way that the boy sees the world, and he is open to the gifts and to the sadness that such a revelation brings with it.

In clock time we rarely have time to host anyone (even ourselves!), never mind someone who does not walk, run, talk, or think at the same speed that we do. However, if we slow down, take time, and open ourselves to the possibility of being guests in the homes and in the lives of people living with profound intellectual disabilities, everything changes. What would it be like to be a guest in the life of a person with profound intellectual disability? To be with him or her in a way that enables both of you together to use your talents wisely? What if, instead of merely including people, we actively sought out and tried to encourage their vocation? What if we intentionally tried to recognize the potential wicked servant within our churches and moved to seek to please God by encouraging the vocation of the *whole* people of God? If the body of Jesus can learn to dwell faithfully with and within the narratives of those disciples who live with intellectual disabilities, we (all of us together) will be given the opportunity truly to become the body of Jesus. In clock time such a form of dwelling together seems odd, dissonant, and uncomfortable.

But in the time of the three-mile-an-hour God, who is gentle and patient and kind and is drawing creation to its timefull conclusion, it just seems, well . . . ordinary. In a world where some desire to kill people with disabilities or prevent their coming into existence, gentle, hospitable, vocational discipleship that is open to the possibility that each one of us is the unexpected guest at the banquet of life offers both a counter to oppressive cultural norms and a beautiful, neatly fitting key that opens a door into a whole new world of time, grace, and being. In that place Jesus waits for us.

IV

RECLAIMING THE HEART

7

Time and Memory
Dementia and the Advancement of Time

> Instead of squeezing people with dementia into complicated systems designed for people who can remember who the president is, we should find kinder, less judgmental ways to be with them.
>
> (Charles Leadbeater)[1]

Earlier in the book, we spent some time looking at how certain ways of perceiving time were highly problematic for people with dementia. So much so that some assume dementia is worse than death and seek to draw out arguments and engage in practices aimed at ending the lives of those living with this condition. In this chapter and the next, we will explore something of what it might look like to understand and experience dementia from within God's time. We will discover that time in general sits at the center of the experience of dementia and that God's time in particular opens up new possibilities for hopeful presence. The journey that we will embark upon in this chapter will take a little bit of time to develop. We will need to visit the worlds of neurology and philosophy to see how and why we have developed a tendency to think about memory in limited and unhelpful ways. However, such time will be well spent if it allows us to see dementia differently and learn what it means to live with this kind of disability in keeping with a time that is not driven by the demands of the clock but is deeply immersed within the time that God has gifted to us.

WORSHIPPING IN FORGETFULNESS

Imagine a church service in a home for people with dementia. You, the chaplain/pastor come into the dayroom. All around you are people with different experiences of dementia. Some are quite chirpy, walking around laughing and talking to one another. Others are watching television. One or two folks are standing at the window watching the traffic. Some of the folks look quite sad and withdrawn. One woman, Elizabeth, sits in her chair gazing at the floor. The care attendant tells you that she rarely talks. "We can't really find a way to engage with her. She does like music and sometimes she responds to that, but a good deal of the time she is just alone in her own little world." You take out the bits and pieces that you plan to use for the service: a music player with recordings of hymns, the elements of the Eucharist, which you plan to give to those who desire to engage with that ritual, a prayer book, and a number of large-print hymnals. You sit down beside a gentleman whose name you know is Graham. "Good morning, Graham," you say. But Graham says nothing. He looks beyond you, through you, but never at you. You smile at him and touch his hand in a welcoming gesture. Graham makes no effort to reciprocate. He seems fascinated by something behind you. You look around but there is nothing obvious to see. You smile, this time a little awkwardly.

The parishioner who has come along with you sets up his little portable piano, and you get the service in motion. You hand out the hymn books and announce the first hymn. It is always a bit difficult worshipping in such a public space where some people want to be involved and others do not. The staff stand in the corner chatting about something. You suspect that the topic is less than holy as you catch one of them pointing in your direction and smiling. The others nod in agreement. The piano sets up the introduction: "What a Friend We Have in Jesus." You are just about to start singing with your usual gusto (a necessary skill when you *are* the choir!) when suddenly from your left you hear Graham begin to sing . . . with unusual enthusiasm!

> What a friend we have in Jesus,
> All our sins and griefs to bear!
> What a privilege to carry
> Everything to God in prayer!

You watch him. His hands are upturned in anticipation of receiving the gift of the Holy Spirit. His eyes are closed, and his voice is strangely strong and focused. The music continues and you look around the room. No one is singing other than Graham.

The music stops and that is the end of the first hymn. You call the room to prayer. It is not a quiet room. You feel certain you saw that staff member pointing at you again. You invite everyone to join you in the Lord's Prayer. "Our Father, who art in heaven . . ." You sneak a peek as you repeat the well-known words. You can see quite a few people mouthing them, hands folded together in the gesture of prayer. You feel yourself deeply moved. "What a shame . . ." But then you catch yourself. "What do I mean 'What a shame?' What exactly do I think is going on here?" You begin to realize that your sympathy comes from your assumption that these gestures are simply bare reflections of what has been. You feel sadness for what these folks must have been. You do not feel comfortable with that feeling, but you do not seem to be able to help yourself.

When it comes to the Eucharist, you bring out the bread and the wine. You ask the staff who among the folks in the room are church people and might find the sacrament useful. The staff just looks at you. "What's a sacrament?" You feel a little exasperated. One of the most important symbols within the Christian tradition has not just been forgotten; it has never been known by a generation of young people. Now that *is* a shame! You feel the urge to comment, but before you do one young carer, Yvonne, steps forward. "Yes, my dad was a minister. A lot of them like the bread and the wine. Elizabeth likes it." You thank Yvonne and begin to administer the sacrament to those within the room. When you come to Elizabeth, you stand before her and look down. She is tiny. Frail, bent, lost. You kneel down and look up at her face. She looks different from down here. As you kneel before her and really look at her, she seems different, more real. "Hello Elizabeth." You reach out gently and touch her hand. She responds, just a little. "Elizabeth, I know that you enjoy communion, and I know that God would like you to participate. I am going to give you the bread and the wine. Is that okay?" Elizabeth makes no response. You sigh a little . . . inwardly. You pick up a piece of bread and reach out to her. She makes no movement. Then you say the words of institution: "This is my body, broken for you, Elizabeth." She raises her head and her mouth opens, just a little. She moves her tongue outward to receive the bread. You drop the bread on her tongue. She swallows it. "This is my blood, poured out for you. . . ." You put a drop of wine on her tongue. She swallows and whispers, "Amen." Suddenly you realize that you are on your knees before Elizabeth, adopting the posture of worship to facilitate her in the frailty of her sacramental life. You feel humbled, sad, and a little confused. You ask yourself, "What just happened?"[2]

What just happened?

There is an apparently straightforward way to explain Graham and Elizabeth's experiences. They have dementia, and they have forgotten most of what used to make them who they are. Their situation is nothing other than a desperately sad tragedy. Within the context of worship, old memories of the past come to mind; like leaves blowing in the wind, they come and then they go. Graham sings, Elizabeth tentatively accepts the sacrament, but the deep tragedy is that they have no real idea of what they are doing. Their behavior is quaint but meaningless. Certainly, the minister's desire that there might be more going on than meets the eye is to be expected. He clearly does not know much about dementia, neurology, or memory. All he has are stories that no reasonable person would believe in this day and age! It is his job to see the world in ways that others do not. But what he thinks he sees is nothing more than wishful fantasy. "We" know pretty well precisely what dementia is, and "we" no longer require explanations that draw us into the unmeasurable realms of the "spiritual." There are better, more accurate and realistic stories to tell about people's experiences of dementia. In the end, what we bear witness to is simply parts of people's old selves popping up as their fragmented memories and damaged brains respond to stimuli that were once important to them but are now no more than vestiges of what was. It all seems so obvious. But what if in framing the issues in such ways, "we" are actually bearing false witness to the experiences of people like Graham and Elizabeth? What if there were a quite different story to be told about their experiences?

FEARING DEMENTIA: A PROBLEM OF MEMORY?

Dementia is a condition that, among other things, affects the memory. Over time what we thought we knew about the world, God, and ourselves begin to fade away. As our recollections fades we can no longer recall those memories that we and others once assumed were central to our lives. Perceived in this way, it is not surprising that one of the primary responses to dementia is *fear*. If we assume that who we are is determined and gauged by what we can remember, the idea of losing one's memory is indeed fearful. That fear is compounded and reflected in the kind of language and metaphors that people use when they encounter those living with dementia, particularly those with advanced dementia. This is so for both laypeople and professionals. People talk about the way in which dementia "destroys memory," "steals memory," "kills memory." People with dementia are described as "lost souls," or are accused of "no longer being themselves" because they cannot remember certain details, or indeed anything, about their friends, their families, themselves, and even God. So apparently "obvious" are such negative assumptions that it is easy to reify them and assume that such speculation is based on facts and verifiable truth.

However, the situation is not quite as obvious as it may seem. At the heart of much of the fear that surrounds dementia is the loss of memory that accompanies it. However, precisely what it means to lose one's memory is not a straightforward matter. The reason it is not straightforward is that the nature of memory is much more complicated than many of us presume. If we are not clear about precisely what we mean when we talk about memory and memory loss, we are unlikely to grasp the intricacies of what it really means to have dementia and what one is required to do and to be in order to accompany people in ways that are creative and timefull.

In general terms, many of us assume that people with advanced dementia are no longer able to recall certain details about themselves, their family and friends, the past, the present, and so forth. At one level, this very often appears to be the case. People do indeed appear to be no longer able to recall certain details. There are, however, at least two reasons we might want to show humility and a degree of reserve with regard to such perceptions and assumptions about people's memory loss.

First, we cannot be sure. Sometimes what happens within the neurological damage that brings about dementia is that the neurons and the synapses that are necessary to form the various connections within the brain become fragmented, separated, or blocked, thus preventing an individual from *accessing* memory. It may be that the memory is still there; it might simply have become inaccessible. This is why such stimuli as music, smell, pictures, and so forth can "bring back" memories. They function as bridges that temporarily "heal" the neurological fracture and enable people to access memories that they are unable to access through other means. While the ability to recall may seem clearly inhibited and damaged, it may be best always to approach an individual by giving him or her the benefit of the doubt, opening ourselves to the possibility that our touch, the sound of a voice, the smell of perfume, or the music that we bring to the individual can actually bridge the gap, even if that bridging lasts for only a few moments. We will return to this suggestion as we move on.

Second, the idea that memory has only to do with *recall*—when we can no longer recall things, we have lost our memory—is mistaken. Memory as recall assumes that memory equals the ability to bring certain events and characters from the past to mind in a logical and coherent way in order to contemplate them, make sense of the present, and plan for the future. Here, memory is perceived primarily as a cognitive process that maps out and holds in place our perceptions of time. Memory has, of course, to do with recall, but that is not the only thing it has to do with. There are other layers to memory that are equally important.

THE STANDARD ACCOUNT OF MEMORY

The evidence for the suggestion that memory is primarily a cognitive event that relates to recall and intentional cognition and comprehension is impressive and at some levels convincing. Scientifically we are able to test people's memories to see whether they are functioning according to a standard norm. Persons who cannot remember the name of the prime minister of the United Kingdom or the president of the United States or produce other "commonsense" and "obvious" pieces of memory knowledge are deemed to have a memory problem (they cannot recall certain facts). The neurosciences reinforce such a "standard account" of memory. Scientific technology provides impressive evidence that enables us to grasp, see, and understand the precise location of the memory-processing areas within particular regions of the brain.

Initially, discoveries relating to the ways in which different parts of the brain are responsible for the production of memory were made by examining damage to various parts of the brain. By correlating the particular symptoms and experiences of individuals with damage to specific areas of the brain, it was possible to work out which part was responsible for the processing of various types of memory. We have discovered that different areas—the hippocampus, the parahippocampal region, the cerebral cortex (including the prefrontal cortex)—all function in harmony to provide us with a broad range of memory functions. Damage to any one of these areas brings about an effect equivalent to its specific responsibility within the overall process of memory formation and retention. Using advanced neurological scanning techniques, we can map all of this out and present it on charts, diagrams, and bright, colorful pictures that show different parts of the brain lighting up (or failing to) as they encounter different stimuli. Such evidence combined with the daily experience of being with people living with dementia and realizing how much they seem to have forgotten ties us into a quite specific understanding of what memory is and also what memory is not.

Such a picture of dementia and memory loss is indeed frightening. If to remember is simply to recall the past—that which has been and can never be again—dementia does indeed clearly involve a significant loss of memory. If the self—who we and others remember us to be—is based on the idea that we are formed by a series of linear, time-based recollections about ourselves, an *autobiographical self*, then losing our memory will mean losing our ability to tell our own stories, which in turn will mean losing our selves. This effectively means that when we cannot recall the past we "disappear," even though we are still physically here.

Tests and diagrams may well tell us something about what memory is, but what they tell us is profoundly depressing. What is even more depressing is that we know exactly how other people will respond to such a diagnosis. They will give up on us. People will talk about our "past self": "Graham is not the person he used to be." "Isn't it a shame, Elizabeth can't even remember her own name." "What kind of a life is that for them?" There will be nothing but negativity about our present self and what people think our future self will be like: "What a shame, Graham's and Elizabeth's lives are hopeless, it's all gone. . . ." Mary Warnock might add to our woes: "Maybe we should kill them?" The fact that people might feel and experience things quite differently and more hopefully is going to be a hard case for people with dementia to make as their voices tend to be stolen by stigmatic assumptions and presumptions of incompetence. Within this "standard account" of memory, it is presumed that the tests and the scans are all we need to know. "They have lost their memory."

Minding our language

Such negativity is frequently reflected in the language used around people with dementia. Charles Leadbeater opens his otherwise wise and thoughtful article on dementia and memory with this deeply fearful description of dementia:

> Dementia is caused by a range of medical conditions (the best-known being Alzheimer's) that eat holes in the short-term memory of sufferers and degrade their capacity to process new information. Memory becomes like a flickering signal from a faraway shortwave radio station: people can do and say things, then promptly forget them, and then do and say them again. They can no longer read obvious social cues. They become easily distressed as a thickening fog descends upon them, causing them to lose track of everything. As the disease progresses, only fleeting glimpses of the once capable person can be seen; for the rest of the time, everyone is stuck with an uninvited guest. Eventually, the sufferer fails to recognise even loved ones.[3]

Well, that is a description that certainly scares me! If proof were needed for the power of malignant social positioning,[4] this statement would be all that was needed. Apparently, if I have dementia, I will live in a fog, with my old "capable" self popping in and out of the haze before it eventually fades forever, leaving . . . well, what? Dementia is portrayed as an active, living "thing" that apparently has the ability to "eat holes" in a person's memory (do diagnostic labels eat things?), thus degrading (an interesting word choice) my capacity to process new information. As I become engulfed in this thickening fog, I find myself dislocated in time and space. The person that I have become, the person who is here in-the-now, is neither wanted nor valued. I am an unwanted guest, as Mary Warnock would put it; I have become a burden. In the end I find myself stranded in a strange and unwelcoming no-man's-land wherein I do not know anyone or anything. Leadbeater's vision of dementia is pretty bleak. But is it accurate?

WHAT IS MEMORY? MEMORY AS A "NATURAL KIND"

Jens Brockmeier observes that, despite the fact that there are many ways in which memory has been understood across cultures and throughout time and history, the contemporary conversation seems to be dominated by the presumption that one particular model should have hegemony over other ways of looking at memory. This, Brockmeier argues, is more than a little unusual:

> Considering [the] stable and wide-reaching consensus on the paramount importance of memory it is astonishing to see that there is actually little discussion about what we actually mean when we speak of "memory." Our fundamental ideas and concepts of memory are amazingly unproblematized, which is to say, they too enjoy a stable consensus and a high reputation. . . . They are so commonsensical, I believe, because they appear stabilized and fixed through this consensus in a way that has turned "memory" into a given substantial entity, a natural kind.[5]

We have seen some of the ways formal tests and scans serve to create a sense of stability, empirical veracity, and an ensuing consensus around what memory is and the parameters within which it should be understood. Brockmeier gestures toward the ways in which, with the rise of medicine and neurology as the primary explanatory frameworks for perceptions of memory, a general consensus has arisen that we know what memory is and that that knowledge is fixed, real, and settled. Such general accord has led to people assuming that memory is *a natural kind*. Ian Hacking describes a natural kind as "a class denoted by a common name about which there is the possibility of general, intelligible and consistent, and probably true assertions."[6] Natural kinds share particular properties and capacities, and often an assumed mode of causality. So a tree is a natural kind, but objects that share the color yellow or green are not. To assume memory to be a natural kind is to presume that it shares particular properties (as defined primarily by neuroscience), has capacities that can be measured (via particular psychological and cognitive tests), and shares certain causalities (the particular areas of the brain that have been identified in processing memory). This kind of assumption about memory has been deeply influential in shaping people's understandings of and responses to memory disorders such as dementia. Brockmeier continues:

> The etiological scenario follows a familiar script: the focus on dementia as memory disorder, and on AD as an eventually fatal memory degeneration, implies that in losing their capacity of autobiographical remembering, people also lose, in due and natural course, their sense of their being in time, that is, their sense of autobiographical time. Ultimately therefore, they lose their sense of self and identity, if not their right to full personhood.[7]

Read in the light of Brockmeier's reflection, it becomes easier to see why Leadbeater's description of dementia might not raise too many eyebrows. Dementia in his (Leadbeater's) understanding is perceived as a memory disorder—a natural phenomenon—that is inextricably interlinked with a person's sense of linear, historical, sequential time, what Brockmeier calls *autobiographical time*. The fragmentation of that autobiographical linearity is thus perceived as a fragmentation of the person *in time*. If you are no longer able to tell your own story, then you have no story to tell.

The autobiographical self

The idea of the autobiographical self as it resides in autobiographical time is interesting. Brockmeier, inter alia, is unhappy that the ethos of John Locke's understanding of personhood has influenced understandings of time and memory in ways that are particularly difficult and dangerous for people with dementia. For Locke, a person is "a thinking intelligent being that has reason and reflection, and can consider itself as itself, the same thinking thing, in different times and places."[8] According to Locke it is our perception of time and our ability to narrate that perception accurately that make us persons. If we can tell our own story as a seamless, continuous autobiographical narrative that moves from past to present to future, we are to be considered persons. If we lose our sense of time and history, we are no longer persons. Locke's perspective on personhood runs implicitly, and sometimes quite explicitly, through many lay and professional versions of what constitutes personhood. When, for example, people use language such as "she is not the person she used to be" or "he has lost his sense of self" or even "she would never have done this before," we are articulating some version of Locke's position. For Locke, Hacking observes, "the person is constituted not by a biography, but by a *remembered* biography."[9] We are who we remember ourselves to be; if we can no longer remember ourselves in that way, then we cannot truly be ourselves.

In summary, memory according to this way of thinking and illustrated by this type of science and philosophy is perceived as a natural kind that is quantifiable, measurable, testable, verifiable, and empirically observable through the methods and procedures of scientific inquiry. It is primarily a neurological process, or a series of neurological processes, wherein information is encoded, stored, and retrieved in particular sequences. The temporal order of these sequences is considered pivotal in terms of whether someone has a memory problem. Experientially, memory is gauged by the presence or the absence of an awareness of the autobiographical self. However, the problem is that, by reducing memory to the biological, the empirical, and the temporal, the impression is given that there is only one kind of "thing" that we can call memory and that, when that "thing" is lost, people are perceived to have lost their memory. The question is: How accurate is such a description?

WATCHING MEMORIES FORM?

One of the quite fascinating recent developments around the area of memory is the suggestion that we can actually *watch* memories being formed within our brains.[10] Not only can we identify the particular areas within the brain where memory is processed; now we can actually see the neurons and synapses coming together to make up a memory. According to a recent article in the British newspaper the *Daily Mail*,

> scientists have discovered exactly how memories are formed in the brain. The US–UK team has managed to pinpoint individual neurons . . . that fire when people file away their experiences.[11]

Apparently, we can now watch chemicals combining with flesh to become memories.[12] This research invites us to watch what is indeed quite fascinating video footage that shows cells coming together in response to particular experiences to form memories within the brain. Now, it is argued, we can actually *see* what occurs when we remember something! We can watch memories being formed.

Fascinating as such research and its accompanying striking visualization may be, it is difficult to see in what sense we are actually watching *memories* being formed. Certainly we may well be seeing the workings of the brain as it strives to encode particular pieces of information relating to the specific external neural stimuli that the human brain has experienced. However, it is not clear how or why this materialistic process that is visualized for us by the new technology should in any sense be understood to be illustrating or explaining memory. When we see a visual representation of the synapses and neurons working together to find new connections that we then refer to as memory, we cannot help but ask precisely how this relates to our memory of last Sunday's family picnic. Are we really watching Aunt Betty scoffing Uncle Jeff's homemade pork pie? As I remember my wife and children last Christmas when we celebrated Jesus' birthday together, surrounded by presents and cake, am I meant to be persuaded that it can all be reduced to these tiny isolated neurochemical movements? It is obviously the case that such neural connections are necessary for me to capture and store certain experiences within my cerebral cortex. Nevertheless, my cerebral cortex alone cannot tell me anything about the past, the present, or the future. For it to do so, it requires another dimension: *consciousness*, and consciousness eludes exclusively materialistic explanation. As I watch these neurons and synapses shift and change, I may be watching a *part* of the process of memory and memory formation, but I am certainly not watching memories form, at least not in any sense that I would normally use the term "memory."

The Question of Intentionality

Memories are not meaningless neurological formations. To reduce them to such is to misunderstand what memory is. Memories are always *about* something. As such they are *inescapably intentional*. I use the term "intentional" here in a technical sense. Intentionality does not simply mean that one intends to do something in the way that I might intend to go shopping on Saturday. The philosopher Jim Baggott describes intentionality in this way:

> Intentionality means more than just intending things, such as I intended to buy a house or you intend to steal a car. Intentionality is the ability of a conscious mind to represent to itself physical objects, people and states of affairs (real or imaginary).[13]

Intentionality means that an action or an occurrence is *about* something and by *someone*. Neurological change understood apart from the whole person who is experiencing it has no intentionality. It is not *about* anything.

In his reflections on the intentionality of memory, philosopher, gerontologist, and all-around polymath Raymond Tallis gives the example of someone smiling at you as you walk through Waterloo Station in London.

According to the standard account, the smile is encoded into the person's neural circuitry. When something happens that reminds me of the smile, this stimulates the part of my nervous system where the memory is encoded and I remember the smile. According to this understanding, the memory of the smile is an aspect of the physical state of my brain. In this sense I can, in principle, watch its formation on video and make a case for using that to explain memory. Importantly, this physical state is assumed to be somehow *about* the original smile I am remembering; that is, it has intentionality. Tallis describes the process of remembering the smile at Waterloo as an act that has double intentionality:

> One arrow of the double intentionality explicitly refers backwards in time to something that is no longer present: indeed, no longer exists. A remembered smile is located *in the past*: indeed in a past world, which is, as John McCrone has put it, "a living network of understanding rather than a dormant warehouse of facts." Thus we see intentionality elaborated: it opens us up to a present world that exceeds our experience; and it opens up the present world to the absent, the actual to the possible. As a result . . . we have our being in a world that is an infinitely extended space of possibilities; we are not simply "wired in" to what is.[14]

Creating such a complex temporal experience of intentionality is a pretty tall order for something that is simply matter! The question is: How can mere material neurological connections be *about* anything? The answer is that they cannot.

THE TENSING OF TIME

Noticing the significance of intentionality and raising the question of how "mere matter" could be about anything draws attention to another issue: the problem of the connection of time, memory, and matter. A commonsense view of memory perceives it as primarily having to do with capturing something of the movement and flow of time. Like time travelers we move backward and forward in time as we remember things, bring them into the present, and use them to plan and point toward possible futures. Central to this process is the observation that memories draw on a sense of time that is *tensed*: it has a sense of past, present, and future.

The suggestion that time is tensed implies that time is a dynamic aspect of conscious experience rather than a feature of the material world. We perceive time as flowing from one period to the next, with experiences moving on and ceasing to be as we encounter the flux and flow of time. There is an ontological connection between our language and our perceptions of the flow of time. This connection is captured grammatically in our language of past, present, and future. The grammar of time creates tense. Tensed time enables me to say, "I was in London yesterday," or, "I am going to buy some new socks tomorrow." Past, present, and future are perceived as quite different and mutually exclusive. We cannot, for example, say, "I am going to talk to you yesterday," or, "What will be was the same yesterday." All events within time, at least as time is humanly perceived, must be one tense or another. (It is, of course, the case, as we have seen and will explore in more detail later, that the idea of tense is radically altered within the strange temporal simultaneity of God's time.)

Tensed time and the material world

There is no tensed time in the material world. When we "watch memories form," in the ways described above, we can see nothing of the tensed nature of time. Tallis puts it this way:

> The physical world is what it is. It is not haunted by what it has been (or, indeed, by what it might become): by what was and will be. There are, in short, no tenses in the material world. . . . Tenses are not of course, illusions, unless the only reality that is accepted is the world as revealed to physics. But they have no place in the *physical* world. And they therefore have no place in a *piece* of the physical world: a material object such as the brain. The only presence that the past has in the material present is in virtue of the contents of the present being the effects of the past.[15]

The experience of tense in time is the product of some*one* rather than some*thing*. We need someone—a person with consciousness—in order to make the claim that there is a past, a present, and a future. Consciousness is, of course, related to neurology (although the nature of that relationship is contentious), but it also transcends neurology, not least because it can do certain things that neurology in its material simplicity cannot, such as tensing time. On its own, matter can make no judgment as to what was, what is, or what will be in the future. Matter may be able to record neural stimulation, but for such stimulation to be perceived as an event that has significance and meaning, an additional temporal-conscious layer is required.

The veracity of this observation becomes clearer when we reflect on research, which has shown that the brain responds in exactly the same way when it relates to data that comes from the past as it does to data that is available in the present or when it is reflecting on the future.[16] The same neurons and synapses fire into action when we think about last year's birthday party as when we encounter occurrences in the present or fantasize about the future. The neurological processing of memory is thus seen to be flat, thin, untensed, and atemporal. It requires *someone* to provide intentionality and a tensing of time. Placing things within a temporal flow is something that *I* do as a whole being, not simply a part of me. It is *I* who have a sense of time and aboutness, and it is *I* who place events within a particular chronological structure. When we see pictures of chemical changes in the brain, we may in some senses be watching the neural basis of the recording of certain events onto the neural cortex of the brain, but we are most certainly not watching memories form in any way that makes sense in terms of our day-to-day experiences of remembering. Memory is something that we do with the whole of who we are, not something that simply occurs at a purely material level.

REDESCRIBING MEMORY

There are clearly significant issues surrounding standard accounts of memory that focus on autobiography and time. Memory is not a natural kind that can be tied down to any single organ or identified with or by any single discipline. If that is the case, the question becomes, Could it be that there are other ways in which memory can be understood that, while including and respecting current neurological thinking, refuse to be confined or defined by it? If the argument of this chapter bears weight, Graham's and Elizabeth's experiences within worship can be seen in a quite different light. Of course, their brains have been damaged, and their ability to recall has been significantly compromised. But they are not lost souls. Their actions, words, and movements may be dislocated in time, but that dislocation does not detract from their intentionality. They are doing and saying things, and these things are *about* something and by *someone*. Their words and actions remain timefull even though they may not accurately be placed within time. They have meaning, purpose, and value, because Graham and Elizabeth are doing them.

All of this will have to be teased out more fully, but for now, we can begin to see the foundations for a quite different interpretation of the nature of the experiences of people with advanced dementia in worship. We can also see the beginnings of a new understanding of memory and time.

8

Time and the Heart
Affective Remembering

> Several years before his death the Swiss theologian Karl Barth came to the United States for a series of lectures. At one of these, after a very impressive lecture, a student asked a typically American question. He said, "Dr. Barth, what is the greatest thought that has ever passed through your mind?" The aging professor paused for a long time as he obviously thought about his answer. Then he said with great simplicity:
>
> "Jesus loves me! This I know
> For the Bible tells me so."
>
> (J. M. Boice)[1]

"JESUS LOVES ME THIS I KNOW . . ."

The other day I watched a fascinating piece of video on the website of the organization Memory Bridge. They offer a perspective of deep hope that speaks into the lives of people with advanced dementia.[2] Their ethos is that, no matter how advanced dementia may be, if we slow down and give people the right kind of time, there is always a bridge that we can cross to enter into communion. The video was of Naomi Feil, the founder of what has come to be known as "validation therapy,"[3] and Gladys Wilson, an elderly woman with advanced dementia. Gladys was deeply withdrawn. At the beginning of the video, she can be seen sitting alone with her eyes closed. Her head is stooped, eyes closed; Gladys is silent. It appeared that this is how she spends most of her life. The impression given is that she is not someone who communicated regularly or easily.

Naomi kneels before Gladys and reaches out and holds her hand. Gladys does not respond. Naomi talks to her gently. Gladys makes no obvious response. Naomi persists. She continues to talk to Gladys softly and patiently, looking intently into her closed eyes and holding a peaceable smile that seems to model the intentions of her heart. Nothing seems to be happening. Naomi begins to sing:

> *Jesus loves me—this I know, for the Bible tells me so.*

Gladys remains silent, eyes closed, unresponsive, impassive. Naomi sings on.

> *Little ones to him belong,*

Naomi moves Gladys' hands to the rhythm of her voice.

> *We are weak, but he is strong. Yes, Jesus loves me . . .*

Eventually, slowly, Gladys opens her eyes and catches Naomi's gaze. She begins to move her hands to the rhythm of Naomi's voice.

> *Yes, Jesus loves me . . .*

Naomi chants on . . . nothing . . . and then, suddenly, Gladys joins her in her song to Jesus by beginning to move her hand in rhythm to Naomi's persistent melody. Gladys' eyes brighten, and she enters into rhythmic communion with Naomi. She does not sing, but her body clearly resonates with the song. She locks into Naomi's persistent gaze. Naomi becomes more forceful:

> *Jesus loves me—this I know, for the Bible tells me so!*

The speed of the song increases. Gladys becomes more animated. She taps her chair and then begins to tap Naomi's arm. Naomi moves from worshipping Jesus to singing to the Father:

> *He's got the whole world in his hands, he's got the whole wide world in his hands,*
>
> *He's got the whole world in his hands, he's got the whole world in his hands.*

She repeats:

> *He's got the whole world . . .*

Suddenly, as if from nowhere, Gladys joins her:

> *In his hands . . .*
> *He's got the whole world . . . in his hands . . .*
> *He's got the whole wide world . . . in his hands . . .*

The viewer is drawn into a picture of the formation and sustaining of deep communion; we are privileged to watch and be gifted a vision of a meeting of hearts wherein the viewers are simultaneously surprised and awestruck by what we see. Naomi's timefull persistence opens up a space wherein both of them together can sing songs of praise to God with their bodies and their mouths. Naomi's presence and perseverance serves as a holy conduit for the movement of the Spirit as it draws the memory of Jesus gently through Gladys' heart.

Sensing from the heart

It would, of course, be tempting to move from this mountaintop experience to the valleys below and begin to reduce Gladys and Naomi's experience to the shape of that which we think we already know. We have already seen what such a move looks like in our initial reflections on Graham's and Elizabeth's experiences. However, our developing picture of memory would seem to militate against reductive interpretations. What we see here is Naomi welcoming Gladys as a *desirable* guest. By inviting her into deep communion and persisting with her even when nothing at all seems to be happening, Naomi enables Gladys to express her memory in a way that seems to resurrect her public persona and bring the deep memory of Jesus into the present, not as a memory to be recalled and temporalized (made sense of in terms of its proper location in time) but as a present reality to be expressed, shared, and enjoyed. Certainly, one could argue that Gladys and Naomi could have been singing absolutely anything. But they were not. It is *God's* names that they are singing with their mouths and enacting with their bodies, not simply the Beatles' "Love, love me do!" It is God the Creator that they sing about and acknowledge as sovereign and providential. If it is the case that there is intentionality in the act of memory and if the apostle Paul is correct that there is power in the name of Jesus—if you declare with your mouth, "Jesus is Lord" and believe in your heart that God raised him from the dead, you will be saved (Rom 10:9)—then the spiritual semiotics of Naomi and Gladys' encounter are not inconsequential.[4] It is true that they could have been singing anything. *But they are not.* As Christians we know that makes all the difference in the world.

PASSING TIME THROUGH THE HEART

In his work on collective memory, sociologist Rafael Narvaez points out that the Spanish word for remember—*recordar*—has a quite different meaning from the kind of accounts of memory that we reflected on in the previous chapter. The word "remember," Narvaez proposes,

> comes from the Latin *re* (to pass back through) and *memor* (mindful, mind): *remember* means passing a segment of time back through the mind. Logical as this seems, it is not, however, the only alternative. In Spanish, *Recordar* (*re-cordis*) means passing a segment of time back through the heart. Implied here is a suturing (Sanskrit *sutra*: string and memory aid), sensuous in nature, that ties me to an otherwise loose past.[5]

Narvaez highlights Marcel Proust's well-known experience:

> Where the taste of a "little piece of madeleine" shoots him back to his childhood. Beginning on the tongue, the madeleine makes its way up to become a nostalgic memory, an abstraction, and part of an identity. Proust can thus speak of how "involuntary memory" becomes a "voluntary" one which implies that a felt memory, something embodied, can become a conscious cognitive memory.[6]

Proust points out that somehow the past is beyond the reach of the intellect and "unmistakably present in some material object (or in the sensation which such an object arouses in us)."[7] The past is not so much past as it is resting, awaiting a stimulus to enable its return. Such a return is not bound to or by the past but instead sutures itself loosely to the present. The verb "remember" is profoundly Cartesian, locating memory firmly within the mind and resolutely within the past. However, such a mode of remembering offers a false impression that "underestimates the mnemonic importance of the body."[8] Memory is sensuous, embodied, and timefully free.

This is a fascinating and evocative observation that provides a beautiful reframing and opening up of the nature and location of memory. Memories embrace *all* of who we are. They are also deeply timefull. In Latin remembering has to do with passing a segment of time back through the mind. The emphasis here is primarily cognitive, with the temporal dynamic moving in a unilineal way from past to present. What has passed is past, and what is past can be made present by recalling the event through memory that is captured in the language of temporal linearity. Such an understanding of memory presumes a form of unchanging progressive chronology that can be destroyed by the failing of a single organ: our brains. It is this kind of memory that comprises the autobiographical self and the perspectives on memory that are given to us within standard accounts of memory as recall.

In Spanish, however, we are offered a quite different way of looking at memory and time. To remember something is to pass a segment of time back through the heart. Such an understanding of memory moves it from being a straightforward cognitive act of recall, solely dependent on a single organ—an act that contains and is defined by a simple linear movement from past to present—toward an understanding of memory conceived as an engagement with time that is tied to the sensations of our bodies and passes through the deepest regions of who we are: *our hearts*.

Narvaez' suggestion that memory is sensuous, embodied, and not bound by forms of time that are tightly and sequentially tensed opens up two dimensions for reflection, one physiological and the other theological. *Physiologically*, this way of thinking about memory draws us into the area of body memory and the suggestion that, even though our minds may not be able to recall them, the whole of our bodies remembers. *Theologically*, his suggestion draws out a revised understanding of memory: memory as a spiritually oriented experience that finds its true home within the human heart. We will address each of these issues in turn.

The memory of the body

In the previous chapter, we reflected on the experiences of Graham and Elizabeth in worship. There we asked the question, "What just happened?" As they were caught up in the words, sound, and tactility of the worship experience, both of them in different ways seemed to encounter aspects of memory and spiritual experience that were not available to them at other points in time. Part of the answer to the question "What just happened?" relates to the physiological phenomenon of body memory. Psychiatrist and phenomenologist Thomas Fuchs describes body memory (also referred to as implicit memory) in this way:

> Memory comprises not only one's explicit recollections of the past but also the acquired dispositions, skills and habits that implicitly influence one's present experience and behaviour. The term body memory refers to all the implicit knowledge, capacities and dispositions that structure and guide our everyday being-in-the-world without the need to deliberately think of how we do something, to explicitly remember what we did, or to anticipate what we want to do. It is the basic know-how that is mediated by the body and that we need for our everyday getting along with the world.[9]

Body memory occurs when through

> repetition and exercise, a habit has developed. Long-trained patterns of movement and perception have been embodied as skills or faculties that we practice as a matter-of-course in our everyday life—the upright gait, the ability of speaking, reading or writing, and the handling of instruments such as a bicycle or a piano.[10]

The temporal dynamic within body memory is quite different from that which we encounter within cognitive memory. Bianca Maria Pirani notes:

> Explicit recollection is directed from the present back towards the past; implicit memory [body memory], however, does not re-present the past, but re-enacts it in the course of the body's performance. What we have acquired as skills, habits and experience, has become what we are today; implicit knowing is our lived past.[11]

Recall memory brings the past into the present in order that we can think and plan for the future. Body memory enables the past to occur in the present. Body memory is the enactment of the past in the present; it is memory that appears before us as an occurrence in-the-now. We can indeed watch memory, but not in the way that the scientific account urges us to consider. As we watch Graham and Elizabeth sing, pray, move to the rhythms of worship, and participate in the ritual of the sacrament, we see memory worked out in the present, before our very eyes.

Body memory and intentionality

Body memory is not "mere reflex" that is carried out by the body in a meaningless machinelike way. It is meaningful, intentional action. Body memory is always *about* something. Fuchs highlights the fact that the body is

> a third dimension between merely imagined movement and motor execution. The memory of the body is an impressive refutation of the dualism of pure consciousness and the physical body, for it cannot be attributed to either of them. When I am dancing, the rhythmic movements originate from my body without a need to steer them deliberately—and yet I am living in my movements, I sense them in advance, and I can modulate them according to the rhythm that I feel: I myself am dancing, and not a ghost in a body machine.[12]

Body memory does not *just happen*. It is something that *I* do. It has a necessary intentionality. Elizabeth's response to the gift of the eucharistic bread when she apparently cannot respond at other times is not the same thing as tapping her knee and getting her leg to jerk. Why? Because it is *Elizabeth* who is doing it. When Graham sings, it is *Graham* who is singing, and not a random bunch of impersonal neurons. When Gladys taps to the name of Jesus and sings worship to the God who holds the world in his hands, it is not a new version of Gladys who is doing this. Nor is it a vestige of the "old Gladys": *it is Gladys!* By drawing our attention to the embodiment of memory, Narvaez provides us with some powerful counterintuitive hermeneutical tools that can enable us understand and reframe the physiological dimensions of the experiences of people with advanced dementia. But there is more.

REMEMBERING THE HEART

The sensuousness of memory highlighted by Narvaez is associated not simply with the body but also with the *heart*. Narvaez' introduction of the language of the heart opens up the conversation around memory, time, and advanced dementia to the theological and the mystical. The suggestion that remembering has to do with drawing time back through the heart moves us beyond, but importantly not apart from, material explanations of the experiences of Graham, Elizabeth, and Gladys and into the realms of the Spirit. The connection between memory and the heart leads us into the very core of the ways in which human beings encounter God and, at least ideally, one another. It takes us to *the place of the heart*.

By suggesting that this dimension is "mystical," I do not mean to imply some kind of Cartesian separation between the spiritual and the material. The mystical is deeply tied in with the understanding of mystery that I outlined in the introduction to this book. By suggesting that the heart is mystical, I simply mean that the heart is not fully bound by material expectations and current assumptions and presumed knowledge about what may or may not be plausible or possible. The heart is mystical because it is the place where the unfathomable spirit of God encounters the materiality of human bodies.[13] It is not mystical because it separates our bodies from our spirits. It is mystical because it reveals the significance and the purpose of their interrelationship.

THINKING ABOUT THE HEART

In drawing out the implications of the association of memory with the heart, we need to begin by thinking through precisely what theologically we mean when we talk of "the heart." Scripture places the heart as the seat of human relationality and desire:

The heart is the wellspring of life.
Above all else, guard your heart, for it is the wellspring of life.
(Prov 4:23)

The heart is a place of trust.
Trust in the LORD with all your heart and lean not on your own understanding.
(Prov 3:5 NIV)

The heart is a work of God.
Create in me a pure heart, O God, and renew a steadfast spirit within me.
(Ps 51:10 NIV)

The heart is sustained by God.
My flesh and my heart may fail, but God is the strength of my heart and my portion forever.
(Ps 73:26 NIV)

The heart is a source of strength.
My flesh and my heart may fail, but God is the strength of my heart and my portion forever.
(Ps 73:26 NIV)

The heart is the source of godly praise.
I will praise you, O LORD, with all my heart; I will tell of all your wonders.
(Ps 9:1)

The heart is not morally neutral.
For out of the heart come evil thoughts—murder, adultery, sexual immorality, theft, false testimony, slander.
(Matt 15:19 NIV)

The heart is the seat of our desire.
Sell your possessions, and give to the needy. Provide yourselves with moneybags that do not grow old, with a treasure in the heavens that

> does not fail, where no thief approaches and no moth destroys. For where your treasure is, there will your heart be also.
>
> (Luke 12:33-34 ESV)

The heart is required to be purified by the Spirit.

Create in me a pure heart, O God, and renew a steadfast spirit within me.

(Ps 51:10 NIV)

The heart is that within and throughout human beings that communes with God and facilitates communion with others. The heart is the place of joy, praise, lament, desire, purification, and connection. The heart is the beginning point for communion. It is not for nothing that Jesus gives the heart primacy in his description of loving God: "Love the Lord your God with all your heart and with all your soul and with all your mind" (Matt 22:37).

Michael Downey observes that according to the Hebrew and Christian Scriptures the heart

> is used to describe the root of all personal life. The term serves a unitive function, insofar as it does not describe emotion or affection as separated from intellect or reason. It describes the whole, total person.[14]

The term "heart" (*leb* and *lebab* in Hebrew, *kardia* in Greek) is used on ten occasions in reference to the physical organ:

> But it is used more than a thousand times to describe the root or source of diverse personal functions. In this early usage, "heart" meant the whole, total person; the individual at this time was not understood as a being with the separate faculties of intellect and will, but as a unity.[15]

The heart thus expresses "the unitive quality of the human person prior to any distinction of acts and intentions; the core of affectivity."[16] Mind, will, reason, cognition, and intellect remain important, but they require the heart in order to function healthily. Mind, will, and intellect are thus seen to be secondary faculties that are built upon the unitive ontology of the heart. The heart is the place where our wholeness is held. Intellect, will, and reason are aspects of the practices of the heart that find their true focus as they receive the faithful mentoring of the heart. Jean Vanier reminds us that the heart is "the deepest most fundamental aspect of the human being that is touched and transformed by the Spirit."[17] To speak of the heart, Vanier continues,

> is not to speak of vaguely defined emotions but to speak of the very core of our being. At the core, we all know we can be strengthened and rendered more truthful and more alive. Our hearts can become hard like stone or tender like flesh. We have to create situations where our hearts can be fortified and nourished. In this way, we can be more sensitive to others, to their needs, their cries, their inner pain, their tenderness, and their gifts of love.[18]

The heart is not just a place of relationality in general, although it is the seat of all of our relationships. More deeply and more particularly, the heart is a place where we come to meet God in the power of the Holy Spirit within ourselves and within others. Vanier puts this well:

> Behind all the barriers built up since childhood, there is the pure and innocent heart of a child where the gift of God resides. The heart is capable of receiving and giving love, of living in communion with another person and with God, capable of being a source of life for others. In the designs of God, it is the heart, which is meant to inspire all human activities.[19]

Christians are always and inevitably a people of the heart.

The seat of affectivity

Central to the notion of the heart is its basic function as the seat of affectivity.

> Affectivity, from the Latin *affectus*, describes that in us, which is open to attraction from outside ourselves. It refers to that in us, which is open to be moved, touched, lured by another. The affective dimension, or affectivity, is not mere sentiment or emotion. It is the deepest part of us, which yearns, longs, thirsts for, and makes possible communion in love with others and God.[20]

The heart is thus seen to be *the place of communion*. As we watch Elizabeth, Graham, and Gladys praying, singing, worshipping, and using their bodies in various ways to express their love for God, so we can watch and see the memory of their bodies and the desires of their hearts. Such memory is intentional; it has the purpose of bringing them into communion with God, *a communion of the heart*. The Spirit is in the words of their singing, the Spirit is in the sacrament, the Spirit is enmeshed within Graham's outstretched hands and Gladys' faithful tapping of Naomi's arm. Through their engagement with spiritual practices over time, their bodies and their hearts have found their proper orientation.

RETHINKING TIME AND DEMENTIA: SUTURING OUR HEARTS TO THE PAST

This, at least in part, reflects something of what Narvaez means by time being *loosely* sutured to the heart. Passing a segment of memory back through the heart is irrevocably a *sensuous* movement. It is, however, also an oddly timefull movement. Memory ties *me*—who I am in all of my wholeness—to an otherwise loose past. Such memory does not simply have to do with *recall*; it also has to do with *impact*. As a segment of memory is passed down through my heart, it impacts me not simply as something that happened in a previous place and time and that I desire to contemplate in the present. Rather, it comes to me as something that has a sensual impact in-the-now. The memory of the heart is not focused so much on the spatial historical location of memory (precisely where it occurred in time) as it is on the ways in which particular memories impact upon our hearts now, in the present. So it does not really matter whether Graham, Elizabeth, or Gladys can place their spiritual experiences within tensed time. The past has come to meet them in-the-now. The past is loosely stitched into their hearts not as past, present, or future but as, in one sense, ever present. They are sutured into time without the need for tense. It is not that they have become reduced to "mere matter." It is rather that tensed time has unfurled and now binds itself loosely and flexibly to their hearts. In one sense, this perception of time resonates with God's timefull simultaneity; a time where a thousand years is like one day and the past comes to meet us in the passion of Jesus.

THE UNTENSING OF TIME

If we think about such a suggestion in terms of Gladys' experience, something interesting emerges. As assessed within the parameters of the standard accounts of memory, Gladys has profound memory loss. If her memory is assessed by standardized tests, she will clearly fail. However, when the memory of Jesus is passed through her heart, it stimulates her to move and to sing, to feel, and to experience those deep, relational aspects of her life that the memory of Jesus brings to her in all of her sensuality. Naomi's timefull presence serves as a holy conduit for the movement of the Spirit as it draws the memory of Jesus gently through Gladys' heart. In the looseness of the heart's time, Gladys can encounter the past in the present in a way that brings comfort and hopefulness. It is not so much that Gladys has lost her sense of time; it is more that she has lost the ability to express and understand her encounters of the world in terms of an accurate perception of *tensed* time. Gladys therefore has not left the world of time. Rather, she has moved beyond the world of tensed time and entered into a world where time is experienced with a simultaneity that has a strange resonance with God's simultaneous presence within time. She has become sutured to the past loosely. She cannot quite place events within their linear space in temporal time. However, it is not that she is regressing, moving backward toward her childhood world of Sunday school songs. Such a suggestion is to misunderstand both experienced time and God's time. It is, rather, that the cognitive and bodily memory of these songs is moving *forward* into the present and doing their work, their spiritual work, in-the-now. The past is not truly past but continues to pass through her heart in a way that profoundly impacts her present experience. Gladys remains acutely aware of time. She has simply lost the means to time travel through it in the ways that she used to. Naomi's timefull presence with Gladys in the present moment models something crucial. *Being in the moment means being with someone when they are out of time.* The intention of being with them is not to try to drag them into "our time" or to force them back into a time that has passed, as some forms of "reminiscence" tend to do. Being in the moment requires that we recognize the looseness of the suturing of time and learn that living in time that is free, radical, and untensed may in fact be indicative of something beautiful and deeply revealing, rather than simply something that is past, partial, and indicative of that which has been lost.

The sensuousness of memory

Memory has a surprising but vital looseness about its temporality. Memory is also intricately sensuous. Graham and Gladys sing their praises to God. Singing is precisely the type of sensuous mnemonic experience that passes through our hearts and relocates us within time. When we hear particular pieces of music, they not only remind us of certain places and times; they move us *into* those places and times. However, this movement is not simply backward. It brings to us people whom we met "back then," helps us to feel events in our lives, and relive the loves we had and the loves we have lost. Music can take us to an experience, a relationship, a time when things were good or when things were bad. Hearing music does not simply remind us of the sequence of notes and the various instruments and voices of which it is composed (unless one is a musician, in which case it might). It touches our hearts and opens our senses now. How we remember the past is determined by how we are experiencing the present. The memory that is evoked by music is filled with emotion, feeling, and sensual experience not just from "back then" but also from right now.[21] It is not necessary for us to place such experiences in linear temporal order for them to be powerful and deeply meaningful. They come to us in a different way because each time we hear a piece of music we are in a different place in time and space. We do not need to name such experiences or place them correctly in the flow of linear time in order to be impacted by them; we *feel* them with our hearts. As the music touches our hearts, the past enters the present in ways that cannot be captured by a simple then-and-now dynamic. As we become enthralled by the rhythm and tempo and caught up in the lyrical beauty of the music, so our hearts are strangely warmed.

Music does not so much take us back into the past as it brings the past into the present and allows us to engage with it in fresh ways. Music transposes our current experience into a particular set of emotions that emerge tentatively from the cadences of the past, not as the past but as the present, a present that mingles and is enmeshed among the now. These feelings are fresh because our memories of the past are deeply impacted by our current emotions and the emotions that we had then. If we are sad in the present, we will remember certain aspects of the past differently than if we are happy, joyful, or mellow. It is in this way that we can say that a segment of memory passed through the heart binds us with and to time loosely. The suturing is loose because within the memory of the heart the past and the present are unstable; they intermingle and move between one another. The past and the present *feel* at one level as if they are linear, progressive, and separate, but when time is passed through the heart they are revealed to be loose and unstable. Such an understanding of time is not pathological; rather, it draws our attention to the closeness of such experiences to the simultaneity that marks God's time.

NEUROLOGIZING THE HEART?

At this stage an objection might be raised. Surely, mysterious, ineffable, and beautiful as the concept of the heart and the memory of the heart may be, it still requires neurology in order to become the place of relationality? Are we not simply spiritualizing neurology? The answer to such a concern is yes and no. *Yes*, the heart has a connection to our neurology, but *no* we need not assume that it is defined by it or confined to it. At one level, the heart inevitably has a neurological dimension insofar as humans require their neurology in order to experience anything at all. Augustine's famous expression, "You have made us for yourself, O Lord, and our heart is restless until it rests in you," indicates that there is an experiential, material, and creaturely dimension to the heart; *the heart feels things*, and feeling something for humans requires neurology. The argument for the heart is not that it is a disembodied aspect of human beings, some kind of holy space within us that functions like a dualistic soul. The heart is a unitive dimension that contains both the fleshiness and the holiness of human existence. As we saw in the previous chapter, neurology alone cannot adequately reflect or explain the fullness of memory. In like manner neurology alone cannot encapsulate or define the nature of the heart even though it may participate in its workings. The heart is, therefore, not defined by neurological processes. Rather, it is the *point* of neurological processes, their raison d'être.

This will, of course, make little sense to those who desire for the world simply to be seen as "nothing but" the material. If we pay attention to the world in ways that view emotions, feelings, and the works of the heart as nothing other than manifestations of the workings of the brain, the heart will inevitably be reduced to material interaction. However, if we shift our attention a little and take seriously the suggestion that our bodies are literally the temple of the Holy Spirit (1 Cor 6:19), then the strange interaction between the neurological and the divine begins to become clearer, if at the same time still remaining fundamentally mysterious. In the end, in like manner to the relationship between flesh and Spirit within the incarnate body of Jesus, the relationship between neurology and our hearts is a mystery: "As you do not know the path of the wind, or how the body is formed in a mother's womb, so you cannot understand the work of God, the Maker of all things" (Eccl 11:5). And yet it is from within the mystery of the incarnation that our salvation is wrought. Mysteries seem to do good work! In God's time the spiritual and the mundane mingle. As we have seen, for something to be a mystery does not mean that we can know nothing about it, only that we cannot know everything.

MOVING BEYOND LINEAR TIME

Standard accounts understand memory as firmly located within linear, autobiographical history. The modi operandi of remembering are presumed to be located securely within the brain; a single organ is charged with the responsibility of bringing the past to us through cognition and recall. Within such an account, the meaning of the actions of Graham, Elizabeth, and Gladys are not particularly important. However, the memory of the heart looks at the meaning of these actions in a quite different way. If we perceive memory as passing a segment of time back through the heart, we do not view it as relating to the work of a single organ but as work that involves all of who we are. In this way we open up memory and reveal it as something that occurs within our hearts, stitching our hearts into a mode of time that is in some senses ever present.

This mode of memory seems much closer to the ways in which God encounters time. The memory loss that the people we have spent time with in these chapters has a strange resonance with the memory and time that we find in the realms of God's time. My point is not that people with advanced dementia are somehow more godly than others. It is just that paying attention to the shape and form of God's time can provide deep and transformative insights into the ways in which memory is working itself out within such lives. "Testing" the memory of the heart for people with advanced dementia has to do with finding those things that touch, stimulate, comfort, and warm their hearts. Of course, people have forgotten things. But, perhaps, if we slow down, find a space of gentleness, patience, kindness, endurance, trust, and faith, we can discover that their hearts have remembered much more than we have given them credit for. In the epigraph to chapter 7, Charles Leadbeater suggests that

> instead of squeezing people with dementia into complicated systems designed for people who can't remember who the president is, we should find kinder, less judgemental ways to be with them.[22]

Grounding our thinking around memory within the idea of the timefull memory of the heart allows us to do precisely that.

V

THE HORROR OF TIME

9

The Horror of Time
Acquired Brain Injury and Personality Change

If only I could turn back time; if only I had said what I still hide.

(Aqua, "Turn Back Time")[1]

I know you're in there but you're just out of sight . . .

(Al Stewart, "Time Passages")[2]

"But what about you?" he asked. "Who do you say I am?"

(Matt 16:15 NIV)

The year 2014 was an interesting one for our family. My mother turned ninety, my eldest daughter celebrated her eighteenth birthday, and my wife reached the grand old age of fifty! (My own age shall remain a mysterious secret. . . .) Three special birthdays in the same year is pretty unusual. We celebrated by heading out into the country to a chalet just outside Dundee in Scotland with the rest of our family: my five kids, my eldest son's wife, my brother and his wife, and my sister. (It was a large chalet!) Everybody who really mattered to me in life was there in that small piece of Scotland. It was a deeply timefull moment as the span of ages that ran across our family was brought to a place of recognition. There was a deep beauty in reflecting on the time markers that had come together in that year. There was an irreplaceable warmth, comfort, and joy about simply being with my family and enjoying the celebration of the passing of time. My mother is ninety and very beautiful. My eighteen-year-old daughter is a dancer (all of my daughters are, actually).

She moves gracefully, rhythmically; she thinks in dance patterns. She is now a woman, and that invokes happiness and dissonance in me, as it must do for all fathers. I feel like I am losing something and gaining something all at the same time. My wife is my rock. Who knows how she has put up with me for so long! Any man who spends more of his life with a computer than with human beings has got to be problematic to live with. She tells me I have no social skills. I can find no reasonable counterargument! We celebrated the passing of time and the blessings and curses of aging.

There was celebration. However, there was also fear and a tinge of sadness. The markers of time that we came together to celebrate were also pointers toward our mortality, our fading presence on planet earth. God's time is beautiful, slow, filled with love and possibilities. But time is also fallen, filled with brokenness, suffering, and lostness. Joni Mitchell once sang,

> Don't it always seem to go, that you don't know what you've got till
> it's gone,
> They paved paradise and put up a parking lot.[3]

Life is a lot like that. But in those moments in that chalet in Dundee, we *did* know what we had, and we knew that one day it would be gone. And herein lies the problem with time as it is lived out within fallen creation. It is both beautiful and ferociously fearful at precisely the same time. It can be slow, gentle, peaceful, and redeemed. But it can also be horrific. The time markers within my family reminded me of the time when I and they will grieve and long for the times we had and would love to have again. There is a horror built into time that we cannot ignore.

THE HORROR OF TIME

Dietrich Bonhoeffer preached a sermon in Barcelona on August 26, 1928. His text was 1 John 2:17: "The world and its desires are passing away, but those who do the will of God live forever."[4] In that sermon he pointed at the horror of time:

> The great philosopher of the ancient Greeks, Heraclitus of Ephesus, summarized his most profound insight regarding the world with the words: all things are in flux. . . . Nothing abides, nothing is secure, nothing is assured in the world. "It is not possible to step twice in the same river," he says elsewhere, . . . meaning that just when you want to seize life, it has already passed by, slipping through your hands, melting away like nothing. There's no stopping it. . . . Life does not live; it dies. To live means to die.[5]

The horror of time is that it moves remorselessly and unstoppably onwards toward death. Nothing stays the same; there is no security; life comes and goes within the unchangeable flow of time. At the core of human life is an inability to control time and a deep awareness that everything that we have and all that we know is temporary, unstable, and deeply fragile. Time draws our attention to uncontrollable change and death. As such, time is fearful. The true horror of time is that it cannot be undone. Bonhoeffer puts it this way:

> The misfortune hanging over the world, however, the misfortune that makes it so vain, is time. Time, a doubly frightful word. First because whatever happens remains something that happened; it can never be undone; not even the smallest bit of what happened can be brought back. Guilt remains guilt, omission remains omission. That is the reality that has and will cost us the most tears in our lives. What has happened, has happened for all time. The other terrible consideration is that nothing stands still, not even for a single moment, everything moves forward in eternal change and towards a specific goal, namely death. . . . The puzzling, unfathomable contradiction in our lives is that only where we experience bliss do we want to be eternal, and yet nowhere are we more transitory than there. Joy in the world passes away because the world itself passes away.[6]

It is the inability to change time that is one of time's most frightening features. What is done is done and cannot be undone; what has happened cannot be "unhappened," so to speak. The powerlessness that accompanies our inability to control or to change time takes on particular poignancy when we experience changes that are deeply negative and for which we desire nothing more than to be able to turn back time to a time where we felt in control and where our current pain and loss was not the primary shaping force that drives our lives. But we can never change time. As David Bowie once put it: "Time may change me, / but I can't trace time."[7]

Being eternal in every moment?

The horror of the unchangeable nature of time is brought into particularly sharp focus within the lives of those who, often over a brief period of time, find their lives and their sense of who they are in the world completely transformed by a blow to the head or the internal neurological devastation caused by a stroke or a brain tumor: those with what has come to be known as "acquired brain damage." What are we to make of the experience of being one person at the top of a flight of stairs and waking up at the bottom of the stairs apparently a very different person? Bonhoeffer informs us that our calling is "to be eternal in every moment . . . beholding God, that is the meaning of our lives."[8] The horror of time is alleviated by the knowledge of the presence of God in time. He urges us to realize that as creatures each moment is filled with the eternity of God; our lives find meaning as we learn to recognize God in the depths and midst of day-to-day time. But how can we be "eternal in every moment" when the moment before we tumble down the stairs is so radically different from the moment that we now find ourselves inhabiting as we look up from the floor? What is it that makes the "me" at the bottom of the stairs the "me" that began my journey at the top? How can we behold God in-the-moment when our brains have been so altered that we struggle to behold even ourselves, never mind an invisible transcendent being? What sense are we to make of such changes? Even within God's time we struggle to find sense in the midst of what seems to make little sense.

The focus of the final three chapters will be on one form of disability and one source of deep human suffering: acquired brain damage. The term "acquired brain injury" includes all types of traumatic brain injury (injuries to the brain that are caused by some kind of external force that occurs after birth), alongside strokes and hypoxic brain injury (lack of oxygen to the brain). Injuries to the brain that are present at birth, such as is the case for many people with profound and complex intellectual disabilities, do not fall into this category. Likewise, other neurological conditions such as dementia or Parkinson's disease are not covered by the category of acquired brain injury. For our purposes, this form of brain damage is quite different from the types of brain damage we have examined thus far.

Current developments in the area of neuroplasticity are showing us what a wonderful and resilient organ the brain is. If we encounter damage to one area of our brain, it can compensate by using other areas and in so doing develop new neural connections to help overcome something of the brokenness of the damaged area.[9] Even so, when our brains are damaged in certain ways, we can never get back that which has been lost. When parts of our brain die off because of a lack of blood supply or are broken off because of traumatic injuries, we are forced unwillingly to learn to face the fact that time has moved on and what was can never be again.

Our practical and theological resources are inevitably stretched when we are faced with the raw reality of brain damage and personality change. Even something so apparently positive as the memory of the heart can be a source of deep unease as certain touches, places, smells, memories take us back not to a place of peace but to the locus of our trauma and the unending presentness of our loss. Brain damage certainly slows us down, but such slowing down is not always perceived as a blessing. In a hyperneurological culture that, as we have seen, has a tendency to assume that all human functioning, including our sense of "self" (who we are) and even our relationship with God can be traced to some aspect of neurology, brain damage and the changes that accompany it can all too easily be translated into "soul damage": the assumption that somehow both the self and the soul are wholly dependent on the state of our brains. Viewed in this way, our inability to change time can indeed be truly horrifying. The question that will be explored in the final three chapters of the book is, *What practical and theological difference does an awareness that we live within God's time make to those who live with acquired brain injury and its accompanying changes in personality?*

BECOMING "SOMEONE ELSE"

> My entire brain, the organ by which my very consciousness is controlled, was reorganized one day ten years ago. I went to sleep here and woke up there; the place looked the same but nothing in it worked the way it used to.
>
> (Floyd Skloot)[10]

On December 7, 1988, Floyd Skloot woke up to discover that the Floyd Skloot who had gone to bed the previous evening was quite different from the Floyd Skloot who woke up the following day. He was on a business trip, attending a conference on national energy policy. When he woke up in his hotel room, everything had changed. He could not remember how to shut off the alarm on his watch. He could not work out why he could not get onto the elevator when the door was closed. He literally developed dementia overnight.[11] Skloot had contracted a virus that targeted his brain. The virus had left lesions in his cerebral cortex that, among other things, seriously damaged his long- and short-term memory and his basic ability to think:

> I used to be able to think. My brain's circuits were all connected and I had spark, a quickness of mind that let me function well in the world. There were no problems with numbers or abstract reasoning; I could find the right word, could hold a thought in mind, match faces with names, converse coherently in crowded hallways, learn new tasks. I had a memory and an intuition that I could trust.[12]

All of that changed in an instant:

> Without prelude and without time to prepare, momentously, the way it does in people suffering strokes or tumors, a bullet to the brain or exposure to toxic substances like carbon monoxide. For me, it was how I

> imagine the day some 65 million years ago when a huge meteorite struck the earth, turning summer to winter in an instant. Not that I noticed right away.[13]

The virus had literally drilled holes into the frontal lobes of his brain. He was unable to remember, to think, or to act in the ways that he had done the day before and indeed in the life he had previously. Part of him had vanished forever, melting away before the assault of the virus as it broke down and destroyed the neurons and synapses that were responsible for key aspects of Skloot's encounters with the world. If it is the case, as Descartes suggests, that thinking and being are deeply interconnected, Skloot asks, "What happens when I cannot think, or at least cannot think as I did, cannot think well enough to function in a job or in the world? Who am I?"[14] The lesions on his brain were, he considered, "lesions in my Self, fissures in the thought process that result from this damage to my brain. When the brain changes, the mind changes—these lesions have altered who I am."[15] Whether the lesions to Skloot's brain actually altered who he was or whether they altered his perception of who he was is a question that we will return to later. For now, the point to note is Skloot's assumption and indeed his experience that changes to his brain constitute changes to his self.

Living differently

The "new person" that Skloot perceived he had become experienced the world quite differently than did the "old person" he believed he had been. Even his most basic functioning had been altered. The normally simple act of walking suddenly became complicated.

> It requires intense concentration, as does maintaining balance and even breathing if I am tired. It is apparent in activities requiring the processing of certain fundamental information. For example, no matter how many times I have been shown how to do it, I cannot assemble our vacuum cleaner or our poultry shears or the attachments for our hand-cranked pasta maker. At my writing desk, I finish a note and place the pen in my half-full mug of tea rather than in its holder, which quite obviously teems with other pens. I struggle to figure out how a pillow goes into a pillowcase. I cannot properly adjust Beverly's [Skloot's wife] stereo receiver in order to listen to the radio; it has been and remains useful to me only in its present setting as a CD player. These are all public, easily discernible malfunctions.[16]

This public transition from who he was into how he is now perceived by others is echoed by a private, personal transition. He thinks differently not just about himself:

> For me, being brain damaged also has a physical, conscious component. Alone with my ideas and dreams and feelings, turned inward by the isolation and timelessness of chronic illness, I face a kind of ongoing mental vertigo in which thoughts teeter and topple into those fissures of cognition I mentioned earlier. I lose my way. I spend a lot of time staring into space, probably with my jaw drooping, as my concentration fragments and my focus dissolves. Thought itself has become a gray area, a matter of blurred edges and lost distinctions, with little that is sharp about it. This is not the way I used to be.[17]

Speech became highly problematic:

> You should hear me talk. I often come to a complete stop in mid-sentence, unable to find a word I need, and this silence is an apt reflection of the impulse blockage occurring in my brain. Sitting next to Beverly as she drives our pickup truck through Portland traffic at 6:00 p.m., I say, "We should have gone for pizza to avoid this blood . . ." and cannot not go on. I hear myself; I know I was about to say "blood tower traffic" instead of "rush hour traffic." Or I manifest staggered speech patterns—which feels like speaking with a limp—as I attempt to locate an elusive word. "I went to the . . . *hospital* yesterday for some . . . *tests* because my head . . . *hurt*." Or I blunder on, consumed by a feeling that something is going wrong, as when I put fresh grounds into the empty carafe instead of the filter basket on my coffee maker, put eye drops in my nose, or spray the cleaning mist into my face instead of onto the shower walls. So at the dinner table I might say, "Pass the sawdust" instead of "pass the rice," knowing even as it happens that I am saying something inappropriate. I might start a conversation about "Winston Salem's new CD" instead of Wynton Marsalis's or announce that "the shore is breaking" when I mean to say "the shower is leaking." There is nothing smooth or unified any more about the process by which I communicate; it is dis-integrated and unpredictably awkward.[18]

Skloot encountered radical change; he does not recognize himself as the person he used to be. He has become, in some senses, a stranger to himself and to others. His thought processes, his communicative interactions, and his sense of who he is in the world have shifted in ways that, at times, make him unrecognizable. It is not that he has in any sense ceased to be a person or even become a lesser person. He is just a different person. He has taken on ways of being in the world that are different from the way he has been previously. That difference is not necessarily for the worse. But it *is* different.

An insult to the brain?

The way that Skloot articulates these changes is important. He does not like them. However, he also does not like the way in which his experiences are often framed within medicine and neurology. The types of experiences outlined above are not, for Skloot, best named in terms of symptoms. The communicative difficulties, his problems with thinking, his difficult gait are not alien to him in the way a fever or tonsillitis might be. He knows where they come from: his damaged brain. But they are also not symptoms or failures; they are not simply broken bits that need to be fixed or corrected. His experiences are much more than mere deficits. What neurology perceives as deficits, Skloot explains, "have been incorporated into my very being, my consciousness. They are now part of my repertoire. Deficits imply losses; I have to know how to see them as gains."[19]

This is a very powerful reframing and renarration of his experience of acquired brain damage. Skloot uses medical knowledge to help him understand his experience, but then he moves beyond the confines of that particular story in order to use that limited explanatory information to reconstruct a powerful counterstory that translates the language of deficit into a language of being. His experiences are not alien to who he is; they are part of who he has become. In this way Skloot integrates neurological understandings with a subtle renarration of his self in a way that holds the tension between lament and grief for what has been, and the reality of the possibilities of what is and what will be in the future. However, this fragile tension is easily broken by outside forces that desire to push to the fore the suggestion that his "symptoms" should be perceived as unfamiliar and alienating rather than consolidating them as aspects of his emerging self.

Skloot observes the way in which practitioners of neuroscience refer to the damage caused by trauma to the brain as an "insult" to the brain. Tracing the etymology of the term "insult," he observes that in common parlance it refers to "an offensive remark or action."[20] It has to do with some kind of break with an implicit or explicit code of manners. To insult someone is to be rude to them and to treat them with contempt. However, when the term is translated into medical language, its meaning changes:

> "Insult" comes from the Latin compound verb *insultare*, which means "to jump on" and is also the root word for "assault" and "assail." It's a word that connotes aggressive physical abuse, an attack. Originally, it suggested leaping upon the prostrate body of a foe, which may be how its link to contemptuous action was forged.[21]

So, medically, an insult to the brain is perceived to be a type of assault, an attack on the brain from forces inside or outside of the brain. However, Skloot wonders how the idea of contemptuousness came to be a part of our understanding of insult. Contempt is, of course, central to the idea of insult. However, viruses, pavements, steering wheels, blood clots, and so forth can hardly be acting contemptuously when they bring about brain damage. Contempt enters the arena by another route:

> I think society at large, medical scientists, insurers, legislators, and the person-on-the-street do feel a kind of contempt for the brain damaged with their comical way of walking, their odd patterns of speech or ways in which neurological damage is expressed, their apparent stupidity, their abnormality. The damage done to a brain seems to evoke disdain in those who observe it and shame or disgrace in those who experience it—I know I refer to a feeling of humiliation when I expose my neurologically induced aberrant behaviors in public.[22]

The insult that brings about brain damage refers not only to the physical. The insult to the brain brings about contemptuousness from those who observe the changes the insult initiates. Shame, humiliation, fear, and rejection can easily overpower the type of more positive reframing that Skloot proclaims and embodies. The rebuilding of the self after brain damage requires much more than attention to basic neurology or even personal reframing. It requires that we pay a different kind of attention and practice a quite particular discipleship of the mind.

Rebuilding

Skloot's response to all of his changes is fascinating, moving, and revealing. He begins by reframing his own and other people's expectations in fundamental ways. Those around him constantly ask whether he will ever recover, whether he will "get better." But such questions seem odd to Skloot because these are precisely the types of questions that he has *stopped* asking. He recognizes and positively acknowledges that there are important developments within brain science that may well help people in his situation in the future. But such brain science has absolutely no meaning for him. Such advances are so far in the future that, in his opinion, it is "best not to think about this sort of thing."[23] The question of whether he will "get better" has no meaning to him. He has another strategy and another frame to place his life within:

> To continue looking outside for a cure, a "magic bullet," some combination of therapies and treatments and chemicals to restore what I have lost is to miss the point altogether. Certainly if a safe, effective way existed to resurrect dead cells, or generate replacements, and if this somehow guaranteed that I would flash back or flash forward to "be the person I was," it would be tempting to try. But how would that be? Would the memories that have vanished reappear? Not likely. Would I be like the man, blind for decades, who had sight restored and could not handle the experience of vision, could not make sense of a world he could see? *I am, in fact, who I am now*. I have changed. I have learned to live and live richly as I am now. Slowed down, softer, more heedful of all that I see and hear and feel, more removed from the hubbub, more internal.[24]

Skloot's strategy is to avenge the insult, not through anger or the use of violence but by seeking ways of exploiting his gifts (old and new) in the strange new world of his revised self:

> The duel is fought over and over. I have developed certain habits that enable me to work—a team of seconds, to elaborate this metaphor of a duel. I must be willing to write slowly, to skip or leave blank spaces where I cannot find words that I seek, compose in fragments and without an overall ordering principle or imposed form. I explore and make discoveries in my writing now, never quite sure where I am going but willing to let things ride and discover later how they all fit together. Every time I finish an essay or poem or piece of fiction, it feels as though I have faced down the insult.[25]

Skloot is at war! But it is a different kind of war. A gentle, slow war that seeks to avenge the insult of brain damage in all of its different forms. When he achieves his given goal, no matter how long it has taken and no matter how trivial others might find it, the insult is avenged. He is not simply resigning himself to his fate or putting an idealistic gloss on a bad situation. Skloot does not pretend that he does not miss his "old self." He leaves plenty of space for lament:

> Certainly I want to be well. I miss being able to think clearly and sharply, to function in the world, to move with grace. I miss the feeling

> of coherence or integrity that comes with a functional brain. I feel old before my time.[26]

He clearly mourns for the lost parts of who he was. And yet he believes that, despite appearances, *he has recovered*:

> In many important respects, I have already gotten better. I continue to learn new ways of living with a damaged brain. I continue to make progress, to avenge the insult, to see my way around the gray area. But no, I am not going to be the man I was. In this, I am hardly alone.[27]

Skloot offers a poignant reframe of the idea of recovery. Recovery has to do with learning to live well with the person we have become. He is not going to be the man that he used to be, but as he astutely observes, who among us is?

HEALING TAKES TIME

Skloot's story does not tell us everything that needs to be known about brain damage. As the old adage goes, if you have met one person with brain damage, you have met one person with brain damage! Nevertheless, there are implicit spiritual dynamics and resonances that emerge from Skloot's story that reverberate across a broader range of experiences and feed into the theological reflection that will form the substance of the following chapter. Skloot's account captures and embodies some vital aspects of the nature and impact of brain damage and personality change, the need to renarrate the self with stories that neurology cannot tell and the possibility that recovery might look quite different from the expected norm. He illustrates and reveals subtle ways to manage the horrors of time and come to terms with the radical instability of the self. Importantly for the purposes of this book, his story draws particular attention to the unrelenting temporality of the experience of brain damage. It has to do with a significant rupture in time, a horrifying break with the past wherein what was can never be again. Time changes, but we cannot change time. Thinking becomes slower; movement becomes tentative and unsteady. Healing is possible even if cure is not. Healing—finding a place in the world where one is comfortable with who one is and what one is in the world for—takes time, a long time, and even then recovery does not mean returning to the place and the perception of time that was held before the accident or trauma. It means learning to live well in a new place with a changed perception of time, past, present, and future. Skloot's experience was spiritual in the sense that it fundamentally changed the meaning of his life. But it also points us in the direction of some fundamental practical theological truths.

10

The Time Before and the Time After
Brain Injury, Human Identity, and the Hiddenness of Our Lives in Christ

For you died, and your life is now hidden with Christ in God.

(Col 3:3 NIV)

A primary motif within Skloot's story is the suggestion that somehow he changed from being one person, with whom he was familiar, to another person who in many ways he perceived as a stranger. There seems to have been a Floyd Skloot before the virus' insult and a different Floyd Skloot afterward. But what could such a "before" and "after" dynamic mean in terms of theology, human identity, and time? At one level, Skloot's experience illustrates well Bonhoeffer's reminder of the horror of time. To wake up one morning and find one's self profoundly changed and unable to go back to the safe, familiar places where one has been before is undoubtedly an experience that is filled with horror. But there is more to the story of brain damage. The presupposition in Skloot's story is that he *really had* become a different person after the insult to his brain. If that is so, it becomes quite difficult to work out who he has become. If he is not who he was back then, then who is he in-the-now? If he *is* the same person, what is it that makes him the same, and how are he and others to understand and manage the changes?

In this chapter, in critical dialogue with the work of Hans Reinders,[1] we will explore the frightening gulf between the before and after of the experience of brain damage. The temporal gap between the before and the after may be miniscule, but the horror that it can bring is immense. We will unpick something of the timefull complexity of the before and the after of acquired brain damage, arguing that it is not necessary to think of these two positions in time as indicative of a radical separation between the "two selves." Drawing on the apostle Paul's "in Christ" language, we will develop a practical theological perspective on time, identity, and acquired brain injury that will serve to open up new ways of reframing and responding to the experience of brain damage. If it is the case that who we are is hidden in Christ and that the process of discovering who we are is *always* emergent, confusing, and deceptive even if we never encounter brain damage, it may be possible to find a solid bridge between the "two selves" and the "two times": before and after. In so doing we will pave the way for an understanding of Christian hospitality toward "strangers" that creatively and liturgically includes the stranger within us and the stranger among us.[2]

PERSONALITY CHANGE

Some years ago my friend Tonya Whaley entered the world of traumatic brain injury when she was involved in a serious car accident. In explaining the impact of the changes, she draws upon the language of personality and personality change:

> *The biggest things that my family and friends have told me is that my personality changed. There was a fracture in who I was and who I had become. I struggle with my self-confidence. I was very self-confident before. I worked in the corporate world. I had no issues with numbers. I did international sales. But right now, the best I can do is basic math. I was fluent in Spanish and French and now I am lucky to pick up a word or two. I came from the Bible Belt. I was very familiar with the Bible. But in seminary I'm having to relearn our Bible. And so there are pieces that I lost with that. I struggle with PTSD. There's fear with that. There's a mourning for that self-confident person that I used to be, someone who was ready to tackle the world. And now I think about everything before I do it. I've lost my desire for risk. I fatigue easily, so when I travel or do a lot I really have to pay attention to my energy in what I'm doing so that I don't crash. Before the accident I could just go and do whatever. I wear different clothing than I did before. I used to wear clothing with patterns on it and now I don't like that. Even how I taste and smell. Before I probably enjoyed the smell of perfume, but now I can't stand it. It's not like, you break an arm and you cast it and it heals. You change.*

There is a clear before-and-after dynamic apparent in Whaley's reflection on her personal changes. She has had to slow down, take stock, and reprioritize. Like Skloot, Whaley reflects on herself and her losses and recognizes that what has changed will remain changed. There is much to grieve. The horror of time has become a lived reality.

One way in which we might frame the types of change that Whaley and Floyd Skloot refer to is by suggesting that they have experienced a change in their personalities following trauma to their brains. They have had a "personality change." The American Psychological Association defines personality as referring to "individual differences in characteristic patterns of thinking, feeling and behaving."[3] In the context of acquired brain injury, personality change is described as

> alteration or discontinuity in personhood post-injury. When considering many survivors of ABI, this alteration is undisputed by most professionals and families involved in the lives of these individuals. For many survivors themselves, there is a subjective discontinuity in their felt, embodied or social experience of who they are now in comparison with who they were. For others around them, there is an obvious change in "something" about them.[4]

Such a description of personality change seems obvious and, taken at face value, relatively uncomplicated. Following injury to your brain, you behave differently, you feel and think differently, and therefore your personality—the particular group of characteristics or qualities that are perceived by you and others to constitute the essence of your identity and character—has changed. Whaley's reflections seem to illustrate this quite plainly.

At one level, the idea of personality change resonates with our experiences of brain damage and does seem to capture some of the dynamics of the postinjury subjective discontinuity that makes brain damage so dissonant, disturbing, and disorienting for all concerned. Key aspects of a person's life clearly do change, sometimes drastically and dramatically. People (or at least aspects of them) do become unrecognizable, or at least strange, to themselves and to others in comparison with the ways in which they were at a previous point in time.

The idea of personality change is very much located within the realm of the temporal. It requires some sense of a before and an after, a then and a now. In its simplest form, this past-to-present dynamic assumes personality changes are temporal, sequential shifts wherein the configuration and quantity of a person's neurological matter is changed by a specific traumatic incident or incidents leading to perceived identity discontinuity within the self-awareness of the individual concerned and those around her. Such simplicity is, however, deceptive for two reasons. First, the before and after of the standard narrative of brain damage and personality change assumes a straightforward sequential movement between the two times. The problem is that if it is the case, as the writer to the Hebrews states, that "Jesus Christ is the same yesterday and today and forever" (13:8 NIV) and if Paul is correct that we have died and our lives are now hidden in Christ (Col 3:3), then the temporal simplicity of before and after is clearly up for challenge. In Christ there is no before and after, at least not in the way that we assume it to be in the world of sequential clock time. If we have died and been raised in Christ, we reside in a quite different kind of time. The kind of time that we think we live in makes all the difference to the ways in which we understand brain damage and personality changes.

Second, the idea of personality change following brain damage assumes that we knew who we were before the accident, that we move from a position where we know more or less precisely who we are into a situation where we are now unsure of who we are. Experientially, it may feel that this is exactly what is happening. However, theologically—within God's time—as we will discover, what is actually happening is quite different. If we respect the experiential and bring it gently into conversation with the theological, we might just be able to see things differently and in seeing things differently discover new ways of practicing faithfully.

THE TIME BEFORE AND THE TIME AFTER

In his fascinating and important book *Disability, Providence, and Ethics: Bridging Gaps, Transforming Lives,* my good friend Hans Reinders explores some of the complex relationships among disability, suffering, and God's providence. The first section of the book comprises a series of narratives of disability, primarily drawn from accounts of families who have members living with one of two types of disability: profound intellectual disability or traumatic brain injury.[5] Here we will focus primarily on Reinders' thinking about issues relating to traumatic brain injury, which, as we have seen, is an aspect of acquired brain injury. Although not explicitly stated, Reinders' account is all about time and the horror of time. The basic rhythm that he tries to capture is the complex temporal movement from before to after following a traumatic incident that leads to neurological damage. He names this temporal dynamic "the time before" and "the time after." Reinders uses sharp, moving, and tragic vignettes that illustrate the impact of brain damage on personality. His focus is primarily on those who offer care to people with acquired brain injury rather than people who are experiencing brain damage. These stories are designed to reveal and illustrate the radical discontinuity between the time before the brain trauma and the time afterward:

> Through all the stories we have been considering so far runs the theme of a shattered life. Whether it is confronted by the birth of a disabled child parents did not know was coming, or with a terrible road accident resulting in brain injury, in all cases there is a "before" and an "after."[6]

For parents awaiting the birth of their child, the discovery that she is profoundly intellectually disabled shifts their expectations toward a new "after" and a new "now," which is filled with quite different content from their expected or desired "after." The sharp, horrific movement of time has brought with it a surprise and, at least initially, a disappointing, an unwanted gift. Reinders suggests that the situation becomes a legitimate source for lament. He moves on to show the ways in which the disappointment of the present moment opens the door for sadness, grief, and lament even if, as is often the case, things change and sometimes become more positive as time moves on. Reinders' purpose is to raise as sharply as possible the context for the "why me?" questions that form the essence of lament and often comprise the basis of modes of theodicy that he believes can be difficult and destructive, yet illuminating for the ways in which we conceptualize and live out our understandings of providence. Providence, then, is Hans' primary focus. There is nevertheless an aspect of his thinking that crosses over into our current conversations around time and disability. Central to Reinders' task is his highlighting of the temporal movement from before to after within the context of traumatic brain injury. Skloot's experience has raised some important issues around the existential dimensions of such a movement. But reflection on the theological dimensions of this shift takes us to a quite different place.

THE PROBLEM WITH THE TIME BEFORE AND THE TIME AFTER

Reinders argues that it is "not inappropriate to think about the event that caused the brain injury as the moment that divides life into two episodes: the time before, and the time after."[7] Here Reinders offers an apparently straightforward temporal movement that reflects an uncomplicated linear movement from one moment in time to another. The changes that occur in that instant split life into "two episodes" that appear to have no obvious connection other than that they simply progress from one into the other. The time before is mere history; it has passed and the new has come.

Importantly, the difference between the before and the after is defined purely in terms of a person's neurological condition. According to this understanding, the movement from "then" to "now" is determined by a physical occurrence that takes place within a brief instant of time and that brings about irreversible changes in a person's neurons and synapses. There was a life before when we had one neurological configuration, and there is life after when we have a different neurological configuration. In Reinders' formulation, the dynamic is dichotomous, flat, linear, and above all neurologically determined. The life before and the life after are shaped, formed, and defined solely by change in a person's brain. People are assumed to be radically discontinuous because their neural formations have become radically discontinuous. Such a neurological formulation of the issue makes it rather difficult to see how the two aspects of a person's life—before and after—can be held together in any way other than through a sense of alienation and feelings of sadness, grief, and lament for what has been. Likewise, the linear temporal dynamic of Reinders' thinking seems to leave no room for the odd simultaneity of God's time, a point that I will return to later in this chapter. There is not a lot of hope within such a formulation of the time before and the time after.

There is no question that life is significantly changed following the accident or incident, but is the division really as firm and separate as Reinders seems to imply? A simple, experiential, and neurologically based explanation leaves people with acquired brain injury in a tricky position. How are they to understand and come to terms with the discontinuity within their lives without simply concluding that "that was then and this is now," as if the two lives were dissociated and unrelated? Put differently, how are they to avoid perceiving themselves and being seen by others as *total* strangers, people of the "then" rather than people of the "then *and* the now"? The danger with Reinders' neurologically determined and timefully sequential before-and-after schema is that, after the trauma, people are effectively left as strangers, with their old lives somehow completely dislocated from their current lives. Now, of course, this might be *exactly* how people feel. Such feelings should be honored, respected, and listened to. I imagine that is at least a part of Reinders' intention. Nonetheless, the experiential dimensions of acquired brain injury also need to be brought, gently, into hospitable conversation with theological perspectives that may offer people different and potentially more hopeful ways of framing their situations. Paul tells us that the gospel is intended to enable us to renew our minds (Rom 12:2). Renewed minds help us to see broken brains differently.

AFTER THE FALL?

A second concern that emerges with regard to Reinders' reflections and analysis of the experience of people with acquired brain injury is the way in which at one point he seems to draw that experience into a rather odd theological framework. After sensitively narrating the stories of a number of people with acquired brain damage, he draws upon a surprising theological perspective to try to help the reader make sense of their experiences. He describes the aftermath of brain damage as being similar to the time "after the fall":

> Given the grief over the experienced loss of a previous life, as distinct from the bleak necessities of the life that remains, it is not uncommon to think about both of these lives as before and after *the fall*. To some the life they used to live appears from a distance as "paradise lost": Sometimes I would like to go back to my old life . . . when I was 16 . . . when life was great, when I was told that I had the world by its tail.[8]

Reinders takes the division between before and after to another level. Previously he had described the split as between "two episodes." Now, he phrases the division between before and after as being between "life now" and "a previous life." The discontinuity is complete. Life after brain damage is a different life from life before—not just a different episode in a continuous life but a different life. The old life has gone and all that is left are the "bleak necessities of the life that remains."

Longing for what was

The idea of longing for life as it was previously is an understandably common trope within people's lives and within the literature that seeks to describe the experiences of people with acquired brain damage. Eric Stewart in his qualitative study of women living with a wide range of acquired brain injuries makes a similar observation:

> The pre-injury self may also loom as a desired once and future self—the "nostalgia for a return to prior functionality" that structures the rehabilitation experience. This is a haunting, mournful presence that continually invokes loss, tragedy and abjection.[9]

Looking back and desiring to be where one used to be in life is common, completely understandable, and to be expected. There are important theological resonances in such longings. For example, in some senses the metaphor of exile captures something of the nuances of this experience. As the people of Israel were taken into captivity, so they lost their identity, their culture, their freedom, their language, their corporate personality; almost everything that made them who they perceived themselves to be was taken from them. Only the presence of YHWH held them in place. They looked and felt very different, but YHWH held them and guided them into new places and new ways of being in the world. The metaphor of exile draws theological attention to interesting ways of losing one's self and coming to terms with the "new self."

The problem with the fall

However, Reinders chooses a different metaphor: the fall. His use of the fall to illustrate people's experiences does different theological work. It is one thing to suggest that there is a tragic temporal transition running from what was to what is. However, to juxtapose such a transition to the fall is problematic. To be fair, absolutely nothing in Reinders' corpus of work indicates his making any kind of connection between disability and sin, so that is clearly *not* his intention. I suspect that Hans simply means to indicate that there has been such a change in people's lives that it *feels* like they are living in a world that has lost its goodness. In other words, he is using the term "fall" metaphorically rather than theologically to make an experiential point. The kinds of tragic narratives he selects to make his case would certainly indicate this as a possible interpretation. Likewise, it may well be that people living with traumatic brain injuries use similar metaphorical language to articulate their experiences. The problem, however, is that such language freezes the theological narration of the story of brain damage in the wrong place. By ending the story at the stage of tragedy and fall, and seeking to explain the transition using—metaphorically or otherwise—the language of sin without the accompanying language of redemption and reorientation, people are left with a somewhat bleak picture of their present state and future possibilities.

The world that they now inhabit is, it would appear, without goodness; it is a world that has fallen, is sinful, filled with suffering without relief. Trapped by the horror of time in a tragic postlapsarian world, people's possibilities appear quite desolate. It is true that Reinders then moves on to provide a theological language through which people can express and make sense of such suffering, namely lament and providence, but the problem remains. Reinders may be correct insofar as some folks may well feel their lives have fallen from grace. However, there is still an uneasy sense of theological nonresolution that inevitably accompanies the language of before and after and its juxtaposition to language about the fall. The story of God did not end with the fall, and neither does the story of people living with brain damage. After the fall came Jesus. With Jesus came redemption. The temporal dynamic of God's redemptive actions is *before*, *after*, and then *after after*: the time of Jesus. Floyd Skloot found not only disruption, change, and confusion (before and after); he also discovered promise and new hope (a time "after after"). If it is true that "God has said, 'Never will I leave you; never will I forsake you.' So we say with confidence, 'The Lord is my helper; I will not be afraid. What can mere mortals do to me?'" (Heb 13:5-6), then there is a richness and a hopefulness about the "after" that requires exploration and theological development. The point is not that the after will become any less painful or tragic. Reinders is right to open space for lament. It is simply that, when viewed from within a different temporal dynamic, it can be seen to be a lot more hopeful.

HIDDEN IN CHRIST: REIMAGINING THE TIME BEFORE AND THE TIME AFTER

In developing the implications of this reflection on Reinders' explanatory schema of before and after for our understanding of time and acquired brain damage, we must begin by thinking through more precisely what might be meant by "the time before." The general assumption within Reinders' thinking and within many other general perceptions of the concept of personality change seems to be that persons encountering acquired brain injury are fairly certain about who they were prior to the accident or incident. Following the traumatic event, they became unsure of who they were. It is, however, not quite that simple.

"In Christ": Jesus and the question of truth

A useful place to begin to reimagine the time before is in relation to Karl Barth's perspective on the nature of truth and the precise way in which the followers of Jesus come to know and identify all things—including themselves—within God's creation. Reflecting on Barth's theology of salvation, George Hunsinger points out:

> Truth in Barth's theology is a category that governs not only our knowing of God's identity, but also God's knowing of our identities in Jesus Christ. Soteriological objectivism, briefly stated, means that there is finally no other truth about us than the truth of who we are before God in Jesus Christ. We have no existence before God that stands in independence of Jesus Christ. "The truth of our existence is simply this—Jesus Christ has died and risen again for us. It is this and this alone which is to be proclaimed to us as our truth" (II/1 167 rev).[10]

Barth's idea of soteriological objectivism opens up a whole new way of viewing the truth about who we *truly* are.

Soteriological objectivism is a way of thinking about truth and salvation wherein any human contribution to salvation is subordinated to what has occurred in the work of Christ. The truth of who we are is not to be found in who we might think ourselves to be (introspection and self-reflection), a way of knowing ourselves that is inevitably fluctuating and dependent on the vagaries and horrors of time and the fragility of our bodies. For Barth, the truth of who we are is found only in Jesus. Salvation is not about what we do or do not do. Salvation has been accomplished in Christ alone. It is a work of grace accomplished for all human beings. Faith is necessary, but it is not the human act of faith that saves us:

> The human act of faith is in no way determinative or creative of salvation, and the divine act of grace is in no way responsive or receptive to some condition external to itself as necessarily imposed upon it by the human creature. Grace therefore confronts the creature as a sheer gift. The human act of faith, moreover, in no way conditions, contributes to, or constitutes the event of salvation.[11]

Salvation is thus seen to be an objective work of grace in which we are included. We are who we are "in Christ." Hunsinger points out that the idea of being

> "in Christ" is the key indicator of Barth's soteriological objectivism. It indicates that salvation is understood to be fully constituted, complete, and effective apart from and prior to any reception of it that may or may not occur here and now in our existence. It indicates that Jesus Christ is the decisive locus of salvation in the sense that his existence is so inclusive of ours that we can recognise our true selves only in him. It indicates that whatever may or may not take place in us, it cannot add or subtract from the actuality of our salvation as it avails for us apart from ourselves in him.[12]

Thus, our existence is redescribed and reinterpreted as we realize what it means to be in Christ. Sin separates us from God. In Christ we are freed from sin and included as we discover to whom it is that we belong. Hunsinger concludes:

> Men and women are therefore summoned to understand themselves as being incorporated "in Christ by Christ." It is his action, and not in any sense theirs, by which they are incorporated into his reality before God and therefore into salvation. The actuality of salvation, which comes to them as a gift complete in itself, depends solely on the mediatorial work of Jesus Christ apart from them, against them, and for them.[13]

Through Christ we are included in Christ. When we come to realize that all that needs to be done has been done in Christ, we come to realize that all that we are and all that we can be is who we are *in Christ*. This has crucial importance for the purposes of this chapter for two reasons. First, it helps us understand certain soteriological concerns that can emerge around the spiritual state of people who have experienced brain damage and personality change. Second, it offers a whole new frame on the nature of human identity. If we are to discover the truth about ourselves and ultimately comprehend (if only through a glass darkly) the implications of our salvation, we need to turn away from ourselves and look toward Jesus. Only in Christ can we discover the truth of who we are.

On losing faith

The first issue we will treat briefly as it requires us only to contextualize the arguments presented thus far. One of the most disturbing changes that can accompany brain damage is the way in which some people seem to lose their faith or interpret and live out their faith in ways notably different from how they did before.[14] For some, the option of expressing their faith is no longer an option because of the devastation of their brain damage. This may raise questions for some people around whether their salvation remains or whether their current behavior somehow jeopardizes their salvific relationship with God. If Barth's soteriological objectivism is accurate, there is no need for people to be concerned. Their salvation has never been a matter of what they could or could not do. It has always had to do with who Jesus is and what Jesus has done. True, faith was and remains important in the sense of the joy that is expressed when one realizes whose one is. Nevertheless, that faith is not what brings about salvation. Salvation is the work of Jesus in which we are included. If we cannot save ourselves, neurological change and damage cannot take away our salvation. The fact that people change or no longer proclaim their faith in the way that they did previously does not impact upon what Jesus has done for them. If it is the case that, with Paul, we are "convinced that neither death, nor life, nor angels, nor rulers, nor things present, nor things to come, nor powers, nor height, nor depth, nor anything else in all creation, will be able to separate us from the love of God in Christ Jesus our Lord" (Rom 8:38-39), we can legitimately put such concerns to one side. Even in the deep spiritual lostness that can accompany brain damage, Jesus communes and travels with us into and through that darkness. It is not for nothing that the writer to the Hebrews can confidently proclaim, "For he has said, 'I will never leave you or forsake you'" (13:5).

Reimagining ourselves in Christ

Our understanding of salvation is secured as we discover that who we are is who we are "in Christ." This way of thinking also helps to secure our identity by locating it as lying outside the boundaries of our fragile bodies. Who we are—our identity—is also found to be secured as we realize that we are who we are only as we come to perceive ourselves as being "in Christ." The nature of that security is somewhat surprising. The standard account of identity change in relation to the experience of brain damage is in terms of a clear-cut movement from before to after: in profound ways we have become unrecognizable to ourselves and to others. It is certainly the case that this may be how things appear and indeed how people may feel. The changes we experience when our brains are damaged are real, alienating, and deeply troubling. My intention is not to downplay such difficulties. Nevertheless, the sense that we are somehow unrecognizable to ourselves is not totally discontinuous with the state of *all* human beings. If we are who we are in Christ, any perceptions of who or what we are that emerge from our self-perceptions and self-oriented assumptions about ourselves will inevitably be flawed. If we are who we are "in Christ" and, more perplexingly, if, as Paul suggests, who we are is in fact *hidden* in Christ (Col 3:1-4), the experience of being "unrecognizable" following brain damage is but an intensification of the mysterious nature of human identity and our false self-perception of who we are.[15]

It will be helpful to think of it in this way. When Christians identify who they are, they identify themselves in relation to Jesus. If I were to say I am John Swinton because I look like this, think like that, can do this, can express myself in this or that way, I would not be acting truthfully according to Barth's way of defining truth. The self I would be presenting would be autonomous, self-constructed, and above all misleading. I would be attempting to define who I am according to who I (or others) *think* I am; I would be creating myself according to criteria that are apart from Jesus. Rather than the truth of my existence being defined according to who I am in Christ—a mode of being in the world that forms the ground of our identity and from which any capacities I may or may not have emerge—my awareness of my self would be idolatrous; that is, I would be placing my self-perception—who I think I am—in the space that only Jesus should occupy. I may (or may not) be able to think clearly, talk smoothly, walk steadily. These abilities are not what makes me who I am. I am who I am in Christ alone. In a real sense I have died and risen with him, and now I can see the world only as I look to him: "We were therefore buried with him through baptism into death in order that, just as Christ was raised from the dead through the glory of the Father, we too may live a new life" (Rom 6:4 NIV).

There is no truth about me other than the truth of Jesus. One dimension of being in Christ is thus very practical. It changes the hermeneutic that we use to read our existence and interpret our experience; it renews our minds (Rom 12:2) and allows us to see ourselves as we truly are: *creatures who know ourselves only in relation to Jesus*. There was therefore *never* a time when who we were was determined by the particular neurological configuration of our brains. We may have thought there was, but we were quite wrong. Who we are is who we are in Christ, and, crucially, *that is hidden*.

HIDDEN WITH CHRIST: RETHINKING THE TIME BEFORE

The idea of our identity being in Christ moves us beyond normal temporal logic and into a world of God's eternal simultaneity, a world of time that is, to say the least, strange. The New Testament is full of odd language about the simultaneous nature of God's time. In Ephesians 1 Paul talks about how we are elected "from before the foundation of the world" (v. 4 ESV). In Matthew 25:34, we are informed that God has had a place for his followers since the beginning of creation—in other words, before they even existed: "Then the King will say to those on his right, 'Come, you who are blessed by my Father; take your inheritance, the kingdom prepared for you since the creation of the world'" (NIV). In Revelation 13:8 we find the rather startlingly enigmatic sentence, "The lamb who was slain from the creation of the world" (NIV). Again in 2 Corinthians 5:14, Paul states, "For Christ's love compels us, because we are convinced that one died for all, and therefore all died" (NIV). This kind of language indicates that time is much more flexible and nonlinear than it often appears to be when viewed from the perspective of humanity. It also and vitally, for current purposes, indicates that somehow we are *included* in the death and the resurrection of Jesus.[16] Even though the death and resurrection of Jesus was an event that happened many years ago, we participate in it in the present. To perceive of ourselves as being "in Christ" in such ways makes the temporal dynamic of a simple linear time before and time after tenuous, to say the least.

In Colossians 3:1-4, Paul states:

> Since, then, you have been raised with Christ, set your hearts on things above, where Christ is, seated at the right hand of God. Set your minds on things above, not on earthly things. For you died, and *your life is now hidden with Christ in God*. When Christ, who is your life, appears, then you also will appear with him in glory. (NIV)

This is truly a mysterious and timefull passage. Somehow, in spite of the huge temporal gap between the crucifixion of Jesus and our present experiences, we who are alive today have died with Jesus and are alive with him in-the-now. The only significant time before and time after is the dichotomy that comes with the entry of Jesus into human history, and that gap is clearly not sequential. We are alive in Christ but in a mysterious way, hidden from ourselves. Who we are is real and present but at the same time inaccessible to us. Hunsinger points out:

> It cannot be known to us directly, but only indirectly as we look to him. "In him we are hidden from ourselves. Only in him can we be revealed. We cannot, therefore, be revealed to ourselves or know ourselves directly, but only indirectly, in relation to the One who for us too is the Mediator between God and human beings" (IV/2, 271 rev).[17]

Only as we come to know Jesus do we learn to know ourselves. And even then the fullness of our selves will remains a mystery until the coming of God in glory. "For now we see only a reflection as in a mirror; then we shall see face to face. Now I know in part; then I shall know fully, even as I am fully known" (1 Cor 13:12 NIV).

The hiddenness of our selves becomes clear when we reflect on what we discovered about ourselves when we became Christians. Before we were Christians, we thought that there was no God. We presumed we were free, autonomous individuals who could write our own life stories in any way we pleased. When we came to know Jesus, we discovered that we were sinful, fallen creatures who needed to be redeemed and reoriented. We found out that we were members of the body of Christ and that who we are is deeply woven in with who our brothers and sisters are. Our old selves, the selves that we had constructed without Jesus, have been proven to be false, indicative of self-sovereignty, and ultimately idolatrous. Much and perhaps all of what we thought we knew about ourselves turned out to be self-deception. Over time we have learned, through our encounters with Jesus in the power of the Spirit, what it means to live and to love as one of his followers: to be gentle, kind, loving, patient, perseverant, forgiving—not because these qualities are what make us who we are but because that is what those who are in Christ do and become as they engage with the Spirit. We are people who are loved and then learn to love, not people who love independently of the love that is given to us in Jesus. Gradually, we are being shaped and formed into our true selves as we encounter the identity-forming power of the Holy Spirit. *We have discovered that we never really knew ourselves before we met Jesus*. There is much about ourselves that we still need to learn as we continue to walk with Jesus. In the end, we will never know who we are until we reach glory, the veil of our current flawed identity is torn away, and we see both God and ourselves face to face. Life in Christ informs us that discovering who we are is not a human quest that is determined by worldly circumstances. Rather, it is a divine gift that is ultimately mysterious, timefull, and unfolding. What we do with our time now matters, but what we can or cannot do is not ultimately definitive of who we are in Christ:

> Our true selves, our reality, is not what we see and apprehend even by faith directly; it's who we are in Christ in God's sight. God does not look upon us except as we are in him because he has embraced us by his grace in Christ already to begin with.[18]

Discovering that our true selves are found in Christ is an aspect of learning to trust God in all things and realizing that what we know, even about ourselves, is limited, fragile, and wholly dependent on Jesus.

The "true self" is not some kind of Platonic ideal, the idea that eventually the things of this world will have passed away and we can enter into the realm of our ideal selves. The self that is hidden in Christ should not be understood to be somehow apart from the self that is currently being transformed and redeemed: "And we all, who with unveiled faces contemplate the Lord's glory, are being transformed into his image with ever-increasing glory, which comes from the Lord, who is the Spirit" (2 Cor 3:18 NIV). In God's divine temporal simultaneity, that which is occurring within our present lives is deeply connected with that which we are in Christ, even though what we are in Christ remains an emerging mystery. There is a crucial Christ-centered continuity and discontinuity with what we have been in the past, what we are now, and what we will be in the future. The time before our trauma was the time when we were who we were in Christ. The time after the trauma is a time when we remain in Christ. *Jesus holds the center*.

The truth of who we are is *real* and *present* (we are who we are now), *hidden* (our true selves are hidden in Christ), and *still to come* (who we will become in glory). If this is so, then that which we know about ourselves has more to do with faith and hope than strictly propositional knowledge, closer to trust than to certainty. Hunsinger points out, "That means we have to take it by faith and not expect to see too much or at least not base our understanding of ourselves on what we can observe or judge about ourselves."[19] Such an understanding of human-identity-in-Christ can truly be grasped only by faith. Such a faith does not claim to contain everything that is necessary for salvation but rather offers itself trustingly to the work of God in Christ with gratitude, joy, trust, love, and faithfulness, sure of what it hopes for and certain of what it cannot see. In the end there is no truth about us other than the truth of who we are before God in Christ. Such a fact can only really be described, rather than explained.

REIMAGINING THE TIME AFTER

The time before we encounter brain damage is thus seen not to be quite as straightforward as it might at first appear. If that is so, the time *after* the traumatic event will also be different. If the theological framework laid out thus far is correct, there is an important difference between someone's *personality*—individual differences in characteristic patterns of thinking, feeling, and behaving—and one's true *identity* in the Barthian sense of the term. One's personality is certainly open to mutability and change. That change can come about in an instant via traumatic brain damage, or it can simply occur as we get older and our attitudes, values, opinions, and behavior change as our brains begin to wear out and slow down. At this level, temporal, historical time as experienced within the day-to-dayness of human experience is open to sometimes radical change. However, when who we are is viewed as hidden "in Christ," the issues of identity and change take on a richer and fuller dimension. Aspects of our personality are open to change, but our identity is stabilized and held within the heart of Jesus. The changes we experience are very real, but God's "job" is to hold the center and to hug us into love. *Our* job (and by "our" here, I mean the whole of the body of Christ) is to trust that this is so (to have faith) and to work to manage the changes in creative, faithful, and healing ways. When we are faced with the painful raw realities of personality change in ourselves or in those whom we love, at a minimum, we can approach one another with hope and certainty that neither we nor our brother and sister are forgotten, alone, or in any sense lost. In the midst of the turmoil, God continues to recognize us and to call us by name: "Do not fear, for I have redeemed you; I have summoned you by name; you are mine" (Isa 43:1 NIV). The "time after" may be tragic and difficult, but it is not without hope.

11

Time and Ritual
Funerals for Friends

With Tonya Whaley

> All things must pass.
>
> (George Harrison)[1]

Such a theological foundation grounded in God's simultaneous time and the mystery of Jesus' redemptive work provides hope in contexts where hope can be hard to find. However, it does not in and of itself make the process of change and reorientation following brain damage easier at the level of our experience. How then are we to hold the critical tension between the theological foundations of our identity (who we truly and immovably are in Christ) and the experiential reality that things have changed, sometimes quite radically? If we lose this tension, either theology will become irrelevant and practice ill informed, or practice will become misaligned and theology will become irrelevant for practice.

This chapter has been written in collaboration with my good friend Tonya Whaley, whose story was featured in chapter 10. Tonya has lived with an acquired brain injury for a number of years. Tonya was kind enough to gift me her story. I believed that it was only right that the giver of the gift should have the opportunity to share in the blessing that the gift brings. There is another reason for inviting Tonya to participate in this conversation. The previous reflections on profound and complex intellectual disabilities and advanced dementia simply could not have been done by those living with that form of disability. People living with such disabilities require theological advocates who can help articulate the complexities of their experiences. Such a role should be approached with trepidation, but it is nonetheless important if the body of Christ is faithfully to imagine life together. However, with regard to acquired brain damage, many people living with this condition can and do speak for themselves. It is clearly not my role to advocate for people who can advocate for themselves. As a practical theologian, I do, however, believe that I have something useful to offer to the conversation. The reader should therefore look upon this chapter as part of a hospitable collaboration between a practical theologian and someone who not only knows about ideas and concepts, but has learned to live with the issues and to befriend them. We hope that the fruits of our friendship will be a blessing for those who resonate with what we have to say.

THEOLOGICAL AND OPERATIONAL EFFECTIVENESS

In her book *Caring Liturgies: The Pastoral Power of Christian Ritual*, Susan Marie Smith notes, "There is always a tension between the churches' theology of sin, humanity, sacrament, the church, and so forth, and the immediate pastoral need in a specific situation."[2] Her point is that the relationship between doctrinal formulations and the pastoral practices of the church can be difficult and uneasy. Smith names this tension by distinguishing between what she describes as *theological effectiveness* and *experiential* (or operational) *effectiveness*. Theological effectiveness relates to "the doctrinal claims of God's power and effectiveness in worship and Christian rituals that are affirmed in Scripture, tradition, and reason."[3] Theological (or doctrinal) effectiveness has to do with the ability of particular doctrines to enable Christians to see God more clearly, to imagine God properly, to use Medi Volpe's perspective, which we explored earlier in the book. We could say that the kind of theological exploration of what it means to be "in Christ" that we have engaged with thus far in this chapter relates to the development of this kind of theological effectiveness.

Experiential or operational effectiveness relates to the empirical consequences or changes that individuals or communities experience as they engage with doctrine and attempt to explore what it looks like in practice.[4] One relates to how the church understands and perceives God to be (God's ways and God's time); the other relates to the way that theology is practiced and lived out within the experiences of the church. Experiential effectiveness informs us of what doctrine *feels* like and *looks* like. We need both modes of effectiveness in order to live faithfully. Still, they can seem, feel, and look as if they are separate. What we believe about God is not necessarily part of our day-to-day experiences. For those of us with brain damage, there is a deep tension between the existential security of the theology of being in Christ and the uncertainty of our day-to-day experience of being strangers to ourselves and to others. We may well believe that our identity is held in Christ, but if our experience is fundamentally different from our belief, then we will inevitably encounter problems. In the midst of a pastoral crisis, operational effectiveness can often appear more obvious and pressing. To hold the tension means to maintain a creative balance between the two. To lose the tension risks developing practices that *look* as though they are effective but that function less than faithfully.

Smith offers the example of baptism. Baptism is a theologically effective doctrine. Its efficacy is not determined by its practical utility but by the promises of God:

> God is the actor in baptism, the giver of the gift. By water and the Holy Spirit, in the name of the Trinity, and by the intentional work of the church through its designated pastors, the one baptized is washed new, freed from sin and united to Christ in his death and resurrection. Baptism is irrevocable. God's powerful, loving action makes the baptizand part of Christ's body, forever. The initiate freely responds to God by receiving baptism. Baptism is effective. Whether or not the newly baptized person feels different does not change the fact of our belief in God's power through the sacrament (or ordinance): the person *is* now different, bonded with Christ in his death and resurrection. This firm faith is *theological effectiveness*.[5]

She tells the story of a young soldier, Dennis, who is about to go into the arena of war. He was baptized as a child but wanted to be rebaptized, as he did not feel that his original baptism was meaningful for him. Despite his knowledge of the fact that God ministers to him in the Spirit through his baptism (theological effectiveness), the original ritual was not embedded within his experiential consciousness and was therefore not available as an immediate sensory experience. The pastor felt caught within the tension between theological and experiential effectiveness. Smith continues:

> The effectiveness of theology is not the same as the effectiveness of experience, however, as Dennis wants his pastor to see. Not everyone remembers her or his baptism. Not everyone is old enough to have felt the water, to have labored and prepared so as to leave their fears and resentments in the depths, to have come out to the joyous song of the congregation's Alleluia! Not everyone has an embodied memory as a reference point to recall, in the bad times, that they in fact belong to God. While baptism is true and powerful whether or not one is conscious of it, still, without the embodied memory as reference, it can be harder to pull

> up the power of one's baptism in times of need. And sometimes, this lack of memory is a source of pain.[6]

The absence of an embodied memory of baptism (and we have seen previously the importance of the memory of the body) makes the experiential effectiveness of the ritual less than effective. Dennis wants to *feel* the theology of baptism, not just *know* it intellectually. Even though he believes in its theological effectiveness, he feels a deep need to have it embedded and embodied within his experience. In this case the pastor yielded to Dennis' concerns and rebaptized him. Smith considers this to be an error. Her concern is that in this situation the theological effectiveness of the baptismal ritual has been trumped by the perceived pastoral needs of experiential effectiveness. It is absolutely right to ritualize change. The pastor simply chose the wrong ritual. He chose the wrong ritual because he was unable adequately to manage the tension between the two modes of effectiveness.

In the case of people living with acquired brain injury and the experience of the changes they go through, we might encounter a similar dissonance between theological and experiential effectiveness, only this time the dissonance arises from the tension between what we know about God and ourselves and what we feel about ourselves and see within ourselves. Despite the fact that God in the power of the Spirit is ministering to us and holding our identity in a place of hiddenness in relation to who and whose we are, we may not *feel* the importance of realizing that we are who we are only in Christ. The theology may be so distant from the experience that it makes little sense. We may have developed a theology that bridges the gap between before and after, but unless it is accompanied by a set of practices that bridges the apparent experiential gap between theological and operational effectiveness, nothing much will change. The question is, What kind of timefull practices can help ensure that our theologically effective perspective on being in Christ is accompanied by ways of being in the world that are operationally/experientially effective?

MANAGING THE CHANGES: FUNERAL FOR A FRIEND

Tonya describes the changes brought on by her traumatic brain injury as *a live death*:

> *Most individuals go through a "live death." They have to go through a process of mourning and a loss of who they were. A lot of us remember who we were before and we can never get back some of those pieces. For me it was*

> *important to take ownership and develop an understanding that you can't go back to who you were. Things have changed.*

The "live" dimension of Tonya's experience of death is frustrating. If we encounter physical death, our bodies are no longer available to ourselves or to others. We may retain our resurrection hope, but for now the person has gone. However, with a "live death," things are quite different. We *are* available and present, albeit in quite different ways from how we were in the world prior to the injurious event:

> *Not everybody has physical markings of their injury, so then you look normal or typical. It becomes a hidden disability. People say, "You look fine!" "You look normal." "I don't understand what's happening." "You look like how you used to but you're not the same."*

The process of grieving is hampered by the fact that, in a sense, you are in the world, but not in the ways that you were before. Your body holds and reveals the shape and form of the life that you led before but can never lead again. The form of your body seems the same, but the content of your life has changed. Your behavior, thoughts, and words are not only different from before but dissonant in ways that cause confusion, frustration, and rejection by others, a form of confusion that easily bleeds over into self-rejection. That sense of estrangement from self and others leads to a feeling that something deep within you has changed.

On becoming a stranger

In his book *Becoming Human*, Jean Vanier discusses the nature of "strangerhood." To be a stranger, one has to be unknown or to have aspects or qualities to one's self that are alien or unknown:

> Those who are different are the strangers among us. There are many ways of being different: one can be different by virtue of values, culture, race, language or education, religious or political orientation. And while most of us can find it stimulating or at least interesting to meet strangers for a short while, it is a very different thing to truly open up and allow a stranger to become a friend.[7]

Vanier's understanding of the stranger urges us to realize that, in some respect, *all of us* are strangers to one another. The status of "stranger" is not something that applies only to the Other. It is an ascription that can be applied to all people in different ways.

Vanier points us toward the ministry of Jesus and the ways in which he spent time with those whom society considered to be strangers: the tax collectors, sinners, prostitutes, and so forth. By spending time with such strangers, he became their friends (Luke 7:34). In this sense the stranger is with Jesus and Jesus is with the stranger. But Vanier wants us to recognize that the connection between Jesus and the stranger is much deeper than simple bodily presence:

> However, there is still a paradox. Those with whom Jesus identifies himself are regarded by society as misfits. And yet Jesus is that person who is hungry; Jesus is that woman who is confused and naked. As I carried in my arms Eric who was blind, deaf and with severe brain damage, I sensed that paradox: "Whosoever welcomes one of these little ones in my name, welcomes me; and whoever welcomes me, welcomes the one who sent me."[8]

For Vanier, as Jennifer Kilps points out:

> To welcome those persons who are considered strange or different, who are set apart or marginalized, or who are vulnerable and weak, is to welcome God. For Vanier, to welcome any person, for all persons are helpless, different, weak and strange, is to welcome Christ.[9]

In our discussions thus far, we have explored what it might mean to understand acquired brain injury from the perspective of being "in Christ." Vanier opens up another dimension to the presence of Jesus: *we are in Christ, but Christ is also in us.* The practice of befriending strangers images the earthly, bodily ministry of Jesus, but it also points toward the mystical presence of Jesus within the stranger. This is very important, bearing in mind that, as we have pointed out, the stranger is all of us. This set of observations has significant implications for the kind of strangeness that Tonya experienced.

The stranger within

Vanier draws attention to Carl Jung's response to a Christian woman wherein he makes an interesting and somewhat disturbing observation:

> I admire Christians, because when you see someone who is hungry or thirsty, you see Jesus. When you welcome a stranger, someone who is "strange," you welcome Jesus. When you clothe someone who is naked, you clothe Jesus. *What* I do not understand, however, is that Christians never seem to recognize Jesus in their own poverty. You always want to do good to the poor outside you and at the same time you deny the poor

> person living inside you. Why can't you see Jesus in your own poverty, in your own hunger and thirst? In all that is "strange" inside you: in the violence and the anguish that are beyond your control! You are called to welcome all this, not to *deny* its existence, but to accept that it is there and to meet Jesus there.[10]

Jung draws upon the imagery of Matthew 25 and the powerful statement by Jesus that "whatever you did for one of the least of these brothers and sisters of mine, you did for me" (v. 40). Christians are called to be loving and compassionate toward the weakest members of our society: strangers and outcasts, those alienated and vulnerable to the quirks of humans and the capriciousness of nature. Why? Because that is where Jesus lives. As we act in such ways toward the poor, the outcast, and the stranger, so we minister to Jesus, who takes up residence within the stranger. As we love one another with the love of Jesus, so we discover that we are loving God and loved by God. If it is the case that "Christ may dwell in your hearts through faith" (Eph 3:17 NIV), then it could be no other way. "Jesus is in my heart" is not a metaphor but a mysterious reality.

Vanier's point in using Jung in this way is not simply to highlight Christian attitudes toward strangers in general. He is pushing us to think about the possibility that the outcast and the stranger are not simply "out there" or "over here." The stranger can be within us. The stranger is thus seen to be both within and without. Vanier points out:

> Jesus calls us not only to welcome the weak and the rejected . . . but also the weak and the broken person within us and to discover the presence of Jesus within us. . . . In order for us to be men and women who give life to others we have to live in the truth of who we are; we have to find an inner wholeness, no longer to deny or ignore our wounds but to welcome them and to discover the presence of God in these very places of our own weakness.[11]

What Vanier pushes us to consider is that the great reorientation for the followers of Jesus who encounter brain damage is the knowledge that Jesus resides in their hearts and rests with them. The disorientation is terrible, but Jesus moves with us into the great unknown. The key question is: How can we make such a stranger our friend? How then are we to go about welcoming the stranger as she comes to us from outside and within? Tonya's story gives us a clue as to how we might begin to move toward an answer.

UNEXPECTED BLESSINGS

Like Floyd Skloot, Tonya encounters strange and unexpected blessings:

> *My brother says to me sometimes that I'm healthier now. I had a stronger demeanor or presence that didn't have a lot of fear before. I used to be a first responder; I used to be a victim's advocate and now—I know it was in my past and I know I did a good job, but it's almost like that was another life; it was another person. I had to go through a process, probably five years after the injury, which I went through with my friends and family. I literally had a funeral for the Tonya that I was. I've helped other friends to do that too, and there's a freeing that happens. A lot of my friends now call me T or TBear; sometimes I even wish that I would change my name. I literally feel like that Tonya died.*

Similar to the experience of Judith Snow, whom we met in chapter 4 (disability is like mindfulness . . . it slows you down), there were gifts to be discovered within her experience even if these gifts were not the sorts of gifts that she might have hoped for before her accident. She has had to slow down, reclaim her fearfulness, and learn to live in the world in a way that was much slower and gentler than before. Tonya has come to terms with the horror of time: the fact that what was is no more. Nevertheless, what she has become continues to have value even in the midst of its strangeness. Her point is not that we should pretend that brain damage is a good thing. It may carry some blessing with it, but no one desires it. When the apostle Paul informs us that "in all things God works for the good of those who love him" (Rom 8:28), his point is not that all things are good. Rather, he directs us to the ways in which God can redeem and bring hope to even the most terrible situations. Tonya's point is that to live with the strangeness brought about by acquired brain injury we must learn how to find ways of befriending the stranger, of moving from strangeness to friendship.

A FUNERAL FOR AN OLD FRIEND: RITUAL, HEALING AND CHANGE

A quite startling moment in Tonya's story is the creation of her own funeral. Funerals are ritualized transitional points in life that are intended to mark a movement in time from one way of being in the world to another. For those who have physically died, funerals participate in the movement of those who grieve, ritually moving them from a state of deep loss through into a state of liminality and from there on into a world that has to be recreated and reimagined in such a way that the persons who have died are held in memory even if they are, for now, lost to physical embrace. The ritual of the funeral is thus designed to transition people through time: from the time then, to the time now, to the time after, and onward into the time after after. Death remains tragic, horrific, and undesirable, but the funeral embodies the fact that it is not the end of the story.

The significance of rituals

A funeral is a particular form of *ritual*. The anthropologist and theologian Gerald Arbuckle describes ritual in this way: "Ritual is the stylized or repetitive, symbolic use of bodily movement and gesture within a social context, to express and articulate meaning."[12] Rituals are bodily, dynamic, operationally expressive, and transitional. They are operationally expressive in that they embody doctrine and enable us to *feel* what we believe to be true. They are transitional insofar as they are intended to move an individual or a community from one state of being in the world with others to another. Rituals are irreducibly timefull. They have to do with creating holy spaces that enable us to experience the simultaneity of God's time: recognizing the past in the present within the context of a future that has already come in Christ. In the practice of Christian ritual, the divine and the mundane come together in the form of human actions in order to locate people faithfully during the marking of specific times and seasons or within particular experiences. The physical act of engaging in a ritual means that we have to take time out of the world's time to try to enter into experiences and ways of being in the world that draw us into a time that is not our own. For Christians the funeral ritual is a physical reminder of the resurrection and the fact that those who have died have died in Christ while at the same time they have been raised in Christ. Rituals help us set apart holy moments; they enable us intentionally to recognize that we dwell within God's time and that through the meaningful bodily gestures of the funeral we can begin to see and feel that things may not be quite as we had thought they were.

Susan Smith informs us that

> ritual is a way of using strategies to set apart, to alter the every day, to make one moment, one instance of an event, special, singled out, and holy, so that it matters and is memorable. Ritual, then, strategically establishes a contrast that privileges one moment over other similar moments, making it special, meaningful, and holy.[13]

Rituals are thus seen to be and to mark out intentional points within time where holy spaces can be created in order that those involved can perceive and connect with something beyond themselves.

Moving beyond liminality

Importantly for current purposes, rituals are identity-forming and transition-facilitating practices. Central to the funeral ritual is the movement from liminality into new possibilities. Liminality is a phase or a set of experiences that occurs in the middle of the funeral ritual.

> In anthropology, liminality is the quality of ambiguity or disorientation that occurs in the middle stage of rituals, when participants no longer hold their pre-ritual status but have not yet begun the transition to the status they will hold when the ritual is complete. During a ritual's liminal stage, participants "stand at the threshold" between their previous way of structuring their identity, time, or community, and a new way, which the ritual establishes.[14]

In this phase, persons are perceived no longer to hold their pre-ritual status, but still have to move into their post-202
ritual status. They are in a period of liminality, neither in "the time before" nor in "the time after." Randal H. Flutur captures something of this dynamic of estrangement and liminality:

> How does one come to understand and live with an injury which leaves a familiar body, but replaces the person inside that body with a stranger? The old, familiar body evokes old expectations, old memories, in others. How does one explain to family and friends that although the person they see before them looks like the person they prayed back from the brink of death, they are not the same person?[15]

The problem for many people with acquired brain damage is that they feel trapped in a liminal state. People feel that they are not who they were before, but it is not clear who they are now or who they will become. From within such liminality, a person's identity as a stranger is almost inevitable. The funeral is intended to bridge this gap between liminality and newness. Smith puts it in this way:

> Coping with life crises is like walking a path and suddenly coming to a lake or river with no way across or finding your way blocked by a long wall or fence. To keep going, you need help. At the lake, you need a boat to carry you across. At the fence, you need some way to climb over.

> Ritual can be the ferry, the ladder, or stile carrying you from the stuck or stranded place to newness of life. Rituals are needed to carry the baptized over transitions and to place them back on the path to healing. In times of suffering, healing rituals can be the boat to carry someone who is languishing on his or her own to the other shore of wholeness. In some cases, a person may just need insight and perspective on his or her situation, enabling her or him to act, change, move forward, or start anew.[16]

Tonya's brain injury had not shaken her assurance that her identity remained in Christ. Her problem was not an existential crisis of faith. Her problem was very practical: how could she faithfully manage the changes? She found the answer to that question in the creation of a ritual: a lived funeral.

A lived funeral

The way that Tonya chose to engage with the fact that in her perception and in the perception of those around her she had quite radically changed, was by creating what she describes as a lived funeral. As we have seen, a funeral is a transition point marking a movement from what was to what is. Through the creation of this ritual she was able to rest in the knowledge that Jesus held her identity in the midst of the transitions and changes, but that these changes were real and required some kind of resolution. She, her family, and her friends gathered together beside a river. As the river flowed past, one by one they began to tell stories about Tonya; stories of the old Tonya who had been lost; stories of Tonya that required lament, sadness, and grief. Together they mourned for those things that had been lost, but always in the hope that the bridge between "then" and "now" was Jesus and that what held together in the midst of the transitions and changes was her status of being in Christ.

At the heart of their testimony was a desire to bear witness to their enduring love for Tonya and to the faithful, sustaining presence of Jesus. Tonya remained loved and recognised, even if that recognition was filled with surprise and new developments, some of which were desirable, others that were not. The shared friendships of that small community of affirmative friends bore embodied witness to their shared humanness and to their enduring love for Tonya in the midst of some very difficult changes. In testifying in such ways they created *a community of belonging*. The community expressed the fact that they missed the old Tonya; it was not a community of escape or avoidance; it was a community of lament and sadness. But it was also a community that sought after fresh hope, hospitality, welcoming, and belonging. Together they realised and expressed that the love for Tonya had not changed even if in many ways, she had. In bearing witness to the blessings of their old friendship with Tonya and welcoming in their new friendship with the "new Tonya," they created a space of belonging within the community where all of them together could begin to move toward an understanding of what this new life meant as it was lived out in Christ.

And then they prayed.

Each of the participants in the service had gathered leaves as they walked to the place of the ritual. At the given time each person threw the leaves into the stream and together watched as they were washed downstream. In this symbolic gesture there was a deep sense of letting go, of cleansing the past, of watching the past move on. There was a deep sadness in this symbolic process of letting go. But the clearness and persistent movement of the water helped them to recognise that something new was beginning; something fresh, something different, something potentially beautiful. In that ritual they encountered the power of timefull friendship in the honest testimony of the community and together they moved toward the possibility of new life together in Christ. In coming together to worship and recognise one another, they were able to find new hope and a new beginning.

For Tonya, the funeral was like a boat that ferried her, her family, and friends into fresh waters and on to new shores of possibility, revised experiential identity, and wholeness. As they waved goodbye to the "old Tonya," so they pledged to get to know the "new Tonya." It was as Tonya's experiences of a changed sense of identity were ritualized within the format of a funeral for a *very* close friend that the possibility of new beginnings and the befriending of the "stranger within" opened up. She recognized, grieved, and mourned for what was, but, through the creation of a transitional ritual, she found a way to put the past into its proper place and begin to work out ways in which she could come to terms with what it means to be who she is *now* "in Christ." The ritual allowed her not only to *know* what it means to be "in Christ" but to *see* and *feel* that she was in Christ. Doctrine and experience were held together in the tender folds of her live funeral. (In the appendix to this book, Tonya and I have laid out more details on this process along with a liturgical structure that illustrates what such a process might look like.)

WORSHIPPING GOD TIMEFULLY

It is in many ways fitting that we should end our reflections on time and disability by grounding our thinking in the practices of worship. Time is for God; God *is* love; *time is for love*. All of the kinds of disability we have looked at in this book lead us to that same place: time properly understood provides us with an opportunity to love God and to glorify God forever. As we do that, so we will come to love one another and, through that love, learn to recognize surprising things about the power of our differences. Embodying that timefull dynamic within the context of worship enables us to *feel* what it means to be loved by God even when life is difficult. Our focus on time inevitably leads us to a place where we can discover who we are and what it truly means to worship the God who in Christ has transformed time. In and through that transformation, God offers each one of us the opportunity for redemption:

> Don't you realize that *all of you together* are the temple of God and that the Spirit of God lives in you? (1 Cor 3:16 NLT)

This is truly the beginning point for a genuine theology of community and belonging that holds all of us together in the same way that Jesus holds us.

Conclusion

Being in Christ, Being in Time
Every Body Has a Place

Our journey into time has taken us to some fascinating and challenging places. As we have explored the nature of God's time and what it might mean to live in such a time, so we have been challenged to pay attention to the world, time, and disability in fresh and creative ways. As we have moved through the various issues raised in the book we have come to realize that recognizing that we live within God's creation makes a world of difference to the kind of time we keep. The time we inhabit is not our own. We are guests in a timefull creation that has been gifted to human beings, and we are participants in a time that is meaningful, directed, and in the process of being redeemed. Within such a generous context of the Creator's giving and the creatures' receiving, time is revealed as a wonderful aspect of God's graceful love. Like all of creation, time is broken and fallen, but through Jesus Christ, the Timefull One, time is being nudged toward its fullness.

> But when the fullness of time had come, God sent forth his Son, born of woman, born under the law, to redeem those who were under the law, so that we might receive adoption as sons. And because you are sons, God has sent the Spirit of his Son into our hearts, crying, "Abba! Father!" So you are no longer a slave, but a son, and if a son, then an heir through God. (Gal 4: 4-7 ESV)

BEING IN CHRIST

As we begin to come to terms with the transformative fact that time is a gift and that our identity—who we *truly* are—is not the product of human possibilities but is, rather, something that is given to us and at the same time hidden from us in Christ, the barriers between so-called able-bodied people and so-called people with disabilities begin to crumble.

Within Jesus' body diversity has become the new norm, and living faithfully in the midst of diversity is the expected way of being in the world. As people are baptized into the body of Christ, so they enter into a space of deep and radical *belonging*. Within the body of Christ, *every body has a place*, and every body is recognized as a disciple with a call from Jesus and a vocation that the church needs if it is truly to be the body of Jesus. Such vocations stretch our ecclesial imaginations in powerful and deeply healing ways. Doing nothing can be an act of discipleship. Being cared for can be a fulfillment of one's humanness. The truth of who we are is held and hidden in Christ. Our lives are always intentional and vocational, even when our brains are broken. Vocation has to do with time, providence, contingency, and trust. When it becomes the norm within Jesus' body to say of a person with advanced dementia not, "She is not the person she used to be . . . ," a statement that makes no sense whatsoever in God's time, but rather, "She has changed. I wonder what her vocation is now? Let's explore that . . . ," we will be sure that we are taking the practice of living faithfully in God's time seriously.

If the only norm is Jesus, then our task is to live well and to live faithfully with our differences. If difference cannot separate us from Jesus, then it should not separate us from one another. All of us together share the same time and all of us together are called to live in ways that redeem the time that has been gifted to us in Jesus. Living faithfully within God's time has to do with recognizing that each moment, every encounter, all that we are is given to us by God for the purposes of timefull love. When we begin to orient ourselves within the slow and powerful rhythms of God's time, we find time to pay the right kind of attention to the world and the right kind of attention to one another.

TIME POVERTY

Before we conclude this book, there is one thing that still needs to be said. *Time is a gift that is intended to be given away.* If we are to take time seriously and respond faithfully to our calling to be timefull people, we need to pay attention to the temporal needs of the *whole* of Christ's body. Time is not a gift that is intended simply for personal edification; it is a gift that is given in order that it can be given away. One of the consistent themes within the Scriptures is the command to care for the poor: "For there will never cease to be poor in the land. Therefore I command you, 'You shall open wide your hand to your brother, to the needy and to the poor, in your land'" (Deut 15:11 ESV).

Looking after the poor and the sick is what faithful Christians do:

> What good is it, my brothers and sisters, if someone claims to have faith but has no deeds? Can such faith save them? Suppose a brother or a sister is without clothes and daily food. If one of you says to them, "Go in peace; keep warm and well fed," but does nothing about their physical needs, what good is it? In the same way, faith by itself, if it is not accompanied by action, is dead. But someone will say, "You have faith; I have deeds." Show me your faith without deeds, and I will show you my faith by my deeds. You believe that there is one God. Good! Even the demons believe that—and shudder. (Jas 2:14-19 NIV)

What James says about caring for the economically poor applies equally to the time-poor. *What good is it to claim that you know what it means to live in God's time and ignore the needs of those among you who are deeply temporally impoverished?* The issue of time poverty is important.[1] In essence, time poverty has to do with not having enough time to rest and engage in leisurely activities. Time poverty occurs when people are forced to work long hours without any choice. If you are a wealthy entrepreneur, you might choose to work long hours, but that is a *choice*, not a necessity. Those who are time impoverished have no option, either because not to do so would be to risk economic poverty or not to do so would affect the welfare of those whom they are called to offer care to. Time poverty is crushing insofar as it grinds people down and destroys their sense of rest. Time poverty leads to stress, despondency, exhaustion, isolation, and loneliness.

The strain of having to care for all of the needs of a spouse or family member living with the kinds of disabilities we have focused on in this book can be deeply isolating and profoundly time consuming. For many people time is an asset that they simply cannot attain or retain. No matter how rich one might be in spirit and good intention, the strain of living with someone with advanced dementia, profound intellectual disability, or personality change inevitably takes its toll. Into such situations Jesus speaks the words "Come to me, all you who are weary and burdened, and I will give you rest" (Matt 11:28 NIV). If it is the case that Jesus promises to help carry the burden of those who are tired and weary, it is safe to presume that those who claim to *be* Jesus' body are also given the task of bearing the burdens of their brothers and sisters. If God is a God who rests and if human beings are commanded to rest, then facilitation of faithful resting is a crucial task for the timefull community that *is* the church. Walking slowly can be an act of faithfulness. It can also be a sign of being ground down over time by the burden of caring.

TIMEFULL FRIENDS: FINDING RESPITE

Those who truly desire to live faithfully within God's restful, timefull community must learn to offer one another the gifts of respite. To offer someone respite is to provide a period of Sabbath rest or relief from a situation or an experience that is difficult or distressing. Respite is a deeply timefull practice. The apostle John informs us that disciples are friends of God and friends with one another (John 15:15). Friends spend time with one another and share one another's burdens. Friends of the timefull God are called to create Sabbath spaces, to create places of respite, safe havens where those who offer care can find comfort, safety, and rest. If it is the case that time is a gift and if disciples are people who have learned to live within God's time, then giving away the gift of time to those who care is central to living faithfully. Offering time, becoming timefull friends, sharing the burden of care opens spaces for respite wherein the possibility of rest and time*full* living becomes a possibility even in the midst of the burdens of care; that is what disciples do.

Offering respite can take the form of giving time to others by spending time with people living with advanced dementia and working to develop sustainable friendships. Such friendship allows carers and loved ones to move out and see the world beyond the boundaries of their home and, in so doing, to reclaim their sense of rest in a world that is often tumultuous and exhausting. Respite may involve engaging with people with profound intellectual disabilities, their families, and care workers not only in terms of hosting them (inviting them and their families into our homes) but also learning what it might mean to be a guest in their lives.

Offering respite is not always a big thing. Often it is a very small thing. Jean Vanier points to the power that can be found in small things:

> If we are to remain faithful to the daily round, we need daily manna. It may be ordinary, a bit tasteless. But it is the manna of fidelity to the covenant, to responsibility, to the small things of everyday life. It is the manna of meetings, of friendship, of looks and smiles that say "I love you" and that warm the heart.[2]

The power of love is to be found in the small things in life: the smile that assures us that there is warmth in the midst of our inner coldness, the simple act of sitting beside someone who reminds us that we are worthy of friendship, the phone call that shakes and undermines our sense of isolation and reminds us that somebody just might care, the offer of a cup of coffee that drags us out of our loneliness and isolation and into a world where communion feels possible. It is in the smallness of our day-to-day encounters that we come to feel love and encounter respite. It is not necessary for us to become spiritual superheroes. We simply need to learn the habit of giving our time away through the practice of small things. As Vanier (reportedly) puts it, "We are not called by God to do extraordinary things, but to do ordinary things with extraordinary love."

There are a multitude of ways in which respite can be delivered that can relieve the burden of care and increase the promises of humanness. All we need is a timefull imagination and an openness to paying practical attention to one another in the spirit of Jesus' words: "Your love for one another will prove to the world that you are my disciples" (John 13:35 NLT). To offer respite is simply to practice the timefullness of God. Our task is to signal the timefullness of God through small gestures that transform the world.

LIVING TIMEFULLY, WALKING FAITHFULLY

God's time is certainly a mystery. But it is not the kind of mystery that makes us stand back wide eyed and silenced by overwhelming awe and wonder. God's time is a mystery that we are called to engage in, to live into, even if we will never fully understand it. As we—all of the members of Jesus' body—reflect on the lives of those whose vocation is worked out within the world that is brought to them through different bodies and damaged brains, we are given a glimpse of what it might mean to live faithfully within God's redeemed and redeeming time. Paying attention to the experiences of the *whole* people of God reveals wonderful truths that we could never imagine if we pay attention to only those people that some presume to represent some version of "normality." Taking time seriously and realizing the fullness of what it means to be in Christ and to *be* Jesus' body enables us to see human difference for what it is: *mere difference*. If the church can begin to live out such a truth, perhaps the world can at least have the opportunity to begin to learn to tell the time properly.

Appendix

Redeeming Time
A Lived Funeral

with Tonya Whaley

What follows is a reflection on the rationale that lay behind Tonya's creation of the ritual of a lived funeral and her experience of it. John and Tonya then present a fictional example of what such a timefull ritual might actually look like. Readers may find it beneficial to reflect on this appendix in the light of all of the different experiences of disability that have been explored in this book. All of them in different ways involve transition and change. It may be that the kind of ritualizing approach that we lay out here resonates with other areas where people are having to deal with profound life changes.

RATIONALE

After my accident I felt a deep sense of displacement and a need to find something that would ground me in my authenticity. I needed to find myself and reground my identity.

PREPARATION

I spent several years intentionally trying to understand, learn from, and accept the ways in which I had changed. This was not a quick and overnight process. It took time to understand and time to heal. For the ritual to be effective, it was necessary for me to involve my family and friends, as well as professionals such as my counselor. I could imagine that not everyone might want professionals present at such an intimate event, but for me the preparation for engaging in the liturgy emerged over time and in the light of counseling. I had been engaged in a process of counseling for several years before

I decided to commit to the ritual, and that engagement was a vital aspect of the process for me. I made a point of choosing the friends who knew me best, and I asked my closest friend to facilitate the ritual along with me.

THE EVENT AND DATE

The ritual was a time of grieving, healing, owning, and celebrating. For me it was important to have the ceremony around the anniversary of my accident. Having the ritual on that date allowed me to mark out this time as a day of brokenness (a marking point that reminded me both of before and after) but also a day of freedom, liberation, healing, and renewal, a marking point that enabled me to see the importance of what John Swinton has called "after after."

LOCATION

I wanted to do it near water. Part of the ritual had to do with visualizing the idea of letting go. As a part of the ceremony, we dropped leaves gathered on a hike into the water. Each symbolized an intentional letting go. Some wrote messages on the leaves of what they were mourning or letting go. Others lifted their thoughts in silence. Many gathered a rock or stone from the water and kept it as a symbol or memorial of the moment. As we watched the leaves drift downstream, they came to symbolize everything that we wanted to let go of. Each of us who took part in the ritual did the same thing; each of us let go of something, and the leaves carried that something away. I guess the water also helped us to get a feeling that our hurts were being washed away and something fresh and beautiful was emerging. This was a time never to forget. Being in the woods with the water was cleansing and healing. It felt like the water was washing over my life and freeing that which had remained trapped from the trauma. It was freeing. Almost like a rebirthing of the woman I was now and the new life. Yet, I still knew elements of who I was before the accident, and, because of that foundation, I was able to have the strength to survive and the determination to find, accept, and own who I was and am in this life. Life did not end . . . it was transformed out of an authentic lived experience of life. I did not do it alone. It took a tribe to navigate this journey and I am grateful.

MEANING MAKING

Probably the most important aspect of this process was the issue of *meaning making*. Making sense and giving new meaning to my situation brought me deep healing. To understand who I was before the accident and who I was after was crucial. I am a strange combination of "the old" and "the new." I know that within me there are still pieces of who I was. These remain important. However, this ritual process helped me to own and live well with who I am now. I do not find myself constantly struggling to be the Tonya I was. I am fine with who I am now. I care for the wounds and hurts from my past, but the invitation to allow me to move beyond was helpful in reorganizing my life and ultimately myself. My decision to create my own funeral was not an easy one. It took much work on everybody's part as we struggled together to understand its importance. In the end, not everybody was comfortable with my choice. Some people wanted the "old" Tonya back. People had to be allowed to grieve in their own ways. There is nothing wrong with lamenting for the loss of "an old friend" as long as your sadness does not blind you to the friend that is before you.

BEING GENTLE WITH ONE'S SELF

Perhaps the most important thing that I learned through all of this is that it is important to be gentle toward myself and toward others. It is not my fault that I have changed. It just happened. I could get angry with God or put myself down as if I was failing in some way. But I have learned not to be too hard on myself. The funeral kind of reinforced that by allowing me, and indeed all of us, to see things as they are and to move on. It helped me to own the intention of my journey and to realize the obvious: *nothing is perfect*.

GRACEFUL GRIEVING

Perhaps the most important thing that the funeral ceremony allowed us to do was to engage in a process of what I would call *graceful grieving*. It brought the grace of God into the realms of my attention and allowed me to see things a little differently. It was such grace that enabled me to face those who were not supportive of my choices in healing with a degree of gentleness and understanding. It was grace that has enabled me to just let it all go. Change is always difficult. Letting go of the things you loved is tough. It takes grace and a little bit of help from therapy!

CREATING RITUALS FOR CHANGE

A fitting way to end this appendix is—in the light of Tonya's experience—to offer a simple ritual framework through which those experiencing brain damage and those living alongside them can begin to understand their experiences in ways that hold together the doctrinal and the experiential dynamics of our journey toward healing. Reflection on this ritual framework, we hope, will help readers to visualize bringing together doctrine and experience in ways that are timefull, healing, and faithful. It will be worth reflecting on how the essential elements of the ritual could be utilized to bring timefull healing to those experiencing the other types of disability that have been explored in this book.

To avoid unnecessary clumsiness and impersonality, we will name the imaginary participant in the live funeral Joy.

A FUNERAL FOR A *VERY* CLOSE FRIEND

Welcome and prayer

Welcome brothers and sisters to what for many of us is an unusual occasion: a funeral for a friend who is still with us. As we all know, Joy received a significant head injury some time ago, and there are things about Joy that seem strange and sometimes difficult for her and for those of us who love her. We would love to be able to go back to the time before Joy's accident, but we cannot. Time moves unstoppably onward, and there is nothing we can do to prevent that. There is an inevitable sadness built into time. We cannot stop it and we cannot reverse it, but we can learn to live well with it. Why? Because our God is the God who created time and who, in Jesus, is redeeming time. We can live well within God's time because Jesus comes to meet us there. In God's time we find time for one another. In God's time we know that we are safe.

We came to know Joy in the time before her accident. As we came to know Joy, so we came to love her. We thank God for those times and the memories that we carry for all of the things we did together: the joys, the sadness, the laughing, and the crying. For those times we give thanks. But time has moved on, and some of the things that we knew about Joy are no more. The time after her accident is with us. Joy has changed, but our love for her remains the same. We have seen the changes that have occurred since her accident. We have grieved and we have lamented for the things that have passed. But now we see the changes as a part of who Joy is for us *now*. After the accident she became a "stranger." But now we move on and pledge ourselves to getting to know her all over again, to making this "stranger" into a dear friend.

The task of our time together today is to move the changed Joy into a new time wherein all of us together can let go of the things in Joy's life that have passed and come to recognize and perhaps celebrate some of the new things that are with us now. So, we have grieved, we have wept, and we now come together as one Body to move on to the next phase in our lives and in the life of Joy, confident in the knowledge that, no matter how much we change, who we are is held firmly within the beating heart of Jesus. It may not feel that way, but in faith we trust that God remains in control and that who Joy was and who Joy is, is gently held together by the spirit of God of the restful, gentle God who lives within our hearts and who has promised *never* to leave us nor forsake us.

Reading

Joy has changed, but God has not. He knows Joy very well. The apostle Paul offers us a mysterious promise:

> Since, then, you have been raised with Christ, set your hearts on things above, where Christ is, seated at the right hand of God. Set your minds on things above, not on earthly things. For you died, and your life is now hidden with Christ in God. When Christ, who is your life, appears, then you also will appear with him in glory. (Col 3:1-4 NIV)

Amen and may God add God's blessing to this reading from God's word.

Brief reflection

In one of his prison letters, Dietrich Bonhoeffer writes:

> Who am I? This or the other? Am I one person to-day and to-morrow another? Am I both at once? A hypocrite before others, and before myself a contemptibly woebegone weakling? Or is something within me still like a beaten army, fleeing in disorder from victory already achieved?
>
> Who am I? They mock me, these lonely questions of mine.
> Whoever I am, Thou knowest, O God, I am Thine![1]

Only you, O God, know who we really are. You are a God who knows us and holds us in who we are. In the midst of the traumas and trials of our lives, you keep us and you sustain us in who we are. Life is confused and confusing. We suffer, we struggle, we strive. But you are faithful and even when we no longer know ourselves, you know us. You are a God who is intimately involved in our lives and our world. You reside within our hearts, infusing our lives with hope and new possibilities, even in the face of tragedy and loss. You embrace our being and hold us steadfastly. Be with us now as we move on together into the next phase of our lives with Joy.

Sharing and remembering time (leader)

[At this point in the ritual those who know Joy share stories and remember happy and sad stories about how Joy was before the accident. The idea is to honor the past and prepare us for a new future. This is a time of gratitude for what has been and of acceptance and, perhaps, of welcoming for some of the new things that have come. It is also a place to express sadness and lament, but always in the light of God's unending love, the source of all hope and the locus of new possibilities even in the midst of tragedy and sadness. It is a time for the expression of new wishes and desires. What are our new hopes and wishes? It is a time when people take intentional steps of commitment toward each other as they pledge to continue forward with hope and trust.]

Sharing by the person

[This section of the ritual works along similar dynamics to the previous one:

Mourning the loss or change in who Joy was raised to be.
Sharing of the struggles along the journey of healing.
The mourning or recognition of that which has changed Joy forever.
The gifts and awareness that have surfaced following the accident, the hard work in healing, and the acceptance of who Joy is now.]

The words of transition

And so we move on. We say farewell to the things that Joy has lost and the person that she thought she was then. We say farewell with sadness and longing, in the way that we grieve, as if for an old friend. But at the same time we welcome Joy just as she is with all of the changes and all of the differences.

Farewell to Joy; hello to Joy.

[At this stage in the ritual, the "mourners" might wish to use some kind of physical symbolism such as dropping flowers into a river, blowing out and relighting candles, putting on and taking off pieces of clothing, or some other way to mark the power of passing.]

Prayer of thanksgiving

In the book of Job we find these words: "Naked I came from my mother's womb, and naked shall I return. The LORD gave, and the LORD has taken away; blessed be the name of the LORD" (1:21 ESV). Today we acknowledge this deep truth but also recognize that while some things have been taken way from Joy, some new things have been given. If we take time to look, perhaps we can find some blessing. All of us together need to learn to look differently at Joy, and Joy at herself, in order that we can see value in new things and promise in small things. We are grateful for God's faithfulness. Help us, O God, in our struggles to live lives that have become very different but that are no less important for that.

The Lord's Prayer

Sending forward

> May the road rise up to meet you. May the wind be always at your back. May the sun shine warm upon your face; the rains fall soft upon your fields and until we meet again, may God hold you in the palm of his hand.
> *Amen.*

(traditional Gaelic blessing)

Notes

INTRODUCTION: TIME, DISABILITY, AND THE FRAGILE BRAIN

1 Iain McGilchrist, *The Master and His Emissary: The Divided Brain and the Making of the Western World* (New Haven: Yale University Press, 2009), 75.

2 McGilchrist, *The Master and His Emissary*, 75 (emphasis added).

3 Augustine of Hippo, *The Confessions*, Oxford World's Classics (London: Oxford University Press, 2008), book 11, ch. 14.

4 Here I am thinking of the definition of practical theology laid out in my book with Harriet Mowat: "Practical Theology is critical, theological reflection on the practices of the Church as they interact with the practices of the world, with a view to ensuring and enabling faithful participation in God's redemptive practices in, to and for the world" (*Practical Theology and Qualitative Research Methods* [London: SCM, 2006], 6).

5 *Westminster Shorter Catechism*, Christian Classics Ethereal Library, accessed November 27, 2015, http://www.ccel.org/ccel/anonymous/westminster1.

6 Stephen Pattison, *The Challenge of Practical Theology: Selected Essays* (London: Jessica Kingsley, 2007), 268.

7 Alison Kafer, *Feminist, Queer, Crip* (Bloomington: Indiana University Press, 2013), 25–26.

8 There is much to be gained by adopting such a position. There is, however, a significant problem with this line of thinking (other than the obvious issue that self-interest is not necessarily the best basis for the development of meaningful community). The idea of the temporarily able body seems to assume that there is such a thing as an "able body." If those who do not have disabilities are classed as having "able bodies," then those with disabilities presumably have "dis-abled bodies." In creating two distinct categories—even if neither is fixed—that are held together only by the ever-changing threads of time, the idea of the temporarily able body seems to turn it into a bodily experience in a way that is oddly paradoxical to the claims of the social model of disability and its assertions that the *real* problem of disability is not the body, be that disabled or able, but social attitudes toward different forms of bodies. In other words, it essentializes disability, even if

there is flexibility, fragility, and temporariness within the essence. If time is the separator between able bodiedness and dis-abled bodies, then disability appears to be more real than socially constructed. Despite the problems with these conceptual issues, the idea of temporarily able bodiedness has done some good work in breaking down barriers and remains indicative of the importance of taking time seriously as an issue for the study and lived experience of disability.

9 Eiesland develops this idea succinctly in her paper "Encountering the Disabled God," *Other Side*, September/October 2002, 10–15, and in more detail in her earlier book *The Disabled God: Toward a Liberatory Theology of Disability* (Nashville: Abingdon, 1994).

10 Eiesland, "Encountering the Disabled God," 10.

11 Frances Young, *Face to Face: A Narrative Essay in the Theology of Suffering* (Edinburgh: T&T Clark, 1990), 22.

12 Susie Parr, Kevin Paterson, and Carole Pound, "Time Please! Temporal Barriers in Aphasia," in *Aphasia Inside Out: Reflections on Communication Disability*, ed. Susie Parr, Judith F. Duchan, and Carole Pound (Berkshire: McGraw-Hill Education, 2003), 129.

13 Parr, Paterson, and Pound, "Time Please!" in Parr, Duchan, and Pound, *Aphasia Inside Out*, 131 (emphasis added).

14 Parr, Paterson, and Pound, "Time Please!" in Parr, Duchan, and Pound, *Aphasia Inside Out*, 131.

15 For a fascinating theological exploration of Moses' experience of being "slow of speech," see Marc Shell, "Moses' Tongue," *Common Knowledge* 12, no. 1 (2006): 150–76.

16 Christine Bryden, *Who Will I Be When I Die?* (London: Jessica Kingsley, 2012).

17 Stephen Post, *The Moral Challenge of Alzheimer's Disease* (Baltimore: Johns Hopkins University Press, 1995).

18 "Belief and the Brain's 'God Spot,'" *Independent*, March 10, 2009, accessed November 24, 2015, http://www.independent.co.uk/news/science/belief-and-the-brains-god-spot-1641022.html. For a full overview of the field and the various ways in which the relationship between neurology and theology is worked out within the field of neurotheology, see Eugene G. d'Aquili and Andrew B. Newberg, *Principles of Neurotheology* (London: Ashgate, 2010). Interesting as such research may be, there is a basic flaw in the assumption that identifying a part of the brain that "lights up" when people have religious or spiritual experiences is equivalent to an explanation of what these things are in and of themselves. It is a bit like suggesting that, because the brain lights up when I eat a piece of cheese, we can therefore assume that the cheese is nothing but the product of neurological functioning. The brain, of course, is important for the ways in which human beings experience the world and God within that world; nevertheless, as will become clear as the book develops, the brain is only one factor in the complex process of being human.

19 Dick Swaab, *We Are Our Brains: From the Womb to Alzheimer's* (London: Allen Lane, 2014).

20 Raymond Tallis, *Aping Mankind: Neuromania, Darwinitis and the Misrepresentation of Humanity* (London: Routledge, 2014).

21 René Descartes, *Discourse on the Method of Rightly Conducting the Reason, and Seeking Truth in the Sciences* (1637), 19–20.

1: Thinking about Time

1 Aristotle, *Physics*, Oxford World's Classics (London: Oxford University Press, 2008), book 4, parts 10–13.

2 Isaac Newton, *Philosophiae Naturalis Principia Mathematica* [*Mathematical Principles of Natural Philosophy*] (London, 1687).

3 Albert Einstein, "Time, Space, and Gravitation," *Times* (London), November 28, 1919.

4 Robert Levine, *Geography of Time: On Tempo, Culture and the Pace of Life; The Temporal Misadventures of a Social Psychologist, or How Every Culture Keeps Time Just a Little Bit Differently* (Oxford: Oneworld, 2006).

5 Michael Ratcliffe, "Varieties of Temporal Experience in Depression," *Journal of Medical Philosophy* 37, no. 2 (2012): 114.

6 "On Madness: A Personal Account of Rapid Cycling Bipolar Disorder," *British Journal of General Practice* 56, no. 530 (2006): 726–28.

7 Cecil G. Helman, "Cultural Aspects of Time and Ageing," suppl., *EMBO Reports* 6, suppl. 1 (2005): S54–S58.

8 James Aho and Kevin Aho, *Body Matters: A Phenomenology of Sickness, Disease, and Illness* (New York: Lexington Books, 2008), 37.

9 Levine, *Geography of Time*, 53.

10 Neil Postman, *Technopoly: The Surrender of Culture to Technology* (New York: Vintage Books, 1993), 14.

11 Jeremy Rifkin, *Time Wars: The Primary Conflict in Human History* (New York: Touchstone, 1989), 97.

12 Rifkin, *Time Wars*, 98.

13 Postman, *Technopoly*, 14.

14 Levine, *Geography of Time*, 56–57.

15 Levine, *Geography of Time*, 57.

16 Levine, *Geography of Time*, 57.

17 Thomas Hylland Eriksen, *Tyranny of the Moment: Fast and Slow Time in the Information Age* (London: Pluto, 2001), 39.

18 Rifkin, *Time Wars*, 109.

19 Postman, *Technopoly*, 14.

20 Rifkin, *Time Wars*, 98.

21 Rifkin, *Time Wars*, 100.

22 Rifkin, *Time Wars*, 103.

23 Postman, *Technopoly*, 15.

24 Jacques Le Goff, *Time, Work, and Culture in the Middle Ages*, trans. Arthur Goldhammer (Chicago: University of Chicago Press, 1977), 29–52.

25 Stanley Hauerwas, *With the Grain of the Universe: The Church's Witness and Natural Theology* (Grand Rapids: Brazos, 2001), 55–56n53.

26 Postman, *Technopoly*, 15.

27 Rifkin, *Time Wars*, 103.

28 Rifkin, *Time Wars*, 61.

29 Jeremy S. Begbie, *Theology, Music and Time* (Cambridge: Cambridge University Press, 2000), 86, 72.

30 Navigators, "Got 7 Minutes for God?" October 1, 2012, accessed October 24, 2015, http://www.navigators.org/Tools/Newsletters/Featured%20Newsletters/Disciple/October%202012/October%202012/Got%207%20Minutes%20for%20God.

31 Eriksen, *Tyranny of the Moment*, 39.
32 Charles Taylor, *A Secular Age* (Cambridge, Mass.: Harvard University Press, 2009), 54.
33 Riyad A. Shahjahan, "Being 'Lazy' and Slowing Down: Toward Decolonizing Time, Our Body, and Pedagogy," *Educational Philosophy and Theory* 47, no. 5 (2015): 490.
34 Shahjahan, "Being 'Lazy' and Slowing Down," 490.
35 L. Tuhiwai Smith, *Decolonizing Methodologies: Research and Indigenous Peoples* (London: Zed Books, 2012), 54.
36 Shahjahan, "Being 'Lazy' and Slowing Down," 491.
37 Eriksen, *Tyranny of the Moment*, 47.

2: Time and Progress

1 "Belgium's Parliament Votes Through Child Euthanasia," *BBC News*, February 13, 2014, accessed October 26, 2015, http://www.bbc.co.uk/news/world-europe-26181615.
2 Michael F. Haverluck, "Majority of Dutch Docs Would Euthanize Dementia Patients," *OneNewsNow.com*, May 1, 2015, accessed October 26, 2015, http://onenewsnow.com/pro-life/2015/05/01/majority-of-dutch-docs-would-euthanize-dementia-patients#.
3 "Belgian Murderer Van Den Bleeken Wins 'Right to Die,'" *BBC News*, September 15, 2014, accessed October 26, 2015, http://www.bbc.co.uk/news/world-europe-29209459.
4 John Bingham, "Elderly Should Be Given Euthanasia 'Rewards', Say One in 10 Britons," *Telegraph*, November 6, 2014, accessed November 30, 2015, http://www.telegraph.co.uk/news/uknews/assisted-dying/11213869/Elderly-should-be-rewarded-for-choosing-assisted-suicide-say-one-in-10-Britons.html.
5 "Belgian Murderer Van Den Bleeken Wins 'Right to Die,'" *BBC News*, September 15, 2014, accessed October 26, 2015, http://www.bbc.co.uk/news/world-europe-29209459.
6 "Down Syndrome heading for extinction in Denmark," CPH Post Online, October 20, 2015, accessed February 2, 2016, http://cphpost.dk/news/down-syndrome-heading-for-extinction-in-denmark.html.
7 Kruti Acharya has noted that while Down syndrome is not the most severe form of intellectual disability, it is the most well known. It is also a label that has accrued a good deal of social stigma. Parents can feel particularly acute forms of social pressure to terminate pregnancies if particular tests indicate its presence. Down syndrome can be the intellectual disability parents want to avoid. Kruti Acharya, "Prenatal Testing for Intellectual Disability: Misperceptions and Reality with Lessons from Down Syndrome," *Developmental Disabilities Research Reviews* 17, no. 1 (2011): 27–31.
8 Dorothy Cummings McLean, "Peace Takes Time and Patience: An Interview with Stanley Hauerwas," *Catholic Register*, March 31, 2009, accessed January 10, 2015, http://www.catholicregister.org/columns/item/11176-peace-takes-time-and-patience. For an expansion of this point, see Stanley Hauerwas and Jean Vanier, *Living Gently in a Violent World: The Prophetic Witness of Weakness*, ed. John Swinton (Downers Grove, Ill.: InterVarsity, 2009), 51.
9 Jean Vanier, *Befriending the Stranger* (Mahwah, N.J.: Paulist, 2005), 12.
10 Jackie Macadam, "Interview with Mary Warnock: 'A Duty to Die?'" *Life and Work*, October 2008, 25.
11 Macadam, "Interview with Mary Warnock," 25.
12 John Swinton, *Dementia: Living in the Memories of God* (Grand Rapids: Eerdmans, 2012), chap. 5; and Swinton, "What's in a Name? Why People with Dementia Might Be Better

Off without the Language of Personhood," *International Journal of Practical Theology* 18, no. 2 (2014): 234–47.

13 "Richard Dawkins Apologises for Causing Storm with Down's Syndrome Tweet," *Guardian*, August 21, 2014, accessed November 21, 2014, http://www.theguardian.com/science/2014/aug/21/richard-dawkins-apologises-downs-syndrome-tweet.

14 "Richard Dawkins Apologises for Causing Storm with Down's Syndrome Tweet."

15 "Richard Dawkins Apologises for Causing Storm with Down's Syndrome Tweet."

16 Douglas C. Baynton, "'These Pushful Days': Time and Disability in the Age of Eugenics," *Health History* 13, no. 2 (2011): 43–64.

17 Baynton, "These Pushful Days," 43.

18 Baynton, "These Pushful Days," 44.

19 Baynton, "These Pushful Days," 45.

20 My point is not, of course, that these were particularly good explanations. My point is that they were explanations that reflected a very different understanding of time from the emerging evolutionary perspective: in time God will rid people of their disabilities, as opposed to through time human knowledge will overcome and eradicate disability.

21 Baynton, "These Pushful Days," 45.

22 Paul Ulasien, *The Corporate Rat Race: The Rats Are Winning* (Baltimore: Publish America, 2006).

23 Douglas Baynton, "Handicap," in *Encyclopaedia of American Disability History*, ed. Susan Burch and Paul K. Longmore (New York: Facts on File, 2009), 420.

24 Baynton, "Handicap," 420.

25 Baynton, "These Pushful Days," 48.

26 Richard Dawkins, *The Selfish Gene* (London: Oxford University Press, 1976).

27 Baynton, "These Pushful Days," 49.

28 Baynton, "These Pushful Days," 51.

29 Steven A. Gelb, "Darwin's Use of Intellectual Disability in *The Descent of Man*," *Disability Studies Quarterly* 28, no. 2 (2008), http://dsq-sds.org/article/view/96/96.

30 Gelb, "Darwin's Use of Intellectual Disability in *The Descent of Man*."

31 Gelb, "Darwin's Use of Intellectual Disability in *The Descent of Man*." Darwin's quote can be found in Charles Darwin, *The Descent of Man: Selection in Relation to Sex* (London: Penguin Classics, 1981), 42. It should be noted that the basis for this way of thinking is not really scientific. Rather, it is a way of attempting to fill a hypothetical gap in a theory without invoking God. This strategy is, of course, remarkably similar to that of contemporary ethicists such as Peter Singer who work with precisely this dynamic in order to downgrade human beings in an attempt to raise up animals. Cf. Peter Singer, *Rethinking Life and Death: The Collapse of Our Traditional Ethics* (Melbourne: Text, 1994); and Singer, *Practical Ethics* (Cambridge: Cambridge University Press, 1979).

32 Charles Darwin, *The Descent of Man: Selection in Relation to Sex* (London: Penguin Classics, 1981), 24.

33 J. P. Lesley, *Man's Origin and Destiny* (Philadelphia: J. B. Lippincott, 1868), 120.

34 Gelb, "Darwin's Use of Intellectual Disability in *The Descent of Man*."

35 Henrietta Emma Litchfield Darwin, *Emma Darwin, a Century of Family Letters, 1792–1896*, vol. 2 (Bel Air: Cook, 2007), 162.

36 David P. Steensma, "Down Syndrome in Down House: Trisomy 21, *GATA1* Mutations, and Charles Darwin," *Blood* 105, no. 6 (2005).

37 Charles Darwin, *The Death of Charles Waring Darwin*, in *The Correspondence of Charles Darwin*, ed. F. Burkhardt and S. Smith (New York: Cambridge University Press, 1993), 7:521, quoted in J. David Smith, "Darwin's Last Child," *Disability Studies Quarterly* 28, no. 2 (2008), https://libres.uncg.edu/ir/uncg/f/J_Smith_Darwin_1999.pdf.
38 "Sarah Palin to Atheist Richard Dawkins on Aborting Down Syndrome Babies: I'll Let You Meet My Son," *Christian Post*, August 27, 2014, accessed November 21, 2014, http://www.christianpost.com/news/sarah-palin-to-atheist-richard-dawkins-on-aborting-down-syndrome-babies-ill-let-you-meet-my-son-125414/.
39 "Sarah Palin to Atheist Richard Dawkins on Aborting Down Syndrome Babies."
40 Baynton, "These Pushful Days," 53.
41 Hacking says, "The first meaning of 'normal' given in any current English dictionary is something like 'usual, regular, common, typical.' The *OED* dictionary says that this usage became current after 1840, and gives 1828 for its first citation of 'normal or typical.' That was in a work of natural history alluding to the French writers." Ian Hacking, *The Taming of Chance (Ideas in Context)* (Cambridge: Cambridge University Press, 1990), 162.
42 Hacking, *Taming of Chance*, 160.
43 Baynton, "These Pushful Days," 53.
44 Hacking, *Taming of Chance*, 160–66.
45 Baynton, "These Pushful Days," 53.
46 Paul H. Mason, "What Is Normal? A Historical Survey and Neuroanthropological Perspective," in *Handbook of Neuroethics*, ed. Jens Clausen and Neil Levy (New York: Springer, 2014), 346.
47 W. J. Reichmann, *Use and Abuse of Statistics* (Middlesex: Penguin Books, 1964), 121, quoted in Mason, "What Is Normal?" 346.
48 Mason, "What Is Normal?" 348.
49 Hacking, *Taming of Chance*, 163.
50 Baynton, "These Pushful Days," 54.

3: Time and Christ

1 Scott Bader-Saye, "Figuring Time: Providence and Politics," in *Liturgy, Time, and the Politics of Redemption*, ed. Randi Rashkover and C. C. Pecknold (Grand Rapids: Eerdmans, 2006), 96.
2 Simon Carey Holt, "Slow Time in a Fast World," *Ministry, Society and Theology* 16, no. 2 (2002): 10–21.
3 Timothy George, "St. Augustine and the Mystery of Time," in *What God Knows: Time and the Question of Divine Knowledge*, ed. Harry Lee Poe and J. Stanley Mattson (Waco, Tex.: Baylor University Press, 2006), 38.
4 George, "St. Augustine and the Mystery of Time," in Poe and Mattson, *What God Knows*, 38.
5 Augustine, *Confessions*, book 11, ch. 6.
6 For Augustine time is a trope to explain God, rather than a distantiated philosophical exploration of the nature of time.
7 John Howard Yoder, *Preface to Theology: Christology and Theological Method* (Grand Rapids: Brazos, 2002), 275–76.
8 Stanley Hauerwas, *The Work of Theology* (Grand Rapids: Eerdmans, 2015), 90.
9 Oscar Cullmann, *Christ and Time: The Primitive Christian Conception of Time and History* (New York: Farrar, Straus & Giroux, 1951).

10 Hauerwas, *Work of Theology*, 91.
11 Hauerwas, *Work of Theology*, 91.
12 I am grateful to Stanley Hauerwas for introducing me to Tran's work.
13 Jonathan Tran, *The Vietnam War and Theologies of Memory: Time and Eternity in the Far Country* (London: Wiley-Blackwell, 2010), 49.
14 George Hunsinger, "Our Lives Are Hidden in Christ," *Grace Communion International: Living and Sharing the Gospel*, accessed October 27, 2015, https://www.gci.org/YI089.
15 Hunsinger, "Our Lives Are Hidden in Christ."
16 Karl Barth, *Church Dogmatics*, vol. 3, part 3, ed. G. W. Bromiley and T. F. Torrance, trans. G. W. Bromiley and R. J. Ehrlich (Edinburgh: T&T Clark, 1960), 186.
17 Tran, *Vietnam War and Theologies of Memory*, 49.
18 Tran, *Vietnam War and Theologies of Memory*, 50.
19 Readers should bear in mind that talking about God as being inside or outside of time is always a spatial metaphor. Both Augustine and Tran could be accused of shifting between the metaphorical and the nonmetaphorical in their conversations around time.
20 Judith Shulevitz, *The Sabbath World: Glimpses of a Different Order of Time*, Kindle ed. (London: Random House, 2010), locations 1853–56.
21 George, "St. Augustine and the Mystery of Time," in Poe and Mattson, *What God Knows*, 40.
22 George, "St. Augustine and the Mystery of Time," in Poe and Mattson, *What God Knows*, 40.
23 Scott Bader-Saye, "Figuring Time: Providence and Politics," in Rashkover and Pecknold, *Liturgy, Time, and the Politics of Redemption*, 98; emphasis in original.
24 Bader-Saye, "Figuring Time: Providence and Politics," in Rashkover and Pecknold, *Liturgy, Time, and the Politics of Redemption*, 91.
25 Eph 1:7: "In him we have redemption through his blood, the forgiveness of sins, in accordance with the riches of God's grace" (NIV).
26 Carey Holt, "Slow Time in a Fast World," 11.

4: Becoming Friends of Time

1 Angus Paddison, *Scripture: A Very Theological Proposal* (London: T&T Clark, 2009), 25.
2 2 Cor 5:18: "All this is from God, who reconciled us to himself through Christ and gave us the ministry of reconciliation."
3 Kosuke Koyama, *Three Mile an Hour God: Biblical Reflections* (New York: Orbis, 1979), 6–7.
4 Koyama, *Three Mile an Hour God*, 7.
5 Shulevitz, *Sabbath World*, location 1853–56.
6 John Hull, "Time and Blindness," *World Religions in Education: Time* (The Shap working party on Education in World Religions 2000–2001), accessed November 9, 2015, http://www.shapworkingparty.org.uk/journals/index_0001.html.
7 John Hull, *Touching the Rock: An Experience of Blindness* (London: SPCK, 2013), 68.
8 Hull, "Time and Blindness," 12.
9 Hull, "Time and Blindness," 13.
10 Judith Snow, lecture delivered at the Summer Institute on Theology and Disability, Perkins School of Theology, Dallas, Texas, June 2014.

11 In Levine, *Geography of Time*, 214. For a fuller development of McCrum's story, see his autobiography: Robert McCrum, *My Year Off: Recovering Life after a Stroke* (New York: Norton, 1998).
12 Andrew P. Klager, "The Vulnerability That Makes Peace Possible: An Interview with Stanley Hauerwas," *Huffington Post*, November 9, 2015, accessed November 9, 2015, http://www.huffingtonpost.com/andrew-p-klager-phd/the-vulnerability-that-ma_b_5579366.html.
13 Jean Vanier, *Community and Growth* (London: Darton, Longman and Todd, 1979), 124 (emphasis added).
14 In Frances Young, *Encounter with Mystery: Reflections on L'Arche and Living with Disability* (London: Darton, Longman and Todd, 1997), 82.
15 Vanier, *Community and Growth*, 134.
16 A version of this narrative was published in my essay "Interiority and Christian Spirituality: Why Our Inner Lives Are Not Quite as Inner as We Might Like to Think," in *Sacrality and Materiality: Locating Intersections*, ed. Rebecca A. Giselbrecht and Ralph Kunz (Göttingen: Vandenhoeck & Ruprecht, 2016), 157–67. Used here with permission.
17 Josef Pieper, *Faith, Hope, Love* (San Francisco: Ignatius, 1997), 164.
18 Michael Fishbane, *Sacred Attunement: A Jewish Theology* (Chicago: University of Chicago Press, 2008).
19 Walter Brueggemann, *Sabbath as Resistance*: *Saying No to the Culture of Now*, Kindle ed. (Louisville: Westminster John Knox, 2014), location 79.
20 Brueggemann, *Sabbath as Resistance*, location 79.
21 Carey Holt, "Slow Time in a Fast World," 14.
22 Brueggemann, *Sabbath as Resistance*, 6.
23 Brueggemann, *Sabbath as Resistance*, 6.
24 Brueggemann, *Sabbath as Resistance*, 6.
25 Brueggemann, *Sabbath as Resistance*, 10.
26 Brueggemann, *Sabbath as Resistance*, 28.
27 Lydia Dugdale, personal correspondence.
28 Koyama, *Three Mile an Hour God*, 6–7.

5: Time and Discipleship

1 The University of Aberdeen's Centre for Spirituality, Health and Disability: http://www.abdn.ac.uk/sdhp/centre-for-spirituality-health-and-disability-182.php.
2 John Swinton and Elaine Powrie, *Why Are We Here? Meeting the Spiritual Needs of People with Learning Disabilities* (London: Foundation for People with Learning Disabilities, 2004).
3 Of course, the inability to fully incorporate Loraine into the community could also be tied in with a general wariness of difference. That does not, however, get us away from the issue of discipleship; it simply raises the question as to whose discipleship is missing.
4 For a further development of this line of thinking, see John Hull, *In the Beginning There Was Darkness: A Blind Person's Conversations with the Bible* (London: SCM, 2001).
5 Stanley Hauerwas, "The Church and the Mentally Handicapped: A Continuing Challenge to the Imagination," in *Critical Reflections on Stanley Hauerwas' Theology of Disability: Disabling Society, Enabling Theology*, ed. John Swinton (London: Routledge, 2005), 59.

6 I recognize that such a description may reveal something of my roots in the Reformed tradition. I realize that other traditions may not be as focused on words. Nonetheless, the conversation around intellect and discipleship is of interest across the traditions.
7 Kathryn Tanner, *Theories of Culture: A New Agenda for Theology* (Minneapolis: Fortress, 1997).
8 Tanner, *Theories of Culture*, 124.
9 Medi Volpe, *Rethinking Christian Identity: Doctrine and Discipleship* (London: Wiley-Blackwell, 2013), 41.
10 Volpe, *Rethinking Christian Identity*, 42.
11 Avery Dulles, *Models of Church* (New York: Image Books, 1974).
12 Medi Volpe, personal correspondence, September 18, 2015.
13 Dietrich Bonhoeffer, *Discipleship* (Minneapolis: Fortress, 2003), 57.
14 Bonhoeffer, *Discipleship*, 57.
15 Bonhoeffer, *Discipleship*, 57.
16 Bonhoeffer, *Discipleship*, 59.
17 David H. Kelsey. "Personal Bodies: A Theological Anthropological Proposal," in *Personal Identity in Theological Perspective*, ed. Richard Lints, Michael S. Horton, and Mark R. Talbot (Grand Rapids: Eerdmans, 2006), 142.
18 Kelsey, "Personal Bodies," in Lints, Horton, and Talbot, *Personal Identity in Theological Perspective*, 142.
19 Kelsey, "Personal Bodies," in Lints, Horton, and Talbot, *Personal Identity in Theological Perspective*, 143.
20 Kelsey, "Personal Bodies," in Lints, Horton, and Talbot, *Personal Identity in Theological Perspective*, 143.
21 For a further development of this argument, see John Swinton, "Using Our Bodies Faithfully," *Journal of Disability and Religion* 19, no. 3 (2015): 228–42.
22 Stanley Hauerwas, *The Peaceable Kingdom: A Primer in Christian Ethics* (Notre Dame, Ind.: University of Notre Dame Press, 1983), 86.
23 Medi Volpe, "Saving Knowledge: Doctrine and Intellectual Disability," paper presented at the DThM summer school, University of Durham, UK, September 2013, accessed November 10, 2015, https://www.academia.edu/12529752/Saving_Knowledge_Doctrine_and_Intelletucal_Disability.
24 Volpe, "Saving Knowledge."
25 Volpe, "Saving Knowledge," 10.
26 Volpe, "Saving Knowledge," 11.
27 Volpe, "Saving Knowledge," 12.
28 Volpe, "Saving Knowledge," 12.
29 Volpe, "Saving Knowledge," 21.
30 Maurice Merleau-Ponty, *Phenomenology of Perception*, trans. Colin Smith (London: Routledge & Kegan Paul, 1965).
31 It is not possible here to rehearse the arguments around the pros and cons of baptizing people with profound intellectual disabilities. Readers who want to follow through on this aspect would be wise to refer to the work of Myk Habets at Carey Baptist College in Auckland, New Zealand, and Jason Whitt at Baylor University in the United States. Myk Habets, "'Suffer the Little Children to Come to Me, for Theirs Is the Kingdom of Heaven': Infant Salvation and the Destiny of the Severely Mentally Disabled," in *Evangelical Calvinism: Essays Resourcing the Continuing Reformation of the Church*, ed. Myk

Habets and Bobby Grow (Eugene, Ore.: Pickwick, 2012), 287–331. Jason Whitt, "Baptism and Profound Intellectual Disability," in "Disability," special issue, *Christian Reflection: A Series in Faith and Ethics* (2012): 60–67.

32 Whitt, "Baptism and Profound Intellectual Disability," 62.

33 Bonhoeffer, *Discipleship*, 221.

34 Bonhoeffer, *Discipleship*, 221.

35 Bonhoeffer, *Discipleship*, 221.

36 Brian Brock, personal correspondence. Brock's point is echoed in Volpe's outline of the nature of doctrine: "It helps us to avoid intellectual sins that only the rationally capacious are likely to commit!" But even with regard to sin, it does not have to be "Jesus and me." After all, what Jesus says to the paralytic is "your sins are forgiven." Much could be said about that, but it certainly gives us warrant to bring other people before the throne of grace when they are unable to take themselves. Jesus does it again when he says, "Father, forgive them, for they know not what they do." We tend to set the bar a lot higher than does God when it comes to repentance: God forgives before we ask and makes the way for us to return—this idea runs through a number of the psalms and the prophets, and also is at the heart of the prodigal son parable. If the father had not *already* forgiven his son, he hardly would have hurried down the road to welcome him home (Medi Volpe, personal correspondence).

37 The Genesis text certainly shows the fall of Adam. However, there is no indication that sin then becomes something that is passed on through procreation. Sin is not like a virus or a meme. As we will see later, sin has to do with disobedience. It is very difficult to disobey your genes!

38 For an excellent exploration of Bonhoeffer's conception of corporate sin and corporate personality, see Tom Greggs, "Bearing Sin in the Church: The Ecclesial Hamartiology of Bonhoeffer," in *Christ, Church and World: New Studies in Bonhoeffer's Theology and Ethics*, ed. Michael Mawson and Philip Ziegler (London: Bloomsbury, 2016), 77–100.

6: Time and Vocation

1 A. J. Conyers, *The Listening Heart: Vocation and the Crisis of Modern Culture* (Dallas: Spence, 2006), 7.

2 Frances Young, *Arthur's Call: A Journey of Faith in the Face of Severe Learning Disability* (London: SPCK, 2014), 76.

3 Scott Bader-Saye, *Following Jesus in a Culture of Fear* (Minneapolis: Baker, 2007), 76.

4 John Calvin, *Calvin: Institutes of the Christian Religion*, ed. John T. McNeill, trans. from the 1559 Latin ed. by Ford Lewis Battles, 2 vols., Library of Christian Classics (Philadelphia: Westminster, 1960), book 1.

5 Bader-Saye, *Following Jesus in a Culture of Fear*, 79.

6 Bader-Saye, *Following Jesus in a Culture of Fear*, 79.

7 Conyers, *Listening Heart*, 12.

8 Conyers, *Listening Heart*, 14.

9 A. J. Conyers, "The Meaning of Vocation," in "Vocation," special issue, *Christian Reflection: A Series in Faith and Ethics* (2004): 13.

10 Gary Badcock, *The Way of Life: A Theology of Christian Vocation* (Grand Rapids: Eerdmans, 1998), 35.

11 Martin Luther, "To the Christian nobility of the German nation concerning reform of the Christian estate," trans. C. M. Jacobs, rev. James Atkinson, in *Luther's Works* (Philadelphia: Fortress, 1966), 44:129–30.

12 Quoted in Badcock, *Way of Life*, 35.

13 Hauerwas offers some interesting arguments as to why it might not be a good idea for all of us to have free reign in interpreting Scripture: Stanley Hauerwas, *Unleashing the Scriptures: Freeing the Bible from Captivity to America* (Nashville: Abingdon, 1993).

14 Gene Edward Veith, "The Doctrine of Vocation: How God Hides Himself in Human Work," *Modern Reformation*, May/June 1999, 5–6.

15 Veith, "Doctrine of Vocation," 6.

16 Young, *Arthur's Call*, 151.

17 Young, *Arthur's Call*, 142.

18 Young, *Arthur's Call*, 145.

19 Young, *Arthur's Call*, 146.

20 "Sturge-Weber syndrome," Great Ormond Street Hospital for Children, NHS Foundation Trust, accessed March 1, 2016, http://www.gosh.nhs.uk/medical-information-0/search-medical-conditions/sturge-weber-syndrome.

21 Makaton is a sign language program designed to facilitate communication for people who cannot communicate effectively through words; for more information, see the official Makaton charity site, http://www.makaton.org/aboutMakaton/.

22 Personal communication via e-mail, Mary, April 2010.

23 Katherine Weber, "Viral Photo Shows Pope Francis' Dedication to the Poor, Vulnerable," *The Christian Post*, accessed February 3, 2016, http://www.christianpost.com/news/viral-photo-shows-pope-francis-dedication-to-the-poor-vulnerable-91892/.

7: Time and Memory

1 Charles Leadbeater, "The Disremembered," *Aeon*, March 26, 2015, accessed November 9, 2015, http://linkis.com/rBfqi.

2 This narrative was first published in my article "Dementia and the Memory of the Body: Moving beyond the Autobiographical Self," *St Mark's Review: A Journal of Christian Thought & Opinion*, no. 232 (2015): 38–50. It is published here with permission.

3 Leadbeater, "Disremembered."

4 For a further development of this idea, see Steven R. Sabat, "Mind, Meaning and Personhood in Dementia: The Effects of Positioning," in *Dementia: Mind, Meaning and the Person*, ed. Julian C. Hughes, Stephen J. Louw and Steven R. Sabat (Oxford: Oxford University Press, 2006), 287–302.

5 Jens Brockmeier, "Memory, Dementia, and the Postautobiographical Perspective," in *Beyond Loss: Dementia, Identity, Personhood*, ed. Lars C. Hydén and Hilde Lindemann (New York: Oxford University Press, 2014), 70.

6 Ian Hacking, "Natural Kinds: Rosy Dawn, Scholastic Twilight," *Royal Institute of Philosophy Supplement* 61 (2007): 203–39.

7 Brockmeier, "Identity, Agency, and Embodiment," in Hydén and Lindemann, *Beyond Loss*, 70.

8 John Locke, *Essay concerning Human Understanding* (New York: Prometheus Books, 1995), book 2, ch. 27.

9 Ian Hacking, "Memory Sciences, Memory Politics," in *Tense Past: Cultural Essays in Trauma and Memory*, ed. P. Antze and M. Lambek (London: Routledge, 1996), 81 (emphasis added).
10 "New Memories Filmed in Action for the First Time," Daily News, *New Scientist*, May 16, 2013, accessed November 9, 2015, http://www.newscientist.com/article/dn23555-new-memories-filmed-in-action-for-first-time.html#.VZToJD8w-M8; see also Mark Prigg, "How Memories are REALLY Made: Incredible New Video Captures Their Formation in the Brain," *Daily Mail*, January 24, 2014, http://www.dailymail.co.uk/sciencetech/article-2545560/How-memories-REALLY-Incredible-new-video-captures-formation-brain.html.
11 Ellie Zolfagharifard, "How Memories Are REALLY Made: Scientists See Neurons Change in Real-Time as Events Are 'Recorded' in the Brain," *Daily Mail*, July 1, 2015, accessed November 9, 2015, http://www.dailymail.co.uk/sciencetech/article-3146271/How-memories-REALLY-Scientists-neurons-change-real-time-events-recorded-brain.html#ixzz3jf4cPiaH.
12 Lisa Winter, "Watch Chemicals Turn into Memories—the First Time This Has Ever Been Recorded," *IFLScience*, accessed November 9, 2015, http://www.iflscience.com/brain/watch-chemicals-turn-memories-first-time-has-ever-been-recorded.
13 Jim Baggott, *A Beginner's Guide to Reality* (London: Penguin Books, 2005), 50.
14 Tallis, *Aping Mankind*, 128; emphasis in original.
15 Tallis, *Aping Mankind*, 124–25; emphasis in original.
16 See, for example, D. R. Addis and R. L. Buckner, "Episodic Simulations of Future Events: Concepts, Data and Applications," *Year in Cognitive Neuroscience, Annals of the New York Academy of Sciences* 1124 (2008): 39–60; and Daniel Schacter, *Searching for Memory: How the Mind Forgets and Remembers* (New York: Basic Books, 1996).

8: Time and the Heart

1 J. M. Boice, *Foundations of the Christian Faith* (Downers Grove, Ill.: InterVarsity 1986), 331.
2 Memory Bridge: The Foundation for Alzheimer's and Cultural Memory, accessed November 9, 2015, http://www.memorybridge.org/.
3 A method for communicating with elderly people who are diagnosed with dementia. For further information, see the Validation Training Institute, accessed December 3, 2015, https://vfvalidation.org/web.php?request=index.
4 In the light of what we have explored thus far in this book and what will be developed below, it is not a stretch to suggest that Paul's demand for oral declaration can be seen in broader, more full-bodied terms.
5 Rafael F. Narvaez, "Embodiment, Collective Memory and Time," *Body & Society* 12, no. 3 (2006): 51.
6 Narvaez, "Embodiment, Collective Memory and Time," 52.
7 Narvaez, "Embodiment, Collective Memory and Time," 52.
8 Narvaez, "Embodiment, Collective Memory and Time," 52.
9 Thomas Fuchs, "The Phenomenology of Body Memory," in *Body Memory, Metaphor and Movement*, ed. Sabine C. Koch, Thomas Fuchs, Michela Summa, and Cornelia Müller (Amsterdam: John Benjamins, 2012), 9.
10 Fuchs, "Phenomenology of Body Memory," in Koch et al., *Body Memory, Metaphor and Movement*, 17.

11 Bianca Maria Pirani, ed., *Learning from Memory: Body, Memory and Technology in a Globalizing World* (Newcastle: Cambridge Scholars, 2011), xxiii. Pirani fails to attribute this quote to Thomas Fuchs, who wrote the same words verbatim in a 2003 article available at https://www.klinikum.uni-heidelberg.de/fileadmin/zpm/psychatrie/ppp2004/manuskript/fuchs.pdf.
12 Fuchs, "Phenomenology of Body Memory," in Koch et al., *Body Memory, Metaphor and Movement*, 11.
13 Oh, the depth of the riches of the wisdom and knowledge of God! How unsearchable his judgments, and his paths beyond tracing out (Rom 11:33)! What is mankind that you are mindful of them, human beings that you care for them (Ps 8:4)?
14 Michael Downey, *A Blessed Weakness: The Spirit of Jean Vanier and L'Arche* (San Francisco: Harper & Row, 1986), 58.
15 Downey, *Blessed Weakness*, 58.
16 Michael Downey, "A Costly Loss of Heart: The Scholastic Notion of *Voluntas ut Natura*," *Philosophy and Theology* 1, no. 3 (1987): 251.
17 Vanier, *Community and Growth*, 13.
18 Jean Vanier, *Becoming Human* (Mahweh, N.J.: Paulist, 2002), 87.
19 Jean Vanier, *Man and Woman, God Made Them* (Mahweh, N.J.: Paulist, 2000), 36.
20 Downey, *Blessed Weakness*, 58.
21 For a further development of this perspective on memory, see Swinton, *Dementia*, chap. 4.
22 Leadbeater, "Disremembered."

9: The Horror of Time

1 Søren Rasted, Claus Norreen, et al., "Turn Back Time," Aqua, *Aquarium*, MCA Records, 1997.
2 Al Stewart and Peter White, "Time Passages," Al Stewart, *Time Passages* (remaster), Rhino Records, 2004.
3 See jonimitchell.com/music/song.cfm?id=13.
4 Robert R. Vosloo, "The Feeling of Time: Bonhoeffer on Temporality and the Fully Human Life," *Scriptura* 99 (2008): 342.
5 Dietrich Bonhoeffer, *Barcelona, Berlin, New York: 1928–1931* (Minneapolis: Fortress, 2008), 516.
6 See www.azlyrics.com/lyrics/davidbowie/changes.html.
7 Bonhoeffer, *Barcelona, Berlin, New York*, 517.
8 Bonhoeffer, *Barcelona, Berlin, New York*, 520.
9 Norman Doidge, *The Brain That Changes Itself: Stories of Personal Triumph from the Frontiers of Brain Science* (New York: Viking Books, 2007).
10 Floyd Skloot, "Gray Area: Thinking with a Damaged Brain," *LOST Magazine*, February 2006, accessed November 10, 2015, http://www.lostmag.com/issue3/grayarea.php.
11 Floyd Skloot, "Wild in the Woods," in *In the Shadow of Memory* (Lincoln, Neb.: Bison Books, 2004), ch. 2.
12 Floyd Skloot, "Gray Area: Thinking with a Damaged Brain," in *In the Shadow of Memory*, 3.
13 Martha Stoddart Holmes, "Writing Neurology: Essays and Poetry by Floyd Skloot," *Journal of Medical Humanities* 10 (2009): 5.
14 Skloot, *In the Shadow of Memory*, 6.
15 Skloot, "Gray Area," 1.

16 Skloot, "Gray Area," 2.
17 Skloot, *In the Shadow of Memory*, 5.
18 Skloot, *In the Shadow of Memory*, 6.
19 Skloot, *In the Shadow of Memory*, 9.
20 Skloot, *In the Shadow of Memory*, 9.
21 Skloot, *In the Shadow of Memory*, 10.
22 Skloot, *In the Shadow of Memory*, 10.
23 Skloot, *In the Shadow of Memory*, 16.
24 Skloot, *In the Shadow of Memory*, 16 (emphasis added).
25 Skloot, *In the Shadow of Memory*, 11.
26 Skloot, *In the Shadow of Memory*, 17.
27 Skloot, *In the Shadow of Memory*, 17.

10: The Time Before and the Time After

1 Hans S. Reinders, *Disability, Providence, and Ethics: Bridging Gaps, Transforming Lives* (Waco, Tex.: Baylor University Press, 2014).
2 I am grateful to my friend Tonya Whaley for allowing me to use parts of a conversation we had around her experience of brain damage. Tonya is the coauthor of the following chapter.
3 "Personality," American Psychological Association, accessed November 10, 2015, http://www.apa.org/topics/personality/.
4 G. N. Yeates, F. Gracey, and J. C. McGrath, "A Biopsychosocial Deconstruction of 'Personality Change' following Acquired Brain Injury," *Neuropsychological Rehabilitation* 18, nos. 5–6 (2008): 567.
5 Reinders does not distinguish between acquired brain damage and traumatic brain damage, although his accounts include both.
6 Reinders, *Disability, Providence, and Ethics*, 39.
7 Reinders, *Disability, Providence, and Ethics*, 43.
8 Reinders, *Disability, Providence, and Ethics*, 43; emphasis in original.
9 Reinders, *Disability, Providence, and Ethics*, 82.
10 George Hunsinger, *How to Read Karl Barth: The Shape of His Theology* (New York: Oxford University Press, 1993), 103.
11 Hunsinger, *How to Read Karl Barth*, 106. This is not the place to discuss the universalist aspects of Barth's position. This has been argued well elsewhere. See Tom Greggs, *Barth, Origen, and Universal Salvation: Restoring Particularity* (London: Oxford University Press, 2009).
12 Hunsinger, *How to Read Karl Barth*, 114. Barth puts it thus:
"'In Christ' means that in him we are reconciled to God, in him we are elect from eternity, in him we are called, in him we are justified and sanctified, in him our sin is carried to the grave, in his resurrection our death is overcome, with him our life is hid in God, in him everything that has to be done for us, to us, and by us, has already been done, has previously been removed and put in its place, in him we are children in the Father's house, just as he is by nature. All that has to be said about us can be said only by describing and explaining it as an existence in him; not by describing and explaining it as an existence which we might have in and for itself. That is why the subjective reality of revelation as such can never be made an independent theme. It is enclosed in its objective reality. . . . For by Christ we will never be anything else than just what

we are in Christ. And when the Holy Spirit draws and takes us right into the reality of revelation by doing what we cannot do, by opening our eyes and ears and hearts, he does not tell us anything except that we are in Christ by Christ. . . . We are invited and challenged to understand ourselves from this and not from any other standpoint" (I/2, 240; cf. II/2, 117).

13 Hunsinger, *How to Read Karl Barth*, 115.

14 It is worth noting that this way of thinking helps challenge those who suggest that the fact that morality seems to be neurologically dependent is indicative of the fact that religion is *nothing* but an aspect of brain function. According to the perspective offered in this chapter, it could be both.

15 This way of thinking offers a challenge to Nancy Eiesland's suggestion that she would be unrecognizable to herself if she did not have her disability when she reached heaven (see the discussion in the introduction to this book). The implication here is that she, like all of us, is already unrecognizable. We can really find out who we are only as we discover what it means to be in Christ. It is not our disabilities that make us who we are; it is Jesus. Neither able bodiedness nor disability (if in fact these terms are appropriate descriptors of human difference) contains or shapes our identity; only Jesus does. Nevertheless, the *lived experience* of one's body does indeed shape one's sense of identity and as such remains important. Eiesland is therefore correct at the level of anthropology and experience, but less so with regard to theology and theological anthropology.

16 George Hunsinger makes these points in a fascinating way in his discussion on the nature of inclusion in Christ in "Our Lives Are Hidden in Christ."

17 Hunsinger, *How to Read Karl Barth*, 120.

18 Hunsinger, "Our Lives Are Hidden in Christ."

19 Hunsinger, "Our Lives Are Hidden in Christ."

11: Time and Ritual

1 George Harrison, "All Things Must Pass," *All Things Must Pass* (remaster), Parlophone/EMI, 2001.

2 Susan Smith, *Caring Liturgies: The Pastoral Power of Christian Ritual* (Minneapolis: Fortress, 2012), 27.

3 Smith, *Caring Liturgies*, 28.

4 Smith, *Caring Liturgies*, 28.

5 Smith, *Caring Liturgies*, 28–29; emphasis in original.

6 Smith, *Caring Liturgies*, 29.

7 Vanier, *Becoming Human*, 43.

8 Jean Vanier, *From Brokenness to Community* (Mahwah, N.J.: Paulist, 1992), 25.

9 Jennifer Kilps, "Hospitality to the Stranger: The Experience of Christian Churches in the Resettlement of African Refugees in the United States" (Ph.D. diss., University of St. Andrews, 2008), 50.

10 Vanier, *Befriending the Stranger*, 63–64; emphasis in original.

11 Vanier, *Befriending the Stranger*, 65.

12 Gerald A. Arbuckle, *Violence, Society, and the Church: A Cultural Approach* (Minneapolis: Liturgical, 2003), 31.

13 Smith, *Caring Liturgies*, 6.

14 Conrad Philip Kottak, *Cultural Anthropology: Appreciating Cultural Diversity*, 15th ed. (New York: McGraw-Hill Education, 2012).

15 In Randal H. Flutur, *The Stranger inside of Me* (London: AuthorHouse, 2013), 1.
16 Smith, *Caring Liturgies*, 11.

Conclusion: Being in Christ, Being in Time

1 Claire E. Wolfteich, "Time Poverty, Women's Labor, and Catholic Social Teaching: A Practical Theological Exploration," *Journal of Moral Theology* 2, no. 2 (2013): 40–59.
2 Vanier, *Community and Growth*, 169.

Appendix

1 Dietrich Bonhoeffer, *Who Am I? Poetic Insights on Personal Identity* (Minneapolis: Augsburg, 2005), 8–9.

Bibliography

Acharya, Kruti. "Prenatal Testing for Intellectual Disability Misperceptions and Reality with Lessons from Down Syndrome." *Developmental Disabilities Research Reviews* 17, no. 28 (2011): 27–31.

Addis, D. R., and R. L. Buckner. "Episodic Simulations of Future Events: Concepts, Data and Applications." *Year in Cognitive Neuroscience, Annals of the New York Academy of Sciences* 1124 (2008): 39–60.

Aho, James, and Kevin Aho. *Body Matters: A Phenomenology of Sickness, Disease, and Illness*. New York: Lexington Books, 2008.

American Psychological Association. "Personality." Accessed November 10, 2015. http://www.apa.org/topics/personality/.

Arbuckle, Gerald A. *Violence, Society, and the Church: A Cultural Approach*. Minneapolis: Liturgical, 2003.

Aristotle. *Physics*. Oxford World's Classics. London: Oxford University Press, 2008.

Augustine of Hippo. *The Confessions*. Oxford World's Classics. London: Oxford University Press, 2008.

Badcock, Gary. *The Way of Life: A Theology of Christian Vocation*. Grand Rapids: Eerdmans, 1998.

Bader-Saye, Scott. *Following Jesus in a Culture of Fear*. Minneapolis: Baker, 2007.

Baggott, Jim. *A Beginner's Guide to Reality*. London: Penguin Books, 2005.

Barth, Karl. *Church Dogmatics*. Vol. 3, part 3. Edited by G. W. Bromiley and T. F. Torrance. Translated by G. W. Bromiley and R. J. Ehrlich. Edinburgh: T&T Clark, 1960.

Baynton, Douglas C. "'These Pushful Days': Time and Disability in the Age of Eugenics." *Health History* 13, no. 2 (2011): 43–64.

———. "Handicap." In *Encyclopaedia of American Disability History*, edited by Susan Burch and Paul K. Longmore, 420–21. New York: Facts on File, 2009.

Begbie, Jeremy S. *Theology, Music and Time*. Cambridge: Cambridge University Press, 2000.

Boice, J. M. *Foundations of the Christian Faith*. Downers Grove, Ill.: InterVarsity, 1986.

Bonhoeffer, Dietrich. *Barcelona, Berlin, New York: 1928–1931*. Minneapolis: Fortress, 2008.

———. *Discipleship*. Minneapolis: Fortress, 2003.

Bryden, Christine. *Who Will I Be When I Die?* London: Jessica Kingsley, 2012.

Brueggemann, Walter. *Sabbath as Resistance: Saying No to the Culture of Now*. Kindle ed. Louisville: Westminster John Knox, 2014.

Burkhardt, F., and S. Smith, eds. *The Correspondence of Charles Darwin*. Vol. 7. New York: Cambridge University Press, 1993.

Calvin, John. *Calvin: Institutes of the Christian Religion*. Edited by John T. McNeill. Translated from the 1559 Latin ed. by Ford Lewis Battles. 2 vols. Library of Christian Classics. Philadelphia: Westminster, 1960.

Carey Holt, Simon. "Slow Time in a Fast World." *Ministry, Society and Theology* 16, no. 2 (2002): 10–21.

Christian Post. "Sarah Palin to Atheist Richard Dawkins on Aborting Down Syndrome Babies: I'll Let You Meet My Son." August 27, 2014. Accessed November 21, 2014. http://www.christianpost.com/news/sarah-palin-to-atheist-richard-dawkins-on-aborting-down-syndrome-babies-ill-let-you-meet-my-son-125414/.

Conyers, A. J. *The Listening Heart: Vocation and the Crisis of Modern Culture*. Dallas: Spence, 2006.

———. "The Meaning of Vocation." In "Vocation." Special issue, *Christian Reflection: A Series in Faith and Ethics* (2004): 11–19.

Cullmann, Oscar. *Christ and Time: The Primitive Christian Conception of Time and History*. New York: Farrar, Straus & Giroux, 1951.

D'Aquili, Eugene G., and Andrew B. Newberg. *Principles of Neurotheology*. London: Ashgate, 2010.

Darwin, Charles. *The Descent of Man: Selection in Relation to Sex*. London: Penguin Classics, 1981.

Dawkins, Richard. *The Selfish Gene*. London: Oxford University Press, 1976.

Descartes, René. *Discourse on the Method of Rightly Conducting the Reason, and Seeking Truth in the Sciences*. New Haven: Yale University Press, 1996.

Doidge, Norman. *The Brain That Changes Itself: Stories of Personal Triumph from the Frontiers of Brain Science*. New York: Viking Books, 2007.

Downey, Michael. *A Blessed Weakness: The Spirit of Jean Vanier and L'Arche*. San Francisco: Harper & Row, 1986.

———. "A Costly Loss of Heart: The Scholastic Notion of *Voluntas ut Natura*." *Philosophy and Theology* 1, no. 3 (1987): 242–54.

Dulles, Avery. *Models of Church*. New York: Image Books, 1974.

Eiesland, Nancy. *The Disabled God: Toward a Liberatory Theology of Disability*. Nashville: Abingdon, 1994.

———. "Encountering the Disabled God." *Other Side*. September–October 2000, 10–15.

Einstein, Albert. "Time, Space, and Gravitation." *Times* (London), November 28, 1919.

Eriksen, Thomas Hylland. *Tyranny of the Moment: Fast and Slow Time in the Information Age*. London: Pluto, 2001.

Fishbane, Michael. *Sacred Attunement: A Jewish Theology*. Chicago: University of Chicago Press, 2008.

Flutur, Randal H. *The Stranger inside of Me*. London: AuthorHouse, 2013.

Gelb, Steven A. "Darwin's Use of Intellectual Disability in *The Descent of Man*." *Disability Studies Quarterly* 28, no. 2 (2008). http://dsq-sds.org/article/view/96/96.

Genova, Lisa. *Still Alice*. New York: Pocket Books, 2007.

Habets, Myk, and Bobby Grow, eds. *Evangelical Calvinism: Essays Resourcing the Continuing Reformation of the Church*. Eugene, Ore.: Pickwick, 2012.

Hacking, Ian. "Natural Kinds: Rosy Dawn, Scholastic Twilight." *Royal Institute of Philosophy Supplement* 61 (October 2007): 203–39.

———. *The Taming of Chance (Ideas in Context)*. Cambridge: Cambridge University Press, 1990.

Hauerwas, Stanley. *The Peaceable Kingdom: A Primer in Christian Ethics*. Notre Dame, Ind.: University of Notre Dame Press, 1983.

——— *With the Grain of the Universe: The Church's Witness and Natural Theology*. Grand Rapids: Brazos, 2001.

———. *Unleashing the Scriptures: Freeing the Bible from Captivity to America*. Nashville: Abingdon, 1993.

———. *The Work of Theology*. Grand Rapids: Eerdmans, 2015.

Hauerwas, Stanley, and Jean Vanier. *Living Gently in a Violent World: The Prophetic Witness of Weakness*. Edited by John Swinton. Downers Grove, Ill.: InterVarsity, 2009.

Helman, Cecil G. "Cultural Aspects of Time and Ageing." *EMBO Reports* 6, suppl. 1 (2005): S54–S58.

Holmes, Martha Stoddart. "Writing Neurology: Selected Essays and Poetry by Floyd Skloot." *Journal of Medical Humanities* 10 (2009): 1–28.

Hughes, Julian C., Stephen J. Louw, and Steven R. Sabat, eds. *Dementia: Mind, Meaning and the Person*. Oxford: Oxford University Press, 2006.

Hull, John. *In the Beginning There Was Darkness: A Blind Person's Conversations with the Bible*. London: SCM, 2001.

———. "Time and Blindness." *World Religions in Education: Time*. (The Shap working party on Education in World Religions, 2000–2001). Accessed November 9, 2015. http://www.shapworkingparty.org.uk/journals/index_0001.html.

———. *Touching the Rock: An Experience of Blindness*. London: SPCK, 2013.

Hunsinger, George. *How to Read Karl Barth: The Shape of His Theology.* New York: Oxford University Press, 1993.

———. "Our Lives Are Hidden in Christ." *Grace Communion International: Living and Sharing the Gospel*. Accessed October 27, 2015. https://www.gci.org/YI089.

Hydén, Lars C., and Hilde Lindemann. *Beyond Loss: Dementia, Identity, Personhood*. New York: Oxford University Press, 2014.

Kafer, Alison. *Feminist, Queer, Crip*. Bloomington: Indiana University Press, 2013.

Kilps, Jennifer. "Hospitality to the Stranger: The Experience of Christian Churches in the Resettlement of African Refugees in the United States." PhD diss., University of St. Andrews, 2008.

Klager, Andrew P. "The Vulnerability That Makes Peace Possible: An Interview with Stanley Hauerwas." *Huffington Post*, November 9, 2015. Accessed November 9, 2015. http://www.huffingtonpost.com/andrew-p-klager-phd/the-vulnerability-that-ma_b_5579366.html.

Koch, Sabine C., Thomas Fuchs, Michela Summa, and Cornelia Müller, eds. *Body Memory, Metaphor and Movement*. Amsterdam: John Benjamins, 2012.

Kontos, Pia C. "Alzheimer Expressions or Expressions despite Alzheimer's? Philosophical Reflections on Selfhood and Embodiment." *Occasion: Interdisciplinary Studies in the Humanities* 4 (2012): 1–12.

Kottak, Conrad Philip. *Cultural Anthropology: Appreciating Cultural Diversity*. 15th ed. New York: McGraw-Hill Education, 2012.

Koyama, Kosuke. *Three Mile an Hour God: Biblical Reflections*. New York: Orbis, 1979.

Leadbeater, Charles. "The Disremembered." *Aeon*, March 26, 2015. Accessed November 9, 2015. http://linkis.com/rBfqi.

Le Goff, Jacques. *Time, Work, and Culture in the Middle Ages*. Translated by Arthur Goldhammer. Chicago: University of Chicago, 1977. Lesley, J. P. *Man's Origin and Destiny*. Philadelphia: J. B. Lippincott, 1868.

Levine, Robert. *Geography of Time: On Tempo, Culture and the Pace of Life; The Temporal Misadventures of a Social Psychologist, or How Every Culture Keeps Time Just a Little Bit Differently*. Oxford: Oneworld, 2006.

Lints, Richard, Michael S. Horton, and Mark R. Talbot. *Personal Identity in Theological Perspective*. Grand Rapids: Eerdmans, 2006.

Litchfield, Henrietta Emma Darwin. *Emma Darwin, a Century of Family Letters, 1792–1896*. Vol. 2. Bel Air: Cook, 2007.

Locke, John. *Essay concerning Human Understanding*. New York: Prometheus Books, 1995.

Luther, Martin. "To the Christian nobility of the German nation concerning reform of the Christian estate," translated by C. M. Jacobs, revised by James Atkinson. In *Luther's Works*. Vol. 44. Philadelphia: Fortress, 1966.

Macadam, Jackie. "Interview with Mary Warnock: 'A Duty to Die?'" *Life and Work*, October 2008, 23–25.

MacIntyre, Alasdair. *After Virtue: A Study in Moral Theory*. London: Duckworth, 1996.

Mason, Paul H. "What Is Normal? A Historical Survey and Neuroanthropological Perspective." In *Handbook of Neuroethics*, edited by Jens Clausen and Neil Levy, 343–63. New York: Springer, 2014.

Mawson, Michael, and Philip Ziegler, eds. *Christ, Church and World: New Studies in Bonhoeffer's Theology and Ethics*. London: Bloomsbury, 2016.

McCrum, Robert. *My Year Off: Recovering Life after a Stroke*. New York: Norton, 1998.

McGilchrist, Iain. *The Master and His Emissary: The Divided Brain and the Making of the Western World*. New Haven: Yale University Press, 2009.

McLean, Dorothy Cummings. "Peace Takes Time and Patience: An Interview with Stanley Hauerwas." *Catholic Register*, March 31, 2009. Accessed January 10, 2015. http://www.catholicregister.org/columns/item/11176-peace-takes-time-and-patience.

Merleau-Ponty, Maurice. *Phenomenology of Perception*. Translated by Colin Smith. London: Routledge & Kegan Paul, 1965.

Narvaez, Rafael F. "Embodiment, Collective Memory and Time." *Body & Society* 12, no. 3 (2006): 51–73.

Newton, Isaac. *Philosophiae Naturalis Principia Mathematica* [*Mathematical Principles of Natural Philosophy*]. London, 1687.

"On Madness: A Personal Account of Rapid Cycling Bipolar Disorder." *British Journal of General Practice* 56, no. 530 (2006): 726–28.

Paddison, Angus. *Scripture: A Very Theological Proposal*. London: T&T Clark, 2009.

Parr, Susie, Kevin Paterson, and Carole Pound. "Time Please! Temporal Barriers in Aphasia." In *Aphasia Inside Out: Reflections on Communication Disability*, edited by Susie Parr, Judith F. Duchan, and Carole Pound, 127–44. Berkshire: McGraw-Hill Education, 2003.

Pattison, Stephen. *The Challenge of Practical Theology: Selected Essays*. London: Jessica Kingsley, 2007.

Pieper, Josef. *Faith, Hope, Love*. San Francisco: Ignatius, 1997.

Pirani, Bianca Maria, ed. *Learning from Memory: Body, Memory and Technology in a Globalizing World*. Newcastle: Cambridge Scholars, 2011.

Poe, Harry Lee, and J. Stanley Mattson. *What God Knows: Time and the Question of Divine Knowledge.* Waco, Tex.: Baylor University Press, 2006.

Post, Stephen. *The Moral Challenge of Alzheimer's Disease*. Baltimore: Johns Hopkins University Press, 1995.

Postman Neil. *Technopoly: The Surrender of Culture to Technology*. New York: Vintage Books, 1993.

Rashkover, Randi, and C. C. Pecknold, eds. *Liturgy, Time, and the Politics of Redemption*. Radical Traditions. Grand Rapids: Eerdmans, 2006.

Ratcliffe, Matthew. "Varieties of Temporal Experience in Depression." *Journal of Medical Philosophy* 37, no. 2 (2012): 114.

Reichmann, W. J. *Use and Abuse of Statistics*. Middlesex: Penguin Books, 1964.

Reinders, Hans S. *Disability, Providence, and Ethics: Bridging Gaps, Transforming Lives*. Waco, Tex.: Baylor University Press, 2014.

Rifkin, Jeremy. *Time Wars: The Primary Conflict in Human History*. New York: Touchstone, 1989.

Schacter, Daniel. *Searching for Memory: How the Mind Forgets and Remembers.* New York: Basic Books, 1996.

Shahjahan, Riyad A. "Being 'Lazy' and Slowing Down: Toward Decolonizing Time, Our Body, and Pedagogy." *Educational Philosophy and Theory* 47, no. 5 (2015): 488–501.

Shell, Marc. "Moses' Tongue." *Common Knowledge* 12, no. 1 (2006): 150–76.

Shulevitz, Judith. *The Sabbath World: Glimpses of a Different Order of Time*. Kindle ed. London: Random House, 2010.

Singer, Peter. *Practical Ethics*. Cambridge: Cambridge University Press, 1979.

———. *Rethinking Life and Death: The Collapse of Our Traditional Ethics*. Melbourne: Text, 1994.

Skloot, Floyd. "Gray Area: Thinking with a Damaged Brain." *LOST Magazine*, February 2006. Accessed November 10, 2015. http://www.lostmag.com/issue3/grayarea.php.

———. "Wild in the Woods." In *In the Shadow of Memory*, ch 2. Lincoln, Neb.: Bison Books, 2004.

Smith, J. David. "Darwin's Last Child." *Disability Studies Quarterly* 28, no. 2 (2008). https://libres.uncg.edu/ir/uncg/f/J_Smith_Darwin_1999.pdf.

Smith, Susan. *Caring Liturgies: The Pastoral Power of Christian Ritual*. Minneapolis: Fortress, 2012.

Smith, L. Tuhiwai. *Decolonizing Methodologies: Research and Indigenous Peoples*. London: Zed Books, 2012.

Snow, Judith. Lecture delivered at the Summer Institute on Theology and Disability. Perkins School of Theology, Dallas, Texas, June 2014.

Steensma, David P. "Down Syndrome in Down House: Trisomy 21, *GATA1* Mutations, and Charles Darwin." *Blood* 105, no. 6 (2005): 2614–16.

Swaab, Dick. *We Are Our Brains: From the Womb to Alzheimer's*. London: Allen Lane, 2014.

Swinton, John, ed. *Critical Reflections on Stanley Hauerwas' Theology of Disability: Disabling Society, Enabling Theology*. London: Routledge, 2005.

———. *Dementia: Living in the Memories of God*. Grand Rapids: Eerdmans, 2012.

———. "Dementia and the Memory of the Body: Moving beyond the Autobiographical Self." *St Mark's Review: A Journal of Christian Thought & Opinion*, no. 232 (2015): 38–50.

———. "Using Our Bodies Faithfully." *Journal of Disability and Religion* 19, no. 3 (2015): 228–42.

———. "What's in a Name? Why People with Dementia Might Be Better Off without the Language of Personhood." *International Journal of Practical Theology* 18, no. 2 (2014): 234–47.

Swinton, John, and Elaine Powrie. *Why Are We Here? Meeting the Spiritual Needs of People with Learning Disabilities*. London: Foundation for People with Learning Disabilities, 2004.

Swinton, John, and Harriet Mowat. *Practical Theology and Qualitative Research Methods*. London: SCM, 2006.

Tallis, Raymond. *Aping Mankind: Neuromania, Darwinitis and the Misrepresentation of Humanity*. London: Routledge, 2014.

Tanner, Kathryn. *Theories of Culture: A New Agenda for Theology*. Minneapolis: Fortress, 1997.

Taylor, Charles. *A Secular Age*. Boston, Mass.: Harvard University Press, 2009.

Tran, Jonathan. *The Vietnam War and Theologies of Memory: Time and Eternity in the Far Country*. London: Wiley-Blackwell, 2010.

Ulasien, Paul. *The Corporate Rat Race: The Rats Are Winning*. Baltimore: Publish America, 2006.

Vanier, Jean. *Becoming Human*. Mahwah, N.J.: Paulist, 2002.

———. *Befriending the Stranger.* Mahwah, N.J.: Paulist, 2005.

———. *Community and Growth.* London: Darton, Longman & Todd, 1979.

———. *From Brokenness to Community.* Mahwah, N.J.: Paulist, 1992.

———. *Man and Woman, God Made Them*. Mahwah, N.J.: Paulist, 2000.

Veith, Gene Edward. "The Doctrine of Vocation: How God Hides Himself in Human Work." *Modern Reformation*, May/June, 1999, 4–7.

Volck, Brian. *Flesh Becomes Word*. Loveland, Ohio: Dos Madres, 2013.

Volpe, Medi. *Rethinking Christian Identity: Doctrine and Discipleship*. London: Wiley-Blackwell, 2013.

———. "Saving Knowledge: Doctrine and Intellectual Disability." Paper presented at the Doctor of Theology and Ministry summer school, University of Durham, UK, September 2013. Accessed November 10, 2015. https://www.academia.edu/12529752/Saving_Knowledge_Doctrine_and_Intelletucal_Disability.

Vosloo, Robert R. "The Feeling of Time: Bonhoeffer on Temporality and the Fully Human Life." *Scriptura* 99 (2008): 337–49.

Volf, Miroslav, and Dorothy Bass, eds. *Practicing Theology: Beliefs and Practices in Christian Life*. Grand Rapids: Eerdmans, 2002.

Westminster Shorter Catechism. Christian Classics Ethereal Library. Accessed November 27, 2015. http://www.ccel.org/ccel/anonymous/westminster1.

Whitt, Jason. "Baptism and Profound Intellectual Disability." In "Disability." Special issue, *Christian Reflection: A Series in Faith and Ethics* (2012): 60–67.

Wolfteich, Claire E. "Time Poverty, Women's Labor, and Catholic Social Teaching: A Practical Theological Exploration." *Journal of Moral Theology* 2, no. 2 (2013): 40–59.

Yeates, G. N., F. Gracey, and J. C. McGrath. "A Biopsychosocial Deconstruction of 'Personality Change' following Acquired Brain Injury." *Neuropsychological Rehabilitation* 18, nos. 5–6 (2008): 566–89.

Yoder, John Howard. *Preface to Theology: Christology and Theological Method*. Grand Rapids: Brazos, 2002.

Young, Frances. *Arthur's Call: A Journey of Faith in the Face of Severe Learning Disability*. London: SPCK, 2014.

———. *Encounter with Mystery: Reflections on L'Arche and Living with Disability*. London: Darton, Longman & Todd, 1997.

———. *Face to Face: A Narrative Essay in the Theology of Suffering*. Edinburgh: T&T Clark, 1990.

Index

abnormal, 31, 39, 48, 49, 51, 52, 70, 87, 173
abnormality, 48, 51, 70, 87, 173
acquired brain injury, 17, 165–69, 179–85, 193, 196, 198, 200
affliction, 40
anxiety, 15, 36, 74–80, 122–23
Arbuckle, Gerald, 201
Aristotle, 21
atavism, 44
atavistic, 43–47, 51
Augustine, 3–4, 15, 57–62, 159
autobiographical self, 16, 138, 141, 142, 151, 231

Babcock, Gary, 118
Bader-Saye, Scott, 57, 63, 64, 116
baptism, 95, 103, 109–10, 118–19, 188, 195–96, 230
Barth, Karl, 5, 17, 61, 147, 185–88, 192
Baynton, Douglas, 39–42, 49–51
Begbie, Jeremy, 30
belonging, 11, 93, 98, 109–10, 115, 124, 203–5, 208
blindness, 69, 94
Bonhoeffer, Dietrich, 5, 17, 100–101, 104, 109, 166–67, 177, 217
Brockmeier, Jen, 140–41
Brueggemann, Walter, 78, 121

capitalism, 29
Centre for Spirituality, Health and Disability, University of Aberdeen, 90
clock(s): mechanical, 25–28; hands, minutes, and seconds, 23–28; with no hands, 26
Conyers, A. J., 115–17

Darwin, Charles, 46–48
Darwin, Henrietta, 46
Dawkins, Richard, 38–39, 41, 43, 48, 88–89
dementia: and euthanasia, 37–38; intentionality, 143–44; and memory, 133–43; memory and worship, 147–62
Descartes, Rene, 13, 170
disability: as formative of identity, 8–9; as a gift, 72–73; and healing, 8–9; and heaven, 8, 32, 35; social model, 10; *see also* time
disablism, casual, 11
discipleship: and belonging, 110; as embodied calling, 98; frenetic, 123; gentle, 121–28; and inclusion, 16; and intellectual disability, 94; intellectualization of, 99; and love, 93; of the mind, 173; as obedience, 100; as personal choice, 99; as receiving a call from Jesus, 102; slow, 69; and vocation, 90
divine simultaneity: time, 58–62, 158, 189, 193; trinity, 3, 15

doctrine: embodying, 201; as function and gift, 105; as gift, 106; and imagination, 105; as saving knowledge, 104–6; of the Trinity, 4, 106

Eiesland, Nancy, 8–9
Einstein, Albert, 21–22
euthanasia, 35–37
evolution, 39–53, 83

faith as trust, 100
filming memories, 59
Ford, David, 74
Fuchs, Thomas, 151–52

gentleness, 74–76
George Timothy, 58, 63

Hacking, Ian, 49, 51, 142
handicapped, 39–43
Hauerwas, Stanley, 5, 29, 36, 59, 73, 94, 103
heart: connection with God, 155; and memory, 153; as mystical, 153; the place of trust, 154; the seat of relationality, 154; work of God, 154
hospitality, 75, 128, 178
Hull, John, 69–71, 94
human nature, 49
humanness, 12–14, 18, 31, 47
Hunsinger, George, 61, 185–86, 190–91
hypercognition, 6, 12, 13, 16, 88–89

identity in Christ/hidden in Christ, 177–92
infirmity, 40–41
insult to the brain, 172–77

Jung, Carl, 198

Kelsey, David, 101–6
Koyama, Kosuke, 68–69

L'Arche, 75, 76, 80, 123
liminality, 200–202
lived funeral, 203, 213
Locke, John, 141–42
Luther, Martin, 118–20

memory: body, 151–53; of the heart, 17, 157–59, 160–61; as a natural kind, 140; as recall, 136–39; standard account of, 138
mental retardation, 43
Merleau-Ponty, 107
mystery, 3

Narvaez, Rafael, 150
neighborly love, 119–21
neuromania, 12–13
neuroplasticity, 168
Newton, Isaac, 21

operational effectiveness, 194

Palin, Sarah, 48
patience, 74
Pattison, Stephen, 5
peace\peacefulness, 64, 79–80, 103
perseverance, 149
personality, 179; change, 178
Pharaoh's anxiety, 78
Post, Stephen, 12
practical theology, 4–6, 16, 18
prayer without words, 124
prenatal testing, 14, 35
priesthood of all believers, 119–20
profound and complex intellectual disability, definition of, 89
progress, 32
providence, 40–42, 63, 116–17, 180
punctuality, 23, 26–27

Reinders, Hans, 177, 180–85
repentance, 112–13
respite, 210
ritual, 201–5, 213–16, 218

Sabbath, 77–80, 210
scheduling, origins of, 27
sin and repentance, 110–12
Skloot, Floyd, 169–75
sloth, 68–71
Smith, Susan, 194–96, 201–2
Snow, Judith, 72, 200
soteriological objectivism, 17, 185–87
speed as violence, 64

speed of love, 68
St. Benedict and monastery time, 25–27
Swinton, John, 188

Tallis, Raymond, 13, 144–45
Tanner, Kathryn, 95–96
temporarily able bodied, 7–9
theological advocates, 193
theological effectiveness, 195
three mile an hour God, 67
time: clock, 14, 15, 17, 24, 25, 30, 32, 39, 63, 70, 83, 88, 128, 132, 180; commodification of, 14, 26, 30, 58, 79; event, 27; fallenness of, 52; God's, 15–17, 57–64; horror of, 163; Jesus is, 75; linear, 33, 138, 159–60, 189; poverty, 208; and productivity, 14, 27, 31, 32, 37, 51, 52, 74, 122; redeeming, 63; and relativity, 22; standard average European, 23, 27, 32, 70; tensing of, 144
timelessness, 58–62
Tran, Jonathan, 60–62
transgenerational sin, 97–98
traumatic brain injury, 168, 178, 180–81, 196
Trinity, the, 3–4, 106, 195
tyranny of normality, 49

Vanier, Jean: community, 73; friends of time, 75; the heart, 155, 156; L'Arche, 75; power of small things, 210; stranger within, 197–99; violence, 36
Veith, Gene Edward, 120
vocation, 115–29
Volpe, Medi, 95, 96, 99, 104–6

Warnock, Mary, 37, 39
Whaley, Tonya, 178–79, 193
Whitt, Jason, 109

Yoder, John Howard, 59–60
Young, Frances, 9, 115, 121